OUTRAGEOUS TEXANS

Also by Mona D. Sizer

Texas Disasters: Wind, Flood, and Fire

Texas Bandits: Real to Reel

Texas Money: All the Law Allows

Texas Politicians: Good 'n' Bad

Texas Justice: Bought and Paid For

Texas Heroes: A Dynasty of Courage

The King Ranch Story: Truth and Myth

and

Before the Wind: Poems out of my Life and Thought

Tales Told at Midnight along the Rio Grande

(Edited by Mona Sizer)

OUTRAGEOUS TEXANS

TALES OF THE RICH AND INFAMOUS

MONA D. SIZER

TAYLOR TRADE PUBLISHING

LANHAM • NEW YORK • BOULDER • TORONTO • PLYMOUTH, UK

Published by Taylor Trade Publishing
An imprint of The Rowman & Littlefield Publishing Group, Inc.
4501 Forbes Boulevard, Suite 200, Lanham, Maryland 20706
www.rlpgtrade.com

Estover Road, Plymouth PL6 7PY, United Kingdom

Distributed by NATIONAL BOOK NETWORK

Library of Congress Cataloging-in-Publication Data
Sizer, Mona D.
  Outrageous Texans : tales of the rich and infamous / Mona D. Sizer.
    p.   cm.
  Includes bibliographical references and index.
  ISBN-13: 978-1-58979-338-5 (pbk. : alk. paper)
  ISBN-10: 1-58979-338-2 (pbk. : alk. paper)
  1. Rich people—Texas—Biography. 2. Celebrities—Texas—
Biography. 3. Characters and characteristics—Texas. 4. Texas—
Biography. I. Title.
CT262.S595 2008
976.4'0630922—dc22
                                                    2007047976

A DEDICATION

To all of you who have ever done an outrageous thing
To all of you who have enjoyed it
To all of you who have regretted it later
To all of you who have never regretted it
To all of you who have lived life on the "cutting edge"
To all of you who have wanted to live life on the cutting edge
To all of you who have spent more money than you should, gambled more money than you should, indulged yourselves more than you should

This book's for you.

And to all of you who simply want to know what can happen to those who do, this book's for you too.

May your cups never be half-empty.

CONTENTS

ACKNOWLEDGMENTS

O*utrageous Texans: Tales of the Rich and Infamous* owes its publication to Rick Rinehart, who has always had faith in the project. Hope this book meets your expectations. It was great fun to research and write.

Thanks to Nicholas Fuller for his help putting the book together.

Thanks to Ruth and Bob Welch for their lifelong friendship and support.

Thanks, as always, to Jim Sizer, my strongest supporter and sternest critic, whose attention and commentaries are always welcome and always serve to make the book better. Love you, sweetheart.

Finally, thanks to librarians, archivists, publicists, and others who supplied information and pictures. And thanks so much to several super cooperative people who thought the book title was a "hoot" and were happy to be able to lend their expertise to the enterprise.

OUTRAGEOUS TEXANS

SMACK AND SOUTHERN COMFORT

June 17, 1967, the Monterey Pop Festival started great. They had over thirty rock groups. You could groove however you wanted. Toward the end of the second day, however, things were beginning to sound pretty much "same old, same old." The crowd was yawning and looking for the exits even before a barely mediocre rock group calling themselves Big Brother and the Holding Company opened up with a few quick licks.

We were all getting pretty restless when this chick bounced out on the stage. She was weird. For one thing, she didn't wear any makeup, and her face sure could have used some. Her hair looked like it hadn't seen a comb or a brush in weeks.

While we were all taking in the shiny silvery-white pantsuit, she jived around while the band fumbled through a sorry up-take for her. Suddenly, she grabbed hold of the mike, stamped the stage, and let loose a note that blew everybody's mind.

Up until that moment, according to the buzz, the festival had been nothing special. The Who had set off smoke bombs and smashed their instruments onstage. Jimi Hendrix had burned his guitar. (Waste of damn fine instruments, if you ask me. Why didn't they just give them to some little kids or something?)

The producers had already filled the list of acts they were gonna film the next day. But damned if they didn't add that sorry band right then and there even before the whistling and shouting stopped. Why? Because their lead singer, this chick from Texas, stopped the show. Woke us all up and then blew us away.

And you could almost hear the stampede going on backstage as record producers, booking agents, concert promoters, and road managers pushed and elbowed each other aside to be first to throw opportunities and money at Big Brother and the Holding Company, so long as they had Janis Joplin.

She couldn't be for real.

Just a few months later, the group performed at the Monterey Jazz Festival. This time *Newsweek* and *Time* raved about her. Columbia Records waved a big contract. Janis Joplin's voice was the talk of the nation. Her wailing, grating, digging-deep sound was beyond different. It sounded more like Odetta or Bessie Smith.

"Imagine a white girl singing the blues like that!"

Big Brother had no idea what to do with all the fame and notoriety. Laid back and barely adequate musicians, they played more for fun than to become a serious performance act. But after the Monterrey Jazz Festival at the end of the summer, one of the agents talking seriously to them was Albert Grossman. When one member of the group—trying to sound like he knew what he was talking about—insisted that they had to clear $75,000 a year, the agent smiled briefly and suggested he might even come up with $100,000.

Albert Grossman was head of one of the best talent agencies in the world. He represented, among others, Odetta; Gordon Lightfoot; and Peter, Paul, and Mary. He had the connections to make Janis an international star. Based on the qualities of the two performances he'd seen and heard, Grossman was sure she had the potential to earn millions. If Big Brother could learn to play adequately, they could come along.

It was her dream. She *should* have been ecstatic.

As a matter of fact, Janis Joplin should never have been in California that summer. In 1963 she'd hitchhiked to San Francisco with the very small-time impresario Chet Helms. Everybody talked about making that trip, but she was one of the few who actually did it. The journey took fifty hours, and she was scared to death most of the time. When they finally made it, she joined the Beat Generation.

If the initial experience had succeeded in killing her, she would have died happy.

Her early life in Port Arthur, Texas, had been the American dream that for her had been a nightmare. Her father was an engineer; her mother, a Sunday school teacher. Janis was a bright, pretty, and artistic child. In addition to writing poetry, she sold original oil paintings while still in high school. To this day a few people in her hometown display the works with pride, especially as their celebrity value has increased beyond anything the owners could have imagined.

Encouraged by her father, Janis became a voracious reader in a town where educating oneself from books was not the norm. This learning and penchant for the arts isolated her from people who might have been close friends. According to Janis's account of her loneliness, "I was the only one I'd ever met. There weren't any others."

Perhaps she could have gone unnoticed except that at the end of junior high school, she began to change physically. She gained unattractive weight and developed the most extreme form of acne. Although almost all people in their teenage years have the disease, no one—especially not vulnerable teens—accepts it gracefully.

Shame, self-hatred, disgust at one's appearance, fear of being ridiculed are the feelings that young people with acute acne live through. Most authorities agree that a severe outbreak of acne can have a deep impact on a sensitive person. The combination of Janis's weight gain and skin condition destroyed her self-esteem and further isolated her from her classmates.

Unacceptable to her peers, Janis was determined to show them she didn't care. In high school, she roamed the halls with the boys who drank and smoked and cursed. Defiantly, she took pleasure in smoking in the bathrooms and in shouting four-letter words girls just did not say in the halls. Even the five "bad boys" she gravitated to thought she was outrageous.

After school she went to their "beach parties" in the abandoned Coast Guard station. She drank a lot of beer and Southern Comfort when she could get it. With those same boys, she climbed the water tower and the Rainbow Bridge 300 feet above the Neches River.

Ironically, none of the boys was interested in Janis as a sexual partner. They simply allowed her to "tag along." Their attitude speaks volumes for her appearance. Her figure was bloated, her face was a catastrophe, and her clothing was outlandish even by fifties standards. Her refusal to behave "the way a girl should" embarrassed them.

Then the boys all graduated and went off to Lamar State College of Technology, leaving Janis alone at the mercy of an unforgiving student body that threw things at her and called her "pig." She was only sixteen and miserable, unable to fight except in unacceptable ways. Her few friends had trouble defending Janis's behavior when the treatment by her other classmates infuriated her beyond any desire to change. The more they hated her, the more she behaved to draw that hatred.

While Janis was suffering in the halls, her teachers could not fault her academic achievements in the classrooms. Unfortunately, they could not understand nor appreciate her talents. Janis continued to make excellent grades while her mother was being called to the school for parent-teacher conferences to discuss her outrageous behavior.

By the last semester of her senior year, Janis no longer needed nor wanted to stay in school all day. She was allowed to take only the classes she needed to graduate. She took part-time jobs, but mostly she stayed home and read and painted. She sold a few of her paintings from the walls of the local coffee shop.

Bored and miserable, Janis began singing along with records of Odetta, who was just beginning to sing the new "folk" music in her powerful mezzo-soprano voice. From Odetta's songs as well as from the songs of Pete Seeger and Harry Belafonte, Janis began to develop her sound. The day she learned she could sing was an epiphany. Finally, something she could do that made her truly happy.

While her talents blossomed at home, she was forgotten by her classmates. No one even suspected until years later how hurt she was that no one asked her to the senior prom.

College at Lamar Tech did not solve her problems. Just down the road in Beaumont, it was a small school with journeyman professors designed to give local high school graduates a taste of higher education. Janis was disappointed with her courses and angry because the classmates who had despised her in high school had all gone to Lamar as well.

A gang of them went drinking one night at Lou Ann's, an infamous hangout for the college and high school wild ones. To get back to the dorm, Janis squeezed in with three kids in the front and four in the back of an Oldsmobile. The driver was drunk. He pushed his foot to the floorboard trying to do 120. He turned the car over three times and ended up in the ditch. One boy swore he heard Janis yell, "I hope we'll all be killed!"

Miraculously, no one was hurt. Shortly thereafter, Janis ran off to Houston. Her parents brought her home and sent her to a psychiatrist in her hometown. Later she saw a psychologist.

Probably in hopes of bringing a little sanity back into their own lives, Janis's parents sent her to live with Mrs. Joplin's sister in Los Angeles. After only a few weeks, however, Janis moved into "more economical" surroundings in the notorious beachfront town of Venice. She had rid herself of the last vestiges of parental control as many disaffected youths were doing in those days.

Janis later claimed that she felt at home in Venice, where she met people just like herself. She told different stories about her escapades, of hitchhiking up the coast to San Francisco, where she is reputed to have gotten her trademark sheepskin jacket. She began to sing in amateur clubs and to listen to Bessie Smith. Most likely, Janis was drinking heavily by this time, her drink of choice being Southern Comfort, swigged straight out of the bottle. Part of her persona began looking and behaving as if she didn't give a damn.

Though Janis protested, her parents insisted that she come home and attend the University of Texas in Austin. There she majored in art and immediately fell into the milieu of coffee houses and counterculture. She was happiest when she could make a little money singing on Wednesday nights at Ken Threadgill's Bar and Grill. The famous converted filling station was a hangout for the "folk music crowd."

Sometimes she would persuade amateur musicians to play while she sang. Sometimes she played the autoharp, also called the "idiot zither," an instrument much favored by amateur folksingers of the day because it required very little musical training or practice. Sometimes she would simply sing a capella. When bar money wouldn't reach, she allegedly dealt "grass" on campus.

The sixties were the time of love and peace and flower children, and Janis was the floweriest one of all. She haunted used clothing shops to find outrageous outfits. She became an instantly recognizable figure with her leis of mostly fake, though sometimes real, flowers; long strings of "love beads" and jangling bracelets; feather boas draped over her shoulders and pinned in her hair; skirts that dragged the ground or hiked up beyond mid-thigh. She wore no makeup. She never combed her hair. She wore huge round-rimmed glasses with different colored snap-in lenses.

She would have probably stayed in that milieu a few more years had she not been the recipient of a particularly devastating insult. One of the university fraternities, a band of not-so-merry pranksters, voted her "The Ugliest Man on Campus."

At twenty she was determined to leave Texas behind forever, so she hitchhiked to San Francisco. For two years Janis sang in the Bay Area, where she fell into the pervasive culture of easily obtainable drugs. At that time she began to use smack—"horse," or heroin, in the street trade.

The dangerously addictive and illegal drug must have felt wonderful to her when she first began using. Not only did it make her forget her troubles, but it blew in the face of the ordinary people she'd left behind in Texas, the people who called her "pig." They were the people who would never dare to come to this wonderful place. Initially, heroin created a sleepy, pleasant feeling of euphoria, but with repeated usage the feeling no longer occurred.

Pictures of her from that time show her dangerously malnourished. Like most heroin users, Janis lost her appetite. Her appearance dramatically changed. She became an emaciated woman with sunken cheeks, a scrawny neck, and hollow eyes, which she heavily outlined with black mascara.

Finally, her friends in San Francisco passed the hat and bought her a bus ticket home. When she arrived, she weighed eighty-eight pounds. Her parents loved her and cared for her. With their help and rehabilitation, they brought her back. Janis even dated enough to think seriously that she might get married. Her mother started sewing on a wedding dress.

But Janis got a call from, or perhaps she herself called, the Eleventh Door night club in Austin. With the promise of a job, she was determined not to stay in Port Arthur and lead their kind of life. She craved the excitement of performing. Singing was really the only thing she wanted to do.

That first night Janis sang, she tore the place apart. Even the half of the audience who expected to hear a sort of Joan Baez guitar-backed, folksy performance was set back on their heels. The review in the *Austin Statesman* the next day read, "Texas has been a hard place for . . . blues singers from Leadbelly on, but . . . it has produced some great ones. . . . Janis Joplin is one of the great ones."

A friend who read it told Mrs. Joplin, "Dorothy, you don't stand a chance!"

Still, Janis remained in Texas until March 1966 because, according to friends, she was afraid to go back to San Francisco. The drug scene was turning deadly. Famous and non-famous were using and dying. She was afraid she would get dragged back into it.

In the end, Janis was more afraid of getting dragged back to Port Arthur or becoming passé with the ever-changing college crowd in Austin. So she decided to go back to San Francisco even though, according to some people, she knew the drugs would kill her.

With a few telephone calls, she learned the West Coast had not forgotten her. Janis received an offer to audition with a new rock band, Big Brother and the Holding Company. In her final act of defiance of expected behavior, Janis started making things up, lying about her behavior, especially her sexual exploits with others. She devised the story that Big Brother and the Holding Company were all about sex, and she had made love with them all. Another time she said that Chet Helms had sent Travis Rivers to bring her back to San Francisco. She said that didn't really want to go, but "he was such a *good fuck*! How could I not go!"

Her friends shrugged their shoulders. No one could change Janis.

In May 1966, doubtless with promises to return if "nothing comes of this," Janis returned to San Francisco. She marked her calendar that she arrived where Ashbury crossed

Haight on June 4, 1966. She was overweight. Her face was lumpy and inflamed. She wore her hair in a ponytail, a sloppy bun, or a wild mess of uncombed tangles.

She began working, but not having sex, with the married and/or more-or-less attached musicians who were Big Brother. They were a rock band of sorts—loud, rhythmic, and not particularly good. Their idea of music was "sonic fury." From the first rehearsal, she realized that she couldn't just stand on the stage and sing "simple." She had to sing at the top of her lungs and gyrate to grab the audience's attention.

They had a four-week gig at the Avalon Ballroom beginning June 10. It did not go smoothly. She and Big Brother were just "too freaky." Janis was dressed head to toe in Beat Generation garb—wrapped in a bedspread with chicken bone jewelry and feathers. But the worst was her voice. It sounded hoarse, and she screeched her high notes.

The manager fielded complaints from the audience. "Get rid of that chick! She's *terrible!*"

Fortunately, Janis learned fast.

In the meantime, Big Brother had somehow gotten a gig at the Monterey Pop Festival. From practically her first note, Janis gripped the audience. The first time she unlimbered her wailing soprano, she told the audience that all she could see was the rain. She rocked and jived and sang how "somethin' grabbed ahold of me, honey," and it felt "like a ball and chain."

She grabbed "ahold" of the audience. And for the rest of her short, turbulent life, she never let go.

Based on Janis's performance, Big Brother was able to book a four-week gig in Chicago at Mother Blues, where people started noticing Janis's "electric style." The minute the group finished their last night in Chicago, they hopped a plane for San Francisco for the Summer Solstice performance at Golden Gate Park. They were living a dream they couldn't quite believe.

They were part of the art and music scene on California's west coast. Backstage and offstage. Man! No limits. No limits at all! The drugs and the booze just appeared like magic. It was all so easy and so much fun.

First came speed—a synthetic stimulant, an amphetamine. College students began using it as a "recreational" drug. Graphic artists boasted that they used it and created the psychedelic posters the era was famous for. Janis used it for an appetite suppressant to control her burgeoning weight.

In keeping with the counterculture of the time, when she wasn't singing, Janis would tie macramé or string beads that she draped around her neck and wrists. She and two friends once made a fifteen-foot-long beaded curtain in record time. They worked so fast they bloodied their fingertips in a fit of nervous energy generated by the drugs.

When the effects wore off, Janis would crash, twice as exhausted as she would have been under normal circumstances. From time to time, she would force herself to leave speed alone; but when her hated weight crept up again as she began to binge on food, she would take it again. She knew what she was doing, but her painful memories of being called a pig drove her to use anything to keep from getting fat.

Janis experimented with LSD as people all around her were doing. Not quite thirty years had passed since it was synthesized by a Swiss laboratory from ergot, a black mold found primarily on rye. Ergot had been recognized as a dangerous substance from medieval times when it was administered by "witches" to induce abortions. The original purpose of the lab's experimentation was to develop a drug to treat schizophrenia. When the world came to know that LSD would generate hallucinations, it became the drug of choice to alter and expand the senses and emotions. The "happy generation" of Haight-Ashbury dosed themselves with dangerous amounts—three and four times as much as is normally given to psychotics today.

Those who "tripped" using LSD for extended periods of time were damaged permanently. A single sugar cube soaked in the clear, odorless, and tasteless liquid could send the user off on a "bad trip" that would generate horrible nightmares. He might "flash back" at unpredictable times and relive the original experience for hours. Habitual use altered a person's personality as the fantasies left permanent changes in the brain.

Though Janis knew what drugs would do and was truly afraid of them, she couldn't resist them. The high was too incredible. Loaded, she could sing—she was sure—like no one had ever sung before. She lived for the notes and the screaming crowds.

In an age when crowds were dancing in the aisles, Janis's audiences were the wildest. She thrived on their adulation. Not for her the sit-and-listen-politely-and-then-applaud groups. She was famous for screaming at them, "Show some life!" At several of her performances, the police were summoned to keep order. They closed down The Matrix in the middle of one of her shows when the screaming and shouting turned to drunken disorder and mayhem.

Back in California, Janis was completely out of control. She began hanging out with Hell's Angels, the most notorious biker gang the country has ever known. Pictures taken of her on their motorcycles became part of her publicity image as a "red hot mama."

About the same time, Janis fell into an affair with Joe McDonald of Country Joe and the Fish, who was amazed to discover that she had no conservative side. The only thing she was interested in was getting "stoned—right now." He didn't know what her life had been like back in Texas, but he got the feeling that she was "the wrong person in the wrong place and got treated the wrong way."

In November 1967, Janis signed a deal with Albert Grossman, one of the most important booking agents in America. He was known for asking outrageous prices for his talents. He asked and got $1,000,000 for Bob Dylan for a small role in a movie.

In December of the same year, Big Brother and the Holding Company hired a road manager. John Byrne Cooke was a Harvard graduate and the son of Alistair Cooke, a legend in television's early days of class and culture. John was tall, slender, regal in bearing with black eyes, black hair, a clipped black moustache, and an air of icy hauteur that could command the sun to stand still. Most important, with his clipped British accent, he could snap everyone within hearing into an orderly line. His was the voice fit to rule an empire. Cooke was exactly the right person to bring order to the motley crew.

In addition to getting the group out of bed in the mornings, Cooke ordered the limousines that took them to their airports and their concerts and back to their hotels. To Janis, despite her beads and hair and weird clothes, he was quite pleasant. He recognized her as the reason the whole tour was successful; but more important, he recognized her as a vulnerable soul. In his orderly fashion, he was devoted to her well-being.

Janis's life began to change almost immediately. She dieted until she was a slim, attractive size. She now had money to afford a decent apartment on Lyon Street in San Francisco. She decorated it to suit the image she had dreamed and cultivated for herself: velvet and satin on her bed, lace and silk on her windows. One wall was covered with the series of posters a photographer friend had created for her. Among them was Janis nude with her chest and belly covered with strings of glittering beads. One breast was bare. Her hair streamed down and covered most of her face. She could not get beyond being embarrassed and ashamed of her scarred, lumpy complexion.

Still, at twenty-four, she had achieved a certain peace within herself. She had a dog named George and a friend named Linda, who shared the apartment. Janis radiated a regal aura. She was never going to be a beauty, but she was perfect for the time of acceptance that was dawning across the United States.

She went home at Christmas to visit her family and show herself off to those who had doubted she would ever become anything more than a drunken wreck. She "partied hearty" in Beaumont and saw her old friends, most for the last time. Unfortunately, Janis partied a little too much with one special someone. When she returned to California, she learned she was pregnant.

She endured a gruesome experience at an abortion clinic in Mexico. The moral sin of what she had done bothered her more than the physical damage it did to her body. The abortion left her hardened in a way she had never been. She withdrew into a protective shell. According to her companions and associates, Janis felt more isolated than ever, more set apart, more without friends.

On February 17, 1968, Janis Joplin, accompanied by Big Brother, was booked for the Anderson on Second Avenue in New York City.

The Big Time, baby!

She looked at herself in the mirror and worried that she looked old at twenty-five. As a palliative to her terror and her self-criticism, she had always carried her bottle of Southern Comfort. The two had come a long way together.

"I ain't so sure we're ready for New York," had been her expressed doubt all day long. Big Brother was beginning to feel the same way. Terrified at this ultimate step they had never dreamed of taking, the group could only worry and fret. Janis stared at herself in her tight satin pants and worried that she might be getting fat.

And they were the headliners.

They were tight-lipped and quaking when John Cooke stalked in. "Okay! Let's go!"

Obedient to the voice of authority, they took their places. The equipment men fooled with the amplifiers and then melted back into the wings. Janis walked out to stand motionless before the mike. She crouched slightly as if digging down deep for the sound she wanted.

Then her powerful voice erupted out of her throat. The entire theater blazed with light. She forced them back in their seats and drove the breath from their bodies in one violent gasp. "Catch Me, Daddy!" and Big Brother opened up behind her with an unearthly inferno of ear-blasting sound and whirling colored lights.

Janis! At her best. As she had never been before or would ever be again. Her violent movements, the incredible range of her voice, her passion—all transmitted itself to the audience above and beyond the scream of Big Brother's instruments.

The next song was a shocker, a complete transformation to display her amazing versatility—"Summertime," American classic opera, George and Ira Gershwin's tribute to black music. Janis's voice yearned for the summer "when the livin' is easy."

Between songs Janis rested, sweating with effort, her heart thudding against her ribs, but smiling, smiling because she was the happiest person on earth to be received with so much adulation, so much pandemonium.

The audience wouldn't stop applauding through four encores. For the last, she gave them her signature tune, first performed in Monterey—that might have been a lifetime or only a few minutes ago. She gave them Big Mama Thornton's "Love Is Like a Ball 'n' Chain."

At the end, as she backed away from the mike into the darkness of the wings, the audience simply stared, stunned. Then they erupted. Not a one doubted that they were lucky to have heard her. And for all their lives they would remember Janis Joplin.

The *New York Times* gave her a rave review. The *Village Voice* ran out of adjectives. Big Brother and Janis herself were caught completely unprepared. They had no press kits, no pictures to hand out for autographs, no t-shirts, not even programs. None of the accessories of a star-driven concert had ever been needed before. The performance had not even been recorded.

The next night, they managed a press party and invited everyone who might conceivably be interested to a Village restaurant called Piraeus, My Love. The place was absolutely jammed. Excitement and speculation ran high. Then it ceased abruptly. Albert Grossman appeared at the door towing like a captive whale Clive Davis, president of Columbia Records.

Their lives were about to change significantly forever.

March 8 they opened at the Fillmore East. Columbia Records wanted to record a live performance, but the audience and the performers were completely out of hand. So excited they could hardly stand, Big Brother was unprepared for what they had generated. Janis was beside herself.

OUTRAGEOUS!

Beads, rings, satins, sequins, her hair wild beyond imagination, she met the press. And they were hers!

Absolutely crazy with enthusiasm for this new Texas sensation, the press listened and recorded as she talked. She gave them everything she had to give and more. Always glib, she drew on her excellent liberal education, mostly acquired from reading since she was a child. Her sentences poured out, filled with big words, big ideas, big dreams, and high hopes. The "lady wizard with words" occasionally dropped a four-letter expletive that delighted them at the same time it slightly shocked them. They must have blinked twice when she would occasionally wet her throat from a handy bottle of syrupy Southern Comfort—and then laugh. While they were blinking, they wrote it all down and urged her to say more.

And the photographers kept taking pictures. The flashbulbs kept popping. For the ugly, despised teenager from Port Arthur and the University of Texas, that night was the closest thing to heaven she could have imagined in her wildest dreams. She had opportunities to pose for *Glamour* and *Vogue*.

Famous photographer Richard Avedon loved her, loved her face. Janis wrote her sister, "I guess I must be happy!"

She also wrote of planning to a buy a house and asked her sister to look for one within the $100,000 to $200,000 range. Her hopes seemed high for a triumphant return to Port Arthur and perhaps a retreat to normalcy. That would be in her future, she promised herself. For now she was enjoying her place on the pinnacle of success.

At the same time, Big Brother was drawing criticism that wasn't lost on Janis even though she had scarcely heard the band. They had always been a performance group, given to individual riffs and flourishes. To play well had never been their goal, even if they had possessed the background and training to do so. No one was a leader or a disciplinarian. They were not known to rehearse exhaustively. Their lapses were acceptable, even laughed about, if they were noted at all.

Janis's style was a frenzy of movement. She swayed, she crouched, she tossed her hair, she rocked her hips. She clutched the microphone as if it might fly out of her hand. She gyrated and howled into it, bare inches from her mouth. She exhorted her audiences to hysterical frenzy. They danced on the seats, they screamed and whooped, they jumped for the stage and had to be dragged back by the guards.

Nothing like her had ever happened. She was a superstar before she had ever recorded anything that could be called a record.

While *Time* was referring to her as "probably the most powerful singer to emerge from the white rock movement," and the *New York Times* called her "in contact with an overwhelming life force," Big Brother was left as mere background noise.

And now a recording was inevitable, immediate; it would save everything for posterity. Big Brother was unequal to the task. Their imprecise rhythms, their poorly tuned instruments, their lack of technical proficiency were all obvious. And bad.

Moreover, everyone intimate with the band and involved in the recording knew that what created Janis Joplin's kinetic energy were the drugs and the alcohol she ingested hourly, before and during the performance. What would she sound like in a recording studio with Big Brother's sound playing in earphones clamped to her head? How would she produce a fabulous performance cold sober without the colors, the noise, and the adulation to drive her?

A live recording seemed the only solution. The producer in charge of making it remarked that he couldn't see Janis, much less the band, as a recording artist at all. He maintained that records were made by "studied" music that could be recorded layer by layer, mixed, re-recorded, blended, sounds added and deleted, and, finally, turned into a sound to be played over and over and enjoyed. He called what Janis did "tribal music." When he tried to record it in concert and brought the tapes back to play for Albert Grossman, nobody was pleased.

By the summer of 1968, lack of confidence had driven Janis into a deep depression. When she wasn't sunk in misery and self-doubt, she exploded in frenzied shrieking and cursing at everyone who came near her. People walked around her and stayed out of her way. At the same time, she faced her own lack of skills with some sort of philosophical resignation.

"Well, man," she wrote her sister, "this can't last forever."

But when Columbia finally put together her album, the mixer was amazed to discover he was wrong. From over one hundred tapes of her concerts with Big Brother—more than two hundred reels—he discovered her screams, her wails, her moans, her hollers were at the same places over and over in the course of the performances. She was "on top of her music." At least for her, nothing was "tribal"; everything was "studied."

Moreover, Janis went with him into the booth and listened and critiqued from two in the afternoon to seven in the morning. He said he had never known an artist to work harder or with more intensity. She was "twenty times more serious" than any of the three men who comprised Big Brother. And she wasn't satisfied.

When she finally had to "let it go," she wanted to call her first important recording *Sex, Drugs, and Cheap Thrills.*

When Columbia flatly refused, she reluctantly altered the title. Her first major record became *Cheap Thrills.*

From that point, Janis's life seemed to shift out of her hands. If she had ever had control, she would never regain it.

In August the concert billing changed abruptly: "Janis Joplin *with* Big Brother and the Holding Company" went to the Newport Folk Festival where *Cheap Thrills* was released. The reviews were mercifully "mixed." Most of them maintained that Janis was great; the band "stinks." In September Grossman announced they would no longer be accompanying her.

Big Brother had been informed before the public announcement. That they'd known it was coming didn't make it less hurtful. They'd been with Janis for over two years. They'd seen her grow and become a star. Unfortunately, they'd had neither the will nor the skills to grow with her.

Perhaps reflecting her own pain suffered over and over from being rejected by friends and classmates, Janis suffered more than the band did. They were merely sad. She sought solace in her ever-present Southern Comfort and less frequently in smack. At about the same time, she persuaded the distillery in Louisville, Kentucky, to buy her a lynx coat. She told friends that she should get something for boosting Southern Comfort sales all over the country. Later Janis boasted, "What a hustle! Can you imagine? Getting paid for passing out for two years."

On December 1, 1968, Janis's relationship with Big Brother officially ended. Her behavior became more and more outrageous and dangerous. After concerts she'd accept invitations to go to the homes of strangers to "party-party" with heroin users. In most American cities, young people enjoyed their highs, drawing at least some of the pleasure from being part of an outlaw culture. "Never trust anyone over thirty" was their mantra as they revolted against their parents' values.

The friends who went to these parties with Janis, to protect her from what could prove to be dangerous escapades, would find her in some "private" room shooting up "God knows what" and sloshing Southern Comfort down her throat. With these same friends, she would fake illnesses, voice problems, sore throats, any number of diseases to get amphetamines to pep her up when heroine and alcohol dragged her down.

At the same time, Albert Grossman had managed to pull a band together for her. She insisted that they call themselves Kozmic Blues. The spelling was her idea. She wrote a song about them. Despite the drugs and booze, her brilliant mind and extraordinary talents were still carrying her forward.

At about the same time, Janis bought herself a Porsche. In keeping with the mood of the country embroiled in Viet Nam, she had a bloodied American flag decaled on one fender. She had a picture of Big Brother put on the other.

Ironically, she wrote her most famous song mentioning that car, a fairy-tale list of middle-class yearnings to be lifted into the company of the wealthy elite: "Oh, Lord, won't you buy me a Mercedes-Benz? / My friends all drive Porsches. I must make amends."

When Albert arranged a February 9 preview concert of Kozmic Blues at Fillmore East in New York City, reaction among the members of the press was mixed. Newspaper reviewers that had once been filled with admiration for her were now cool or simply disappointed.

Her reputation and what appeared to be her psychic meltdown were drawing national attention. As if Janis were a lightning rod, CBS TV had come uninvited to interview and film her for *60 Minutes*. Ambushed by Mike Wallace, Janis did not appear at her best. He had no intention of helping her since she had told him to just say "fuck" if she got out of line. The only saving grace of the entire fiasco was that the crew was not allowed to photograph the live performance.

In the middle of March, *Rolling Stone* did a cover story that said it all: "Janis: The Judy Garland of Rock," alluding to Garland's well-known struggles against addictions and their subsequent destruction of her career in films, on television, and on stage. Though Judy was more than twenty years older than Janis, many recognized the title as a frightening prophecy.

Ignoring any problems with his singer—and determined to make her pay for the time and effort he had invested in her—Albert arranged for her to appear on the *Ed Sullivan Show*. Sullivan, an American icon, was famous for introducing new talent, including Elvis Presley, to the same middle American audience that Janis had come from. She was no longer a mere concert performer; she belonged to an audience of millions.

Before she could realize fully appreciate what was happening to her, Albert booked April and May for a European Tour—Stockholm, Amsterdam, Copenhagen, Paris, London, Frankfurt. The Kozmic Blues had finally found their music—London in particular adored Janis—and the tour was brilliant. The Frankfurt concert was filmed. Wherever she went, the "white American blues singer" drew rave reviews.

And then her own strange quirks came close to destroying her. Direct from the stage of London's Albert Hall, she "shot up some junk." Who knew what it might have been. A guest at the same party went into a coma. The whole thing was enough to frighten Janis straight and sober for a time. More horrible news came in the following bulletin: "June 22, 1969, Judy Garland was found dead in London. An autopsy revealed 4.9 milligrams of Seconal in her bloodstream."

The deaths of people she knew or had heard about brought Janis to her senses at least momentarily. She vacillated between trying to control her addictions and shrugging helplessly while giving in to them. As an intelligent person, she could not help knowing what they would do to her eventually. On the other hand, her successful career made the unrestrained life so sweet. She didn't try very hard.

Returning in triumph, Janis enjoyed a whirlwind summer and fall. Her concerts generated enormous amounts of money for her bank account. She made a successful appearance on *The Dick Cavett Show*. She sang a duet with Little Richard at the Atlantic City Pop Festival. (Imagine being on the stage with that wild man and managing to upstage him.) In November she appeared onstage with the Rolling Stones (famous for their lack of control), Ike Turner, and the queen of wild performances, Ike's wife Tina. Janis even sang a duet with Tina but had no memory of the event. She was so stoned, so drunk, so out of control.

At that time, at Albert's insistence, Janis went to an endocrinologist. Though the doctor tried to help her, Janis spent the visit denying everything, protesting that she couldn't see why everyone was worried about her, playing games with him to shock, to control, to test him—anything and everything to turn the conversation away from herself and throw it back on him. She gave a performance in front of the doctor, talking about "balling" men and "shooting up" and drinking. But with each story, she'd back away from him if he tried to suggest that she look at herself. She was flippant about all the serious habits, not wanting to take them out and look at them honestly. She insisted time and again, even as she walked out of his office forever, that nothing could be done for her. Only she could and would make it all beautiful.

Changes in her music were Janis's attempt to do just that. She had left folk music as well as the shouting, screaming rock behind. She wanted to be known and remembered as a serious singer of that most American of sounds—the blues. Rather than adapt old material, she was writing her own with the help of Gabriel Mekler, who remembered, "God! Did she ever want to sing rather than just scream it out." Their song "Kozmic

Blues" exemplified what she continued to feel about herself: "They ain't never gonna love you any better, babe. . . . So you better dig it right now, right now."

She also seemed bent, at least at times, on changing her lifestyle. Janis was aware of the problems she was developing with drugs and alcohol. She became more serious—except when she was driving around in her crazy Porsche. Then she wore her silks and velvets, her gold shoes, her feathers, her flowers, her beads, and her bangles. "Do you think they really love me?" she asked Gabriel over and over as she drew the attention of fans. "Do you think they really love me?"

As she herself was finding out, it wasn't easy living up to Janis Joplin.

While Janis was in New York for a concert in Madison Square Garden in December 1969, the papers linked her romantically with "Broadway" Joe Namath, arguably the most famous football player in America. The quarterback had taken his New York Jets team to victory over the highly favored Baltimore Colts in Super Bowl III. That win in itself was a miracle, but America was still talking about how the cocky so-and-so had predicted that he'd make it happen.

Whether Janis and Joe ever hit it off or even met will never be known. The fact that they were supposedly an "item" announced her rising status as an American icon also.

At the beginning of 1970, Kozmic Blues disbanded. Professional musicians all, they felt no particular attachment to the group.

Back in California, Janis bought a house that she called Larkspur. It was supposed to be her haven where she would find ways to return to sanity and peace. Unfortunately, she could no longer control her impulses. Janis could not sit still. She would jump up and drive like crazy to a supermarket. Then, with a supply of groceries, she would whiz all over Marin County searching for things to do. Even her body was not her own. It would not cooperate with her desire for peace.

In February Janis went to Brazil for Carnival. It was the first vacation she had ever had, and she was determined to make it spectacular. She took a large apartment with a glassed-in porch that faced the beach. She had left her dope behind, and she with a woman friend splashed in the Atlantic in the mornings. They enjoyed the strolling samba bands in the afternoon and went to the Municipal Ball. If this was the life that money provided, Janis knew she wanted more of it.

For a few weeks, she was free from the drugs and the alcohol and, above all, the pressure of constantly being Janis Joplin. She told people that she had asked Albert how long she needed to work to have enough money to live on. He reportedly told her two more years. Whether that conversation ever took place was a question in the minds of those who knew her. The agent, who had come to love his creation like a daughter, never gave her secrets away.

In April they put together a new band, Full-Tilt Boogie, and John Cooke came back to be their road manager. Around the same time, Kris Kristofferson, fellow Texan from Brownsville, blew into town and into Janis's house. Previously, he had composed the song that became one of her big hits: "Me and Bobby McGee." Kris claims he never intended to move in, but Janis was good at fixing piña coladas for breakfast. Under her influence, he was seduced to stay for longer than he intended.

Her friends noticed that Kris didn't protest too much. In fact, they believed that her "keeping" him was just a symbol to add to her myth of carnality. They both liked each other well enough, but it wasn't love, nor was it permanent. Kris left just before her concerts were scheduled to start in May.

His presence had been a hiatus, a time when her life somehow approached normalcy, except for the drinking. When he left, Janis returned to her old mode. The drinks and the drugs were always in the house, always on her mind, never far out of her reach.

Unfortunately for her self-esteem, after a five-month hiatus from the concert trail, Janis returned to half-filled halls. Proving herself a trouper, she gave the scattered audiences her very best, although it hurt her badly. She was used to singing to screaming, exploding crowds who were dancing in the aisles, climbing onto their chairs. The present audiences were more polite—probably because they felt slightly uncomfortable for having bought the tickets when their friends had not.

Janis became almost paranoid that Albert was going to desert her. She sent him a telegram begging him to care about her as much as he cared about his other acts. She didn't understand that he loved her. She didn't feel confident that anyone loved her.

Her confidence was shaken to the roots when she appeared on *The Dick Cavett Show* June 25, 1970. Douglas Fairbanks Jr. was also a guest. She wondered aloud whether it was a show with a has-been theme. When Cavett asked Fairbanks why he quit his successful film career, he shrugged and said he had quit while his career was going well—at the top of his game. He didn't want to wait until someone asked him, "Why don't you quit?"

Janis's performance of "Get It While You Can" reflected her lack of confidence and her unhappiness. At twenty-seven she was a has-been. Clearly upset, Janis later asked one of her friends, "Will you tell me when I get far enough ahead, so I can quit?"

In July Albert arranged for Janis and Full-Tilt Boogie to tour Canada on a special Festival Train. The Grateful Dead went along, as well as other groups. The audiences that greeted her and the rest of the entertainers were very receptive but small. At the same time, *Newsweek* published an article about the declining festival phenomenon.

Janis read it and became more upset. On at least one occasion, the festival promoters cancelled the performances because they hadn't sold enough tickets, although there were thousands of kids sitting up on the hill above the arena and the stage. The White Panthers, a professional protest group, had sent letters to all the households in the area saying that folk music should be free or not performed at all. When the promoters cancelled the performances because of low sales, of course, they did not pay the performers.

Stories blossomed in the press that kids were vandalizing the grounds, urinating and defecating in the grass outside and inside, smoking pot, and dropping acid. Cocaine addicts, called "Cokeheads," were supporting their own habits by frequenting the venues and selling some of their wares cut with corn starch. Other festivals simply disappeared. Parents refused to allow their kids to go to rock concerts.

When the train arrived in Vancouver, Janis invited Full-Tilt Boogie to her home in San Francisco. From there they flew to Hawaii, drinking all the way. Even John Cooke got crocked, an unusual occurrence for the Englishman. They were all leaning on each other when they arrived, too drunk to stand on their own. Because of his own happy condition, John had a hell of a time herding the group into the hotel and keeping them from getting kicked out again before the concert. The seven thousand people who attended got their money's worth, and the *Honolulu Advertiser* proclaimed the show "Dazzling Delirium."

From there Janis flew to Austin for Ken Threadgill's birthday party. Announcing she had left her band in Hawaii, she nevertheless sang "Me and Bobby McGee" and "Sunday Morning Coming Down." She had not forgotten how Ken Threadgill had been her friend through her aborted college days. By the end of her part of the program, the old friendly, happy Janis seemed to reappear. She felt good being among friendly people who loved her. She presented the honoree with a wreath of flowers. "I brought the one thing I knew he'd like from Hawaii. A good lei."

The crowd laughed approvingly.

Ken Threadgill mourned her sincerely after her death, which he maintained was due to alcohol. He "knew" that she never took "to no drugs."

Still problems continued to occur with her performances and appearances. She was becoming virtually uncontrolled and uncontrollable. Even John Cooke could not rein her in sometimes. She was in the depths of depression when she showed everyone a newspaper story about how she had contributed to a tombstone for blues singer Bessie Smith.

To the relief of her friends and her band, Janis went home to Port Arthur August 13 for her high school class reunion. Because she was an international celebrity, a local television station filmed parts of her appearance at the party. It was later used in a documentary made of her life. Though she was drinking moderately, many of her classmates later told stories about her behavior and maintained that she was drunk out of her mind and doped as well. Amid a pretense of pleasant greetings, many made cruel remarks that hurt her because she wasn't drunk enough to blow them off. "She was a pig in high school," one woman said rather loudly. "She's still a pig."

The Port Arthur Police Department had assigned a special squad to the reunion in the hopes they could draw a splash of publicity by "busting her" for being drunk and disorderly. Her behavior was generally irreproachable, but the lies went out— a testament to how much her hometown hated her for doing what none of them would ever do.

She had set herself a goal and reached it. She had become rich and famous.

When she returned to the West Coast to her home, she had a new will drawn requiring that her ashes be strewn over California soil. Never would she return to Texas.

Janis needed a new record desperately. She had not made one since *Kozmic Blues* in 1969. In September Janis, Full-Tilt Boogie, and John Cooke went to the Landmark Hotel in Los Angeles, where she threw herself into recording sessions with her usual energy mixed with self-doubt. The title *Pearl* was already decided. On it were two songs composed and recorded by Janis for the first time: "Down on Me" and "Get It While You Can."

On October 1, 1970, Janis recorded, almost as an afterthought, the song most associated with her, her own composition "Mercedes-Benz."

On October 3, she listened to the final tracks with her usual attention to detail and declared that they sounded good.

On October 4, John Cooke escorted her to her room in the Landmark Hotel and left her at about 1:40 a.m. He closed the door and walked away.

Inside the room, Janis took possibly two steps and fell face down. When Cooke found her the next morning, her nose was broken. She had made no attempt to save herself. She had died before she hit the floor from an overdose of heroine and alcohol—smack and Southern Comfort.

In retrospect:

- *Pearl* debuted at Number One on the charts.
- *The Rose*, based loosely on Janis's life, was released in 1979. It starred Bette Midler, who was nominated for an Academy Award for her performance that captured Janis's relentless descent into self-destruction.
- A bust of Janis is displayed in the Port Arthur Public Library.
- Recently the Museum of the Gulf Coast in her hometown has added an installation including some of her paintings and a Porsche identical to Janis's original in the Rock and Roll Museum in Ohio. The town that never accepted her in her life, now trades on the memories of her celebrity.

"YOU MUST REMEMBER WHEN SHE SHOT HER HUSBAND!"

Divorces in Texas generally tend to be civilized—that is, as civilized as any other dispute that triggers some of the strongest, most violent emotions to be found in human relationships. Truth to tell, some are less civilized than others, some are rancorous, and then occasionally, one partner or the other will push the wrong button, and mayhem and murder erupt.

When those divorces occur, either the last man or woman standing needs a lawyer.

Such a lawyer is Richard "Racehorse" Haynes, whose nickname originated with his football coach at a Texas high school. (Who else but his coach would have given it to him?) He kept the name and adopted it as part of his persona—fast, sleek, and able to go the distance. He served in World War II as an army paratrooper and was decorated for action on Iwo Jima. Always a daredevil, Racehorse has always been absolutely fearless and not necessarily a model citizen. Besides riding his motorcycle through a motel lobby, he once talked his way out of a drunk-driving ticket by doing a back flip off the bumper of his Porsche.

Since the inception of his practice, he has schooled himself to be a splendid actor who can and will summon a wealth of different emotions on cue. He likes to say that "he owes everything to clean living and constant prayer."

For most of his professional life, Haynes has circulated the rumor that he has performed the ultimate lawyer trick (a legend rather than a witnessed fact). He claims to have paid a doctor to give him a shot in his hand. Then at a strategic moment in his argument when he was maintaining vociferously that it wouldn't hurt much to be nailed to a tree, he dragged out a hammer and a nail, slapped his hand down, and nailed himself to the table.

Law students talked about the "crucifixion case" forever, although none knew anyone who had actually seen him do it.

When closely questioned, Haynes will reluctantly admit with a smile, "I have always regretted that my case was so strong I was able to win without doing that."

As part of his permanent ego trip, Racehorse has spread the story that with enough time and money, he could win any lawsuit, anywhere. He maintains that if Richard Nixon had hired him, the disgraced president would have left office at the end of his term rather than being forced to resign. Haynes further states that since reasonable doubt exists in all things human, he could have gotten Hitler off on a reduced charge of malicious mischief. Of course, Haynes laughs when he makes these outrageous statements, but the underlying steel in his expression makes one wonder.

Racehorse has now passed his eightieth birthday but still practices law in Houston. Because of his emeritus position today, he chooses his cases, though to do so is not exactly a new practice for him; Haynes has been very selective almost from the beginning of his career.

When Haynes made the list of ten best criminal defense lawyers in Texas, a reporter asked him, "Do you agree with their estimation?"

Racehorse replied straight-faced, "I believe I am." Then he smiled slightly. "I wonder why you restrict it to Texas."

He loves to tell the story of the first felony case he ever won. It was an acquittal for a poor black man. His fee was $300, but when the words "not guilty" were spoken, "ol' Jesse was hugging me, his big fat wife was hugging me, his eight kids were hugging me, his relatives were slapping me on the back and saying thanks for saving Jesse and inviting me home to dinner. You don't get that feeling winning money from an insurance company."

Haynes' ability to turn a jury to his way of thinking was never more apparent than at the child custody trial of Vickie Daniel, who had just fatally shot her husband. The former Dairy Queen waitress had summoned the police to the scene. She readily admitted to the crime, although she protested she had not meant to kill him on the night of January 19, 1981.

From the outset Vickie repeated her statement. By accident, as she shot her husband twice with a .22 bolt-action rifle, one of the bullets traveled upward into his abdomen where it nicked his aorta. Price Daniel Jr.—scion of a former Texas governor and lineal descendant of General Sam Houston, victor of San Jacinto, first president of the Republic of Texas, and likewise its first governor—bled to death on the floor of their home in Liberty.

The custody trial for the couple's two children began within a month. Bringing suit to secure for the Daniel family was Price's only sister, Jean Daniel Murph, whom his will named as executrix. She had been given power over the million-dollar estate, which was to be used for the couple's children (two with Vickie as well as Vickie's child by a previous marriage adopted by Price). No provision was made for Vickie, and her share of the estate would have been a negligible amount since they had lived in Price's home.

The prosecution thought that proving the defendant an unfit mother and taking her children away legally would make the murder trial itself a "slam dunk." The defense believed it to be a golden opportunity to win outright or at least to practice the winning argument before a jury of the townsfolk.

Racehorse Haynes, observing the proceedings from Houston, only 50 miles away, probably smiled like a hungry predator. He loved a trial where "everybody knew" the defendant was guilty as sin. In such a case only a few years before, he had proved that what everybody knew counted for "nothing" in a court of law. Always plead the alternative.

Before an American Bar Association seminar in New York City, Haynes revealed how a good defense lawyer went about doing that:

> Say you sue me because you say my dog bit you. Well, now this is my defense: My dog doesn't bite. And second, in the alternative, my dog was tied up that night. And third, I don't believe you really got bit. And fourth, I don't have a dog.

Racehorse, with the astounding nerve of a practiced "ambulance chaser," appeared and took the Daniel case out of the hands of Andrew Lannie of Baytown, whose practice was comfortably over the Liberty County line. Vickie had hired Lannie to sue Price for divorce on December 31, 1980.

Happy New Year!

When Racehorse "offered" the "black" widow his services, Lannie could do little but grit his teeth, smile, and agree to give up the most important case that was ever likely to come his way.

The court expected to handle the custody case in an afternoon. With Racehorse Haynes running the show, however, "the expected" went right out the window. He immediately called a press conference and assumed his patented "shocked demeanor" for the reporters and photographers. It was his standard ploy. Speaking slowly and clearly, he waited for them to record every word for the jury, all of whom read Houston newspapers and watched Houston television stations.

"I don't know what happened to the presumption of innocence," he complained sadly. "Just because someone has been charged with a crime, including murder, does not rob that individual of all their treasures, including children."

The reporters stirred and muttered eagerly. This was great stuff.

His voice deepened as he drew his rather short frame to its full height and foretold his summation speech. "Take heart. Every time I drive into town I see its name—and it is Liberty!"

Every single reporter got the "sound bite," the flashbulbs exploded, and another Texas star was added to Haynes' already illustrious crown.

His most famous victory had been the 1976 acquittal of T. Cullen Davis, to be discussed later in the chapter. Davis was, at that time, the richest man ever tried for murder in Texas. That trial took place in big Cowtown Fort Worth. This trial was in a small Texas town, defending a very ordinary and certainly guilty waitress. Yet with Racehorse at the helm, Texas and the nation turned from their football games to watch the show.

Because the famous defense lawyer was by this time a millionaire several times over, he gallantly reduced the amount of his $250-per-hour fee. Oh, he expected to be paid, but Vickie's funds were tied up at this point in probate court. The generosity gained him sympathy in the press and with the eager public, where he was not especially popular. The business of setting guilty rich people free does tend to offend people's moral sensitivities, especially when they hear about courtroom shenanigans.

Racehorse could live with a less than lily-white image. When all is said and done, the business of the defense attorney is not to win popularity contests. It is to win the hearts and minds of the jury, to create reasonable doubt.

The facts in evidence were these:

The call had come in to the Liberty Fire Department from a sheriff's deputy at 7:30 p.m. An ambulance was needed at the Daniel home on Governor Road. In the background the emergency medical technician (EMT) heard a woman's voice yell, "Price, get up!"

Ten minutes later the ambulance arrived at the scene. Vickie Daniel met the men at the door. She pointed. "He's back there."

They found Price sprawled face down next to the pantry, a few feet from the door to the carport. When they turned him over, his face was ashen. Blood bubbled out of his mouth and nose, but a check by both techs for vital signs discovered neither pulse nor breathing.

His wife called from the hallway, "He's okay, isn't he?"

While one tech called for the coroner and the sheriff, the other started to tell her that the man was dead. To their shock, Vickie attacked them both with her fingernails—scratching, screaming, spitting furiously. All three went down in a struggling heap. The techs were genuinely afraid they wouldn't be able to restrain her before she hurt them or caused them to hurt her.

When the first lawman arrived shortly thereafter, Vickie was still out of control. She fought like a madwoman, screaming and finally muttering gibberish. She was like a woman possessed.

While the EMTs struggled, the wail of sirens disturbed the local school board meeting. Bill Buchanan, owner of KPXE Radio, considered himself an investigative reporter. Leaving the meeting, he followed the police to the Daniel house. Price was a friend of his, so he followed the police into the house in violation of every principle of crime scene investigation.

While Vickie lay growling and moaning on the floor restrained by three EMTs, Buchanan asked, "Where's Price?"

One of them gave a jerk of his head, indicating the next room, and Vickie screamed, "Go help Price! Leave me alone! *Go help Price!*"

Buchanan hurried into the crime scene, eager to help with the investigation. Both policemen were searching the darkened area by the staircase. A .22 bolt-action rifle with two casings ejected lay in the middle of the floor in plain sight. The bolt was in the extract position, ready to lever another shell into the chamber.

The policemen called for him to come and help them. He turned and stepped on one of the shell casings with his heel, crushing it and moving it out of position. Dimly realizing what he'd done, Buchanan nevertheless reached down and used his finger to moved the casing back to its approximate place.

When a nurse arrived, Vickie was chewing on one of the EMT's clothes in an effort to get at his knee. It took all four of them to strap her to a gurney to transport her to the hospital.

In the meantime Price's brother Houston, who also lived in Liberty County, had received a telephone call that something was going on at his brother's house. He arrived with his wife, Charlotte. They too entered the house and went upstairs to look after the children who were screaming and crying, but Houston swiftly came back downstairs and began to poke around the house. Finally, he went into the kitchen. Until that moment he did not know that his brother was dead.

He hastily retreated up the stairs where the police heard thudding and assumed that Houston was pounding on the wall in anger and frustration. No one investigated.

By the time Sheriff Buck Eckols arrived, Vickie had been wheeled away. In the house at that time were friends, relatives, neighbors, and other townspeople who had heard the noise and confusion and were simply curious. Unauthorized people picked up and moved objects that might or might not be important to the case, and more and more members of the press as well as onlookers tramped through. Only tardily, as if he suddenly realized the potential damage, did Eckols give the call that the crime scene should be preserved.

At 7:30 a.m. the Harris County medical examiner reported that Price had been shot once in the stomach. The bullet in and of itself was not life threatening, but it had nicked the aorta. The victim had died with fifteen minutes. The coroner also found bruises and scratches on the body similar to those found on people who had been in fights. No drugs were found in his system. His blood revealed only .03 percent alcohol content, normal for someone who had had one drink. Daniel was healthy except for a dozen kidney stones and blackening of the lungs associated with heavy smoking. Since identification was agreed upon, the examiner concluded his report without taking fingerprints.

Immediately, the good citizens of Liberty split over what Vickie's fate, as well as the fate of the children, should be. Hearing their views discussed and argued over and over, Racehorse became more and more certain that Vickie was going to walk away a free woman with her deceased husband's children, his possessions, and his money. The people discussing the case at every street corner, drug store, café, and the post office were the jury pool. Reasonable doubt was everywhere.

The jury selection was a problem for the prosecution from the get-go. The idea that an aunt—even Price's sister, with the support of his grandmother, grandfather, and brothers—should have custody of a woman's children—an innocent-until-proven-guilty woman—did not sit well with the conservative members of the town. Besides, Jean Murph was an outsider from New Orleans, representing high social station, wealth, and political power. Vickie, the little Dairy Queen waitress, was "one of their own."

Even though Price Daniel had been coming down the stairs with a bag in his hand, ready to leave the house, who could say what he might have done before he left? He might have set the bag down and attacked her. Vickie herself had called the EMTs to the scene. Obviously, she had not "felt" guilty.

Likewise, the prosecution had not done its homework. Expecting a "slam dunk," they had hired a psychiatrist who testified under oath that the defendant suffered from "histrionic personality disorder." Did that mean that she was insane? Could she be considered guilty if she wasn't responsible? While the jury did not really understand what that problem might entail, Racehorse's clever questions forced the man to admit that "Vickie Daniel's children" were not in danger from her.

Oh, well.

The Liberty Police Department had never dealt with a high-profile crime before. They had scarcely dealt with any crimes except those committed on weekends by people who got a little out of hand with their celebrating. Consequently, their handling of the crime scene was unbelievably crude.

In the final days of the trial, Racehorse, totally versed in the Houston Police Department's far-superior crime lab and crime scene investigation techniques, delivered a primer in all the things that the Liberty Sheriff's Department had done wrong or—worse—simply failed to do.

1. The house had not been properly sealed after the shooting; thus, no one could know how much damage and dislocation of property had been done during the fight between Vickie and Price *or* how much had been done by the careless investigators and others such as Bill Buchanan, who had no genuine authority to be on the premises.
2. No fingerprints had been taken from items around the house.
3. No log was kept of when photographs were taken, so no chronology of events could be constructed, and the photographs were not labeled and categorized. Therefore, they could easily represent the photographer's bias against Vickie and for Price, especially since there was an unbalanced number of photographs—several of certain subjects, those that might incriminate Vickie, and only one of others. Where were the pictures

of the fifty bottles of liquor Price Daniel had in his house? Evidence of ashtrays had been discarded without photographs; therefore, no substantiation for marijuana use could be proved or disproved.

4. The cars had not been thoroughly searched, and no official reports of their contents had been filed.
5. The ejection location of the two shell casings had not been recorded—and one had been crushed and admittedly handled by Bill Buchanan, who had changed its location.
6. Price's torn jacket might not have been torn by Vickie but perhaps have been caught in the hinge of the folding staircase. No proof existed either way.
7. But the worst of all, the lapse that set the town back on its heels, came in a shame-faced admission from the coroner. Unbelievably, no fingerprints had been taken of the dead man's hands. And now Price Daniel was buried without *ever* having been fingerprinted in his life. No proof could be obtained that he had ever, as Vickie claimed, grabbed the gun and tried to pull it away. Furthermore, there was no proof that he had not because the gun also had been handled incorrectly.

While the citizens of Liberty listened in amazement, and whispered ominously among themselves to this recital of the shortcomings of their own embarrassed officials, said officials cringed, twisted in their seats, turned red, and generally behaved as if they were what Racehorse had proved them to be—a bunch of rubes, incompetent to handle even a minor infraction of the law, much less a major homicide.

The big city lawyer had come to town and made them all look like fools—and they had absolutely no defense. The manuals for crime scene investigation were in their desk drawers, but they had either never been read, or they had been ignored for the very reason Racehorse Haynes had accused them: they had gone into the crime scene with their minds made up about Vickie's guilt. Their preconceptions allowed them to ignore important data and overemphasize objects that may have had no bearing on the case.

Even testimony by Vickie's ex-husband that she was given to screaming attacks when she became frustrated was negated when the man explained that he just held her down until she calmed down and then she was fine. To demonstrate how Vickie's ex might have done so, the irrepressible Racehorse instructed the ex-husband to restrain him while he rolled around the courtroom floor in his $1,000 suit, giving the jury a good laugh.

In short, every argument that might have found Vickie Daniel guilty was aired and refuted by the defense. Everyone was entertained, but one of Price Daniel Sr.'s ex-partners criticized the prosecution severely for letting the custody suit precede the murder trial. "It's just plain dumb. They're givin' away the goldang store."

If the coffin had needed a final nail, it was pounded in when Jean Murph went to pick the children up at Vickie's sister's home in Beach City outside Baytown. Vickie was there, as were the cameramen and reporters from KTRK and KPRC, although they maintained they were independent and uninvited.

When Jean came up the walk, the boys yelled from the door that they didn't want to go. They sobbed and held onto their mother's hair when she carried them outside in full view of the cameras. They screamed as she put them in the car. The whole of the Houston area saw and heard the performance with little Franklin screaming, "I don't want to go, Mama! I don't want to go."

Finally, even the Daniel family themselves were so overwhelmed by the entire fiasco that they began to express doubt and to maintain privately that Vickie was not now and never had been a bad mother. Though the prosecution presented witnesses and bank records and some substantive evidence, Racehorse cast doubt in almost every case.

In the end, the trial took more than six weeks, but jurors deliberated less than an hour and a half to deliver the verdict that Vickie Daniel should retain custody of her children. The jury foreman maintained that the panel could find "no evidence that she was an unfit mother."

Zeke Zbranek, the lead lawyer for the Daniel family, shook his head in dazed surprise. "I truthfully don't understand it. We had our problems back there, sure. But I really thought we'd win it in the end."

In the stated opinion of most townspeople, reporters, and many Houstonians who had followed the trial with avid interest, the prosecution team was "never even in the ballpark on this one."

The murder trial proved to be a waste of time and money. Vickie Daniel waived her right to a jury, testimony of witnesses produced no new information, and the judge ruled her "not guilty" beyond a reasonable doubt. Racehorse Haynes did not bother to participate. His work was done for the time being.

That the Daniel case was a "slam dunk" for the defense was a foregone conclusion in Houston, if not in Liberty. Racehorse had made his reputation in Houston more than a decade earlier by defending another spouse who had come out of rural poverty to marry into a very rich family.

On March 18, 1969, Olive Robinson, wife of oilman Ash Robinson, entered her daughter's bedroom in the mansion on Kirby Drive in the elegant River Oaks district west of downtown Houston.

Joan Robinson Hill was lying in a miasma of vomit and excreta in her bed. Her husband, Dr. John Hill, stood at the foot of her bed. He appeared to be staring impassively rather than trying to help her.

Olive hurried to her daughter's bedside and took her hand. She was burning with fever. She looked back at her son-in-law, who shrugged.

"I think we'd better take her to the hospital, Ma," he said.

Instead of calling an emergency ambulance, Hill insisted on driving his semiconscious wife, not to the world-famous Texas Medical Center, only fifteen minutes away, but to a new suburban hospital with—as it proved—extremely limited facilities. Located miles away in Sharpstown, it was a forty-five-minute drive. He insisted that they were expected.

During the drive, Joan told Olive she was going blind, but John said she was having a "blackout." Olive said he drove like a snail and kept the radio on as high as it would go for the entire time. When they arrived, the nurse took Joan's blood pressure twice. It was so low—60/40—that the woman thought she had made a mistake. Six hours after admission, Joan was perceived to be in septic shock. She was put on dialysis.

When Ash Robinson came to visit her in the evening, Joan was unrecognizable. Her body had swelled as her kidneys had failed. Capillaries had begun to rupture, leaving her skin mottled. Helpless, Ash promised to fill her room with yellow roses the next morning.

Her last words to him were, "I'd like that, Pa."

Later, John Hill came to spend the night at her bedside. A half an hour after midnight, the doctor on call checked her. She seemed stable. Her blood pressure was rising. At 1:30 a.m. the doctor left the small hospital.

An hour later the nurse reported that the patient's vital signs indicated sudden heart failure. The resident brought the cardiac arrest equipment on the run.

Joan raised her head slightly from the pillow. "John!" she begged.

Then a torrent of blood splashed out of her mouth. The resident plunged adrenalin into her heart. Too late! She was dead—a lovely young woman of thirty-eight, who had attended Houston's annual wild game dinner less than a week before.

John Hill did not telephone Ash Robinson. Instead he called mutual friends who came at 5:00 a.m. to find the widower sobbing hysterically. While Jim Oates tried to console him, Dotty walked to the bedside. She was appalled. So ill-prepared and ill-staffed for this type of case was Sharpstown Hospital that Joan's body still lay in a welter of soiled bedclothes. Her own blood and body fluids had been allowed to dry about her.

While Dotty tried as best she could to clean Joan's face, John continued to sob loudly and bemoan the loss of "my beautiful wife" until Jim said sharply, "Knock it off!" All of Houston knew of their ongoing marital troubles. That he had kept a mistress for several years was also well known.

In the middle of the next morning, the three went together to tell Olive and Ash. To their consternation, Jim and Dotty had to do it. John refused to get out of the car.

He need not have been afraid. The couple came back with their task half done. On hearing their news, Olive pleaded with Jim not to wake Ash. "Let him sleep," she sobbed. "This is the last night he ever will."

Thereafter, Ash Robinson became obsessed. He "knew" that John had "murdered" Joan, and he was determined that everyone in town would know. He would have refused to let John ride home from the cemetery with them if John had not forced his way into the car beside Olive. Then John came over to the house with their only grandchild, Robert Ashton "Boot" Hill, as leverage to be accepted back into their company. Furious, Ash sent him packing. Not for anything would he countenance this man in his house. Moreover, the millionaire oilman carried enormous weight in Houston society. John Hill had not counted on the implacability of his dead wife's father.

Within a week, the failure of the little hospital was known to all. No autopsy of any significance had been done on Joan's body. No body fluids had been analyzed. Indeed, the whole body had been drained and all the fluids flushed away.

Sharpstown Hospital listed the cause of death as hepatitis but did not record any symptoms of hepatitis—no sign of jaundice, no elevated levels of bilirubin, and Joan's death within hours was contrary to the course of the disease even in its most acute form.

Not quite three months later, around the first of June, John Hill married his mistress, Ann Kurth. That same month he hired Racehorse Haynes to be his attorney. Marital bliss did not last long as Ann became afraid of her new husband. After much unhappiness and strife between the newlyweds, Hill told Racehorse to file for divorce. The lawyer objected strenuously in the light of autopsy results, charges and countercharges, rumors and innuendoes appearing almost daily in the Houston newspapers. His most reasonable argument was that if Ann Kurth were married to John Hill, she could not testify against him.

But Hill was adamant. He did not seem to realize that he and Ash Robinson were engaged in a blood feud. Despite his lawyer's advice, Hill wanted out of this marriage. Indeed, he had already met the next Mrs. Hill.

Houston loved it. If only the two men would stage a gunfight on Rusk Street in front of the Houston Club, everyone's summer would be complete.

When the law would not act against the death certificate's listed cause of death, saying it was too hard to prove beyond that, Ash Robinson hired the next best thing: the former district attorney, Frank Briscoe, fresh from his term of office and into private practice. Despite Ash Robinson's demands and Briscoe's efforts, two grand juries met and found no wrongdoing in the death of Joan Robinson Hill.

When the third was convened, things went differently. An old friend of Ash Robinson had been impaneled. In February 1970, before Racehorse presented the case to this third grand jury, he argued strenuously about the prejudice on the jury panel. In turn Ash's friend made no bones about his special interest in their deliberations. "Put yourself in Ash Robinson's shoes. Here is a father who lost his only child, a good man, a decent man, and a man about to go crazy. We must take this case up again and settle it forever."

The jury stood as impaneled.

At this time, Racehorse began to play poker. He first called for a court of inquiry in the Hill case. The district attorney recognized that petition as a grandstand play to the newspapers and disallowed it. Racehorse then filed a lawsuit for $10,000,000 against Ash Robinson in the name of John Hill. He informed Ash that the threat would go away when the case was dropped. The old man refused to be intimidated.

At the same time, Racehorse was able to issue nuisance subpoenas to nearly "everybody in town," hoping the people receiving them would be angry and create community pressure on Joan's father. While Ash was undeterred, volumes of testimony began to grow. The Joan Robinson Hill case became an industry while Ash Robinson came to be regarded as an obsessed old man.

He didn't falter. His daughter had been murdered; his grandson was taken from him forever. He had nothing to look forward to except revenge.

At last, testimony from Ann Kurth, Hill's now-ex-wife, a woman scorned and betrayed though not murdered, shocked and horrified the jury, although more than half took it with a grain of salt. More sane, and less like a furious woman overstating horror out of a desire for revenge, was the testimony from a professional pathologist hired by Ash Robinson. In particular, the pathologist described how a responsible physician would under no circumstances let his wife's condition—pain, high fever, vomiting, diarrhea—go untreated for several days. The grand jury declared enough evidence existed to warrant a trial—Houston's trial of the century.

And Ernie Ernst, a lawyer who had been skeptical of the entire proceeding and who eventually took second chair prosecution, began going around the courthouse in front of members of the press saying, "I wouldn't let a dog die the way that doctor did his wife."

Racehorse knew his client was in peril. In the case of Dr. John Hill, he reasoned that the state of Texas would have to prove without reasonable doubt the following items:

Item 1. John Hill was a licensed medical doctor.
Item 2. That he undertook to be the physician to his wife.
Item 3. That he deliberately and *with malice* failed to treat her properly and also failed to obtain the best treatment in the best facility.

Haynes began to look at his famous alternatives:

Item 1. There was simply no way they could prove anything but Item 1.
Item 2. A gray item depending upon the husband-wife relationship.
Item 3. How is the state of Texas going to convince a jury that John Hill, a gentle, churchgoing surgeon in good standing, deliberately killed his wife through medical negligence?

In the meantime, a new will had surfaced, one that John Hill had known nothing about. Instead of the will Hill offered for probate that left him all their community property (valued at $400,000) and left their son the bulk of her estate, the new will, drawn up after Joan found out about her husband's escapades with Ann Kurth, cut him off without a penny. The will was duly dated, witnessed, and signed in November the year before.

Another motive was clear to Houstonians. Since Hill had not known about the will but had guessed that she might be ready to divorce him, he might have killed her to prevent her from doing so. When John Hill offered to take a lie detector test, the DA insisted that he could do so only after staying in jail for forty-eight hours, so that he couldn't "bomb himself" with tranquilizers. Racehorse nixed the idea immediately.

While the grand jury moved implacably through the evidence, questioned those subpoenaed, and deliberated at taxpayers' expense, John Hill announced that he was going to get married—again. Racehorse threw a sheaf of papers at the ceiling. His purported words were, "Then just drive yourself out to Huntsville and spend the wedding night so you'll be close to the state prison."

Knowing the importance of jury selection, Racehorse wanted a majority of women on the panel, figuring that he would tell them over and over that John Hill was not on trial for a bad marriage. But in the end, the panel contained only one woman and eleven men.

As the questioning of witnesses began, the judge kept overruling Racehorse's objections to the prosecution asking what might be construed as leading questions. A glance to his side showed John Hill sitting ashen faced and looking as guilty as sin.

Finally, when Ann Kurth began to testify, the case blew open. She testified that she actually saw an experiment in progress in John Hill's apartment before his wife died. Three petri dishes containing tiny amounts of liquid were being warmed under a gooseneck light. Racehorse leaped up maintaining the witness was lying, declaring that she didn't even know what petri dishes were. The judge overruled him. Later in her testimony, Ann declared that Hill came at her with a syringe, which she was able to knock out of his hand.

As the story grew wilder and wilder, men on the jury began to shake their heads. Ann Kurth was crazy. The defense was right. Finally, as "hypodermic needles flashed through the air," the judge declared a mistrial.

Racehorse was ecstatic. He had considered putting Ash Robinson on the stand as a last resort, figuring his ranting and raving would drive the case further toward complete dismissal of all charges. But Ash Robinson, though furious, was an unknown. Racehorse could not count on the old man to give the answers that would improve John Hill's position. And he knew better than to put a witness on the stand and ask questions when he didn't know what the man might answer.

Ash Robinson did not intend to let his daughter's death go unavenged, but he was seventy-five years old. At the rate things were happening, he could not just wait around for the next trial. He began to think of "alternative" strategies.

John Hill married his third wife, Connie Loesby, who moved into Joan Robinson Hill's house, which he had continued to occupy because the situation was unresolved. His medical practice picked up again, although the couple was never accepted in River Oaks society. The case was passed around the DA's office like an old shoe.

Because of the mistrial and then the subsequent delays instigated by Racehorse, the case rocked along until November of 1972. When the lawyer approached Ash Robinson to persuade him to "call it quits" and to remind him that his former son-in-law still had a $10,000,000 damage suit hanging over Ash's head, Robinson said, "Hell, no! Have you people forgotten that my daughter is dead?"

Haynes remarked, "He reminds me of a crocodile. Old. Mean. He sits there sleeping in the sun . . . about ready to pass on. But just you step on him, and he bites your head off. Snap!"

John Hill had forgotten the jaws of the crocodile.

Two years went by. John and Connie Hill returned from a plastic surgeon's convention in Las Vegas. While John paid the taxi driver, Connie walked to the door and rang the bell for the maid to answer. When no one came immediately, she peered through the glass panes. Suddenly, the door opened and a masked man jerked her inside by her gold chain necklace. She screamed. John raced up the walk to her aid. As the taxi drove off, he plunged into the house.

Seconds later, Connie ran out screaming. At the edge of the drive, she heard a shot and screamed, "My husband's been murdered!"

From the neighbors' house, she telephoned the police. They burst in the front door to see Robert Ashton "Boot" Hill hopping up and down beside the body of his father, both feet and arms bound. A piece of adhesive tape hung from the side of his mouth.

He was sobbing. "They've killed my daddy. They've killed my daddy."

In the end, a man believed to be the killer was shot trying to escape the police in Longview, Texas, taking to his grave the identity of the person who had hired him. Houston society never even speculated about who that might have been.

Ash Robinson later died in Florida. He never admitted anything at all, but when he was questioned as to what he would like on his gravestone, he replied, "Here lies Ash Robinson. He lived and he died, and he didn't give a damn what people thought of him."

The events of this trial were turned into a 1981 made-for-television movie, *Murder in Texas* (based on Ann Kurth's book *Prescription: Murder*), starring Andy Griffith as Ash Robinson; Farrah Fawcett (a Corpus Christi gal) as Joan Robinson Hill; Sam Elliott as her husband, John Hill; and Craig T. Nelson as Racehorse Haynes. You can be sure that the real Racehorse served as technical advisor.

While the Daniel case exemplifies Haynes's ability to turn a jury and the Hill case showcases his ability to drag out a case until it can no longer be equitably tried, there is another that constitutes the pinnacle of his career.

"The One" came in 1976 and is widely considered Racehorse's greatest—the trial that made him famous and put him at the top of the legal world.

T. Cullen Davis, the Fort Worth billionaire, was accused of murder and attempted murder by his wife Priscilla—the bleached blonde with an outrageous boob job—who had commissioned the gold necklace with letters spelling RICH BITCH in pavé diamonds.

Someone in a black wig had gone on a shooting rampage in the mansion in the exclusive Arlington Heights section of Fort Worth. Dead in the basement was Davis's twelve-year-old stepdaughter, Andrea. Dead on the stairs was Priscilla's boyfriend, Stan Farr. Seriously wounded and fleeing to the neighbors screaming was Priscilla. The doctor who removed the bullet reported that she would have died instantly had not the silicone breast implant, paid for by Cullen Davis, slowed down and cushioned the impact of the bullet.

Also running into the street screaming was Bev Bass, a daughter of the wealthy Bass family and longtime friend of the Davises. Shot in the back and lying paralyzed in the driveway was Bev's boyfriend, Bubba Gavrel. Both had strolled up the drive assured of a hospitable welcome by Priscilla. Unfortunately, they had arrived at exactly the wrong time. Priscilla, Bev, and Bubba, with absolute certainty and under repeated questioning by the officers arriving at the scene and later, identified the shooter as T. Cullen Davis. Gravely wounded, Priscilla still managed to advise the police to send somebody out to Cullen's brother's house. Everyone knew the brothers hated each other.

At 4:00 a.m. Davis walked out of the house of his mistress, Karen Masters, and surrendered. While five pistols were found on the premises, none of them was the murder weapon. *No* physical evidence linked Davis to the crime.

He was put in jail without bail. As the prosecutor Tim Curry pointed out, no matter how outrageous the bail, the oilman could make it. From his private cell Cullen continued living his life—valet, gourmet chef, and barber seeing him daily, as well as a string of secretaries and a bank of telephones to allow him to conduct his business. The jailhouse records show that in six months, approximately 195 days, he had 399 visits to his cell.

When questioned, the sheriff shrugged and pointed out that Davis had to oversee the running of eighty-three companies. The man was innocent until proven guilty. He was also getting bags of fan mail, which he faithfully answered. Also, Priscilla's outrageous behavior was well-known. She had not been a popular figure. Obviously, the law was impressed with the money rather than the possibility of a crime.

Fort Worth rubbed its hands in anticipation. Cowtown loved a circus as much as Houston. Maybe more.

Racehorse spent $30,000 to determine what types of people would make the best jurors in the Cullen Davis case. After months of an exhausting selection process that had not produced a full jury panel, the judge learned that one of the eight selected had actually had contact with Davis. She had been in the same jail and had made several unauthorized phone calls. The judge had no choice but to rule a mistrial.

Meanwhile, Bev Bass and Bubba Gavrel had recanted their stories that they had actually "seen" their friend the billionaire T. Cullen Davis doing murder. They had only "heard" Priscilla screaming that the shooter was Cullen. Bubba was improving nicely thanks to very expensive physical therapy. Unfortunately, his legs were paralyzed and withering and would require care for the rest of his life. Shortly after her most recent statement, Bev left town for an extended vacation.

Disgusted with the time, money, and effort spent, the Fort Worth judge made arrangements for a change of venue. The whole circus moved to Amarillo, 350 miles northwest, to a land so isolated that he doubted they had ever heard of T. Cullen Davis.

He was wrong.

Racehorse Haynes brought with him droves of reporters, cameramen, and artists. He also brought T. Cullen Davis's mistress, Karen Masters, whose father had lived in Amarillo and had excellent connections among the townspeople. Karen was a hometown girl. Even though she was a high school dropout, she was a distinct asset. Likewise, she had two handicapped children, always good to garner sympathy, especially since Cullen was contributing to their support. At Racehorse's instruction, Karen took plenty of time to chat with friends, who chatted with friends, who chatted with other friends.

As before, Cullen gave his attorneys free rein to spend whatever they needed to have a jury declare him a free man. Ray Hudson, Karen's father, became a paid consultant to help the lawyers in the selection process. He received $45,000 for expenses incurred.

Though eight lawyers were working on the jury selection, Racehorse decided they needed two more, men who would do nothing but discover personal information about the jurors. When a prospective juror looked less than promising for the defense, Haynes would step forward with an item of personal information. For example, "Oh, by the way, Mrs. Jones, how's your uncle doing with his hernia operation?"

The prosecution would immediately object and waste one of its strikes in an effort to keep a "friend" of the defense off the panel.

Finally, in August 1977, more than a year after the massacre, the trial began and went on and on and on. Cullen Davis was tried for the murder of Andrea Wilborn, his twelve-year-old stepdaughter who had been found in the basement of the mansion. In a month the entire proceeding descended into "he said, she said." The prosecutor even went so far as to say that only two people knew what really happened that night—Priscilla and Cullen—and one of them was lying. He continued, "Every once in a while their eyes make contact. And they *know*."

All the while, people were meeting at Rhett Butler's restaurant and bar in Amarillo. Jury members had to eat somewhere before they spent the night in a downtown hotel. Everyone, of course, had been instructed not to discuss the trial. Casually, they mingled with witnesses, the lawyers, the press, Cullen himself with lovely hometown girl Karen Masters at his side. Cullen was a good fellow, paying the liquor bills for everyone, jury members included. Occasionally a press corps member would speculate on the advisability of Cullen's being allowed to pay the jurors' liquor bills.

One woman was heard to say that she knew Cullen couldn't be guilty because she knew Karen Masters personally. Karen was a good woman. She wouldn't associate with, much less love, a murderer.

On September 22 Cullen's first wife Sandra flew his three children from Fort Worth for a visit. Karen Masters brought them to the jail. The press corps was there to hear Cullen Jr. sob, "Daddy, I just want to be with you alone."

Cynical members of the press maintained that Racehorse had arranged this display of family loyalty and pain. The prospective jurors all heard about the rumors of a staged scene, but most believed that "children were basically honest and could not be bribed."

The trial went on into the fall and the jurors themselves began to wear down. One juror caused a delay because of an impacted wisdom tooth. He had to take Percodan, the very drug Priscilla had foregone despite her pain, so she could be clear-headed for the trial. The trial was delayed because the juror might not be in his full senses.

Meanwhile, Cullen, suave and charming as he could be, became the darling of the women of Amarillo. At Racehorse's suggestion, women of the Menopause Brigade, as the jailers called them, came to the jail to visit with him, to bring him cookies, to scold the jailers if things were not right in his cell. He behaved to one and all as if they were "just like his Momma."

Priscilla, on the other hand, was vilified and condemned as a whore and a bitch, a crime against decent society. The joke circulated that she was writing an autobiography to be titled *Silicone and Sex*, in reference to her breast enlargements requested and paid for by Cullen. "I can tell she's guilty just by looking at her," one woman was heard to say, completely forgetting that Priscilla was the victim. She was not then nor ever would be on trial.

At this point Racehorse began to have serious doubts. Despite the carefully planted bad impressions the jury had of the victim, she was *not* on trial. Her husband *was*. The fact remained that she had survived a bullet wound in her chest and had sworn that he had put it there, screaming to other potential witnesses to run for their lives, warning the police to take care of Cullen's brother. Worse and worse was the body of the twelve-year-old girl shot in cold blood on the floor of the basement with a bullet from the same gun that had shot Priscilla, Stan Farr, and Bubba Gavrel.

Bubba testified that he had distinctly heard Priscilla scream Cullen's name. Hit in the spine as he tried to flee and unable to move his legs, he realized he was helpless as the gunman came after him. His only hope had been to lie still and play dead. A year later, the contrast in his body was obvious and terrible. From the waist up, Bubba was built like a linebacker, but his legs were paralyzed and withered. When he dragged himself into the witness box, he had been unshakeable as to what he knew and believed. Above all, the defense had no real argument to counter Andrea's cold-blooded murder in the basement. The child had no defensive wounds on her arms or hands. She had been shot in the heart by someone she knew.

Meanwhile, the jurors were incarcerated in their hotel rooms except for their stints in the courtroom and their meals. Ironically, Cullen Davis was in jail, but his life was not nearly as terrible as theirs. He had a double-bunk on the floor of a private cell, which was left unlocked. People could visit him as if they were walking into his home. At one time he was seen talking with the mother of one of the jurors, who incidentally was allowed phone calls to her juror daughter. He had a color TV and catered meals. He had a barber, manicurist, and a valet, so that he might look freshly groomed. At 6:00 p.m. several days a week a deputy drove him to a chiropractor.

In the courtroom no effort was made to keep him seated behind the defense table. Cullen moved among his admirers like a movie star, shaking hands, signing autographs, posing for pictures, talking football. He was handsome, soft-spoken, pleasant, and Texan. Everyone loved him—and despised his ex-wife, who had caused him so much "inconvenience."

What a perfect defendant! What a "slam dunk" of a case—if Racehorse had had one shred of evidence to combat the testimony of the witnesses. The only thing to do was "go after Priscilla Davis." If her testimony could be discredited because of people's perceptions of her behavior and reputation, then he would win the case. Priscilla was the only one who had actually *seen* Cullen in his black wig. She was the one to whom he had spoken and said, "Come on, come on," as if inviting her to follow him, perhaps to the cellar where he could show her Andrea's body before he murdered her too.

Her testimony remained unshakeable.

Racehorse's aces in the hole were the three women on the jury. They were enough to hang it, even if there would be no acquittal.

Therefore, he could "hardly find words strong enough to describe her," her actions, and her associates. He produced image after image in his vocabulary: "Dr. Jekyll and Mrs. Hyde" and "Queen Bee." He spoke of her "bringing scalawags and thugs into the big house," of the "skuddies, rogues, brigands" with whom she had associated. He brought some of them in to defame her from the witness stand. In the process, they defamed the murdered Stan Farr as well.

Finally, with "mud slung inches thick on all the victims and their testimonies," the defense rested.

The prosecution responded with the irrefutable fact that "if you believe that Cullen Davis shot Stan Farr, then you have to believe that he murdered Andrea Wilborn also.

"What you've seen in this court is an attempt to run over everyone that gets in this man's way. People were in his way and he *fixed their twats*—that's exactly what he did. Their whole defense has been ABC—*Anybody but Cullen!*"

He played his last card in his concluding statement. Everyone including the jury was informed that the man weeping softly but audibly in the back of the courtroom was Andrea's father, Jack Wilborn.

On Thursday, November 17, 1977, at 9:20 a.m., the nine men and three women chosen for the jury began its deliberations. At 2:23 p.m. the same day, they filed back in. The verdict was read. "We, the jury, find the defendant, Thomas Cullen Davis, not guilty."

Let the revels begin!

Ray Hudson, Karen Master's father, was buying the drinks at Rhett Butler's where the party commenced. As the Scotch and bourbon flowed, the celebration grew to resemble one happening in the dressing room of the Super Bowl winner. In attendance from the first were Cullen's attorneys. Then in a steady stream came a dozen reporters, five jurors, several groupies, three bailiffs, and a "partridge in a pear tree" in the form of the judge who had presided over the trial. He knew he shouldn't be there, but he didn't have anywhere else to go. His girlfriend had left him during the trial.

Someone passed Racehorse a guitar, and he gave them a couple of verses of a Willie Nelson song. Then he and Cullen got together under the glare of the "live from Amarillo" TV lights to do slap palms-bump asses like a couple of rookies who'd scored a winning touchdown.

Then Racehorse made a speech for the TV cameras that he possibly regretted later. He gave the audience his rundown of Priscilla Davis: "She is the dregs. She's probably shooting up right now . . . shameless, brazen hussy . . . charlatan, harlot, liar . . . snake . . . dope fiend. . . . Someone ought to put a barbed-wire fence around her and keep her there."

Racehorse, whose fee for the victory was later "guess-timated" to be an astronomical $3,000,000, proposed toasts to money well spent, although Cullen Davis was only temporar-ily free. He could still be arrested and tried for murdering Stan Farr, for shooting Bubba Gavrel, and for shooting Priscilla Davis. Even now in Fort Worth, judges and district attorneys were deciding whether or not to do so.

In the meantime, juror Betty Blair discussed the reasoning behind her "not guilty" verdict. "It seems like if somebody that rich wanted it done, he'd hire somebody."

For Cullen Davis, the ordeal was over for the time being. He and Karen Masters boarded a Learjet for skiing in Colorado. For Racehorse Haynes, it was the sweetest victory he could ever have imagined.

Still in the end he too paid a price for his outrageous and frequently illegal behavior. His brilliant victory added to his fortune and certainly to the fame he sought. His name came to be ranked along with nationally famous defense lawyers F. Lee Bailey, Percy Foreman, and later with Alan Dershowitz and Johnnie Cochran. But from that time on, he had a much harder time picking a jury. Many jurors excused themselves immediately on the grounds that they had "heard of Haynes," whatever that might have meant. Some came right out and said they were prejudiced against him.

Prospective clients in some cases steered clear of him for various reasons. Some, because they did not want their cases tried in the same glare of the spotlight that Racehorse seemed to attract. Some, because they feared that to hire him would be a signal that they were guilty as sin—the opinion that almost all of Texas shared with regard to T. Cullen Davis. Though the reputed $3,000,000 fee was more likely half or a quarter of what he truly earned, William Randolph Hearst is said to have considered Racehorse to defend Patty, but he gave up the idea and settled for F. Lee Bailey, whose fee was considerably less.

The trials of T. Cullen Davis themselves became an industry for Texas courts and Texas lawyers for the next several years. Juries were deadlocked. Juries declared him not guilty. Finally, everyone gave up out of sheer exhaustion. Priscilla and Cullen were divorced in April 1979. She got $3,400,000 tax free. She has since died of breast cancer.

He got the mansion and the right to marry Karen Masters. Cullen and Karen are still alive under much poorer circumstances. In the eighties he was forced to file for personal bankruptcy. Though he sold the "murder mansion" for a reputed $32,000,000, his debts were too astronomical to pay. At age seventy-three, Cullen has "gotten religion." His brother Kenneth pays him a lagniappe of $25,000 yearly, a salary from the business Cullen is no longer a part of.

And what of the innocent life taken and lost forever in the haze of deceit, lawyer tricks, lies, and misdirection? Everyone has forgotten about her.

No one will ever pay for the death of Andrea Wilborn.

"ART IS ... INSANITY, AND I DO IT VERY WELL"

Stanley Marsh 3—the Amarillo millionaire, philanthropist, and eccentric who has produced some of the Southwest's most memorable art gave a party for his billionaire "friend," T. Cullen Davis of Fort Worth. The festivities were held on Saturday night, November 19, 1977, two days after Davis had been found "not guilty" by an Amarillo jury. Toad Hall, the Marsh mansion, saw a gathering of the whole cast—lawyers, jurors, the press, the best of Amarillo society, the judge, and his ex-girlfriend who had allowed herself to be persuaded to come to the party. Honored guests were the newly freed citizen and his mistress, Karen Masters.

Not invited were Cullen's wife, Priscilla, who claimed he had tried to murder her; Bubba Gavrel, the young man who had been crippled in the homicidal rampage; and Bev Bass, the friend who had run down the driveway screaming, "Cullen don't shoot me! Don't shoot me! It's Bev!" Not even considered was Jack Wilborn, the father of the murdered twelve-year-old Andrea, who had been shot dead in the basement of the Cullen mansion.

Not present also were the Mad Hatter, the White Rabbit, and the Red Queen, although the party at any minute might have evolved into a Mad Tea Party.

Entertaining a man whom anyone and everyone with any common sense knew was guilty as sin of cold-blooded murder was Marsh 3's "cup of tea." With his tongue pressed firmly in his cheek, he led Cullen around to show him some of Toad Hall's objets d'art. The other guests followed avidly or pretended to talk among themselves while they watched and listened to their host's idea of entertainment.

Marsh 3 knew full well that Cullen knew nothing at all about art and cared even less than he knew. Everyone in Texas had heard the story of the art-buying expedition for the mansion at 4200 Mockingbird in Fort Worth. When their new home was finished, Cullen and Priscilla had gone to New York City on a buying spree. They had acquired hundreds of thousands of dollars worth of French Impressionist paintings. The estimated number of acquisitions ranged as high as 115 works whose artists—among them Matisse, Monet, Van Gogh, even Renoir—meant nothing to the Davises. Priscilla liked it or she didn't. Cullen didn't give a rap.

Of course, at the first gala thrown by the couple, many guests found occasions to use the much-talked-about upstairs bathroom to discover that Priscilla had indeed hung a $400,000 Renoir in the same room with the bath, shower, bidet, and sink as well as floor-to-ceiling mirrors to reflect the light from every angle. Her reasoning: the scene had bathers in it. Apparently, the "rich bitch," as Priscilla's pavé diamond necklace proclaimed her, neither appreciated nor understood the painting's value nor how much the dampness of a bath would damage it or how the excessive light from the mirrors and chandelier would fade its colors.

No one can doubt from Marsh 3's boisterous remarks, overheard and repeated by practically everybody, that he despised Cullen Davis and had given the party to humiliate him without the billionaire ever knowing he was being humiliated. Jaws dropped and eyes widened when Marsh 3 greeted Cullen with, "It's always nice to have an ex-accused murderer at Toad Hall."

Marsh 3 then expanded the tale of his friendship and support with lots of false joviality. He maintained he had been with Cullen all the way. Marsh 3 related how he had followed the trial from the very first; that, in fact, one night when things looked sort of bad, he had taken the trouble to call every airline serving the city and book reservations for two for Rio de Janeiro—in Cullen's name, of course.

Cullen hesitated but shook hands and said he was glad to be there. The other guests drank their cocktails, or pretended to. They didn't want to miss a word of what their host would say next or what he would do. One and all were sure the evening would be an adventure to tell their children.

Next, Marsh 3 asked if Cullen had noticed the surprise appearance of the Phantom Pool Table one morning during his trial. When Cullen looked puzzled and shook his head, Marsh 3 told how he had pulled the huge piece of "soft art" literally right out of the pasture and moved it onto the roof of the building across the street from the county jail. It was one of Marsh 3's more famous pieces, commissioned after he had viewed an exhibit of the genre in a New York gallery. Made of canvas, wood, and foam rubber, the pool table was constructed a gigantic twenty times larger than life.

Cullen was forced to admit he had not noticed.

Marsh 3 looked disappointed. Then he suggested that maybe Cullen's cell had been on the wrong side of the building and apologized for not checking more closely.

He then escorted his guests out to the back and showed Cullen the huge ART sign: three eight-foot-high, plastic-covered, free-standing foam letters—a red *A*, a yellow *R*, and a blue *T*. Marsh 3 just "knew" that because Cullen was a patron of art himself, he'd appreciate it.

Cullen looked the sign up and down and nodded. What else could he do?

Marsh 3 then recounted the tale of how he had improved on nature by having his pet pig, Minnesota Fats, tattooed with wings like an Assyrian idol. He then showed his guests the pig he'd had stuffed by the best taxidermist in the Panhandle. Marsh 3 explained that "Pigasus," his poor pet, had "ate himself to death with a whole box of chocolate Easter eggs."

By this time the "ex-accused murderer" must have been wondering if he had somehow slipped into another dimension or fallen down a rabbit hole. If Cullen knew he was being made a spectacle of, he didn't snap at the bait.

During the course of the evening, Marsh 3 showed Cullen his dogs. The two hairless, yapping, leaping creatures had been tattooed in the same manner as Pigasus. Their owner claimed they were the ugliest dogs in the world. Not a soul disputed him.

Then, before "God and ever'body," Marsh 3 asked Cullen about Priscilla. If she was such a hussy and harlot, why had Cullen married her in the first place?

Cullen explained with admirable patience that when he married Priscilla, she changed for the better, but when Fort Worth society refused to accept her, she went back to being bad.

Marsh 3 turned to the onlookers. "I told him," he declared loudly. "'A tiger can't be expected to change her spots.'"

In an effort to gain the upper hand, or at least come out even, Cullen corrected him. "Tigers have stripes."

When the party at Toad Hall was over, the guests all departed in various stages of satisfaction and inebriation. Cullen and Karen drove back to Fort Worth, where they boarded his private Learjet for a Thanksgiving vacation skiing in Colorado. Racehorse Haynes, Cullen's excessively high-priced lawyer, flew off to Boston where he was to give a speech. All the bankers, lawyers, and politicians agreed among themselves not to tell any more Cullen Davis stories. The judge made up with his girlfriend, who had allowed herself to enjoy the party. A happy man, he planned to get back to work on his badly neglected docket.

And a reporter asked Marsh 3, "What do you think of Cullen now?"

"Let me put it his way. I don't think Minnesota Fats would have enjoyed drinking with Cullen."

"Can I quote you on that?"

"I insist," Marsh 3 said. "Fats was just a pig, but he had standards. Blood will tell, I always say."

As the door closed on the last guest, Marsh 3 and his wife, Wendy, regarded themselves with satisfaction.

Another successful evening of craziness!

The first Stanley Marsh, grandfather of Marsh 3, was born in Cincinnati in 1882. When he married his wife, Ida Davis, the first woman in Ohio to be awarded a Phi Beta Kappa key, he told her they would be moving to Amarillo, Texas. She opened a geography book that showed the town in the middle of great blank area on the map labeled the "Great American Desert." Being a trouper, she went anyway.

They didn't arrive in Amarillo immediately. Instead, they followed the oil boom through Oklahoma from Coalgate to Ardmore. From there they went to Wichita Falls and then to Burkburnett, Texas, where a well that was drilled for a few thousand dollars with used equipment blew in, and oil ran down the dried-up cotton rows. Moving on, they finally arrived in Amarillo, where Marsh acquired oil leases from drought-stricken farmers. These he and his investors developed into major oil and gas properties in the new Panhandle field. During World War II, their refinery was a leading producer of natural gasoline, a product made from natural gas.

In the development of their field, Marsh and company discovered something else exceedingly important. A highly profitable by-product of natural gas is helium, a colorless and odorless gas with 92 percent of the lifting power of hydrogen without that gas's obvious drawback. Hydrogen is highly flammable. (It was responsible for the infamous explosion of the dirigible *Hindenberg.*)

Helium, on the other hand, is an inert gas. With two positive charges in its nucleus and two negative electrons surrounding it, it is perfectly balanced. It will not combine with any other elements to form compounds. This second most common element in the world was virtually unknown until World War I when three small experimental plants were built for its extraction and harnessing for use by the U.S. Navy in barrage balloons.

Besides lifting power for lighter-than-air ships, liquid helium is used as a coolant. NASA considers it essential to create the oxygen/hydrogen rocket fuel to continue the missions into space.

The three grandsons of Stanley Marsh have amassed great wealth through the production of oil and natural gas, which the world now knows will be in short supply in the near future. Through the extraction and storage of liquid helium, which they siphon from underground rock formations in the Caprock plateau, their income will be steady for centuries.

Being the grandson of a pioneer cattleman and oilman of the Panhandle, with millions of dollars at his disposal, Marsh 3 has been able to do outrageous things. While his saner brothers run the business, which he admits he has no head for, Marsh 3 is most famous for creating pieces of outlandish art—some of them gigantic and famous nationwide. He has lived his life with an eye to doing what pleases him. Nothing and no one had better be serious around him. He long ago adopted the Arabic number three after his name, rather than using the Roman number. He claims "III" would be pretentious.

The name of his rambling mansion, Toad Hall, is taken from Kenneth Graham's children's book *The Wind in the Willows.* As a reminder to readers, Mr. Toad of the green-skinned variety represents wealthy Englishmen. He is an eccentric to such a degree that he gets arrested, loses his estate, and then has all sorts of adventures before his home is restored to him. The comparison to Marsh 3 may have been truer than he meant it to be.

Marsh 3's father sent him east to college at Wharton School of Finance and Commerce at the University of Pennsylvania. It provided the requisite education for the heir apparent to the family fortune. He completed the courses in managing money, but while he was about it, he decided that he needed to be "cultured."

He read voraciously, an act in itself extremely suspect in rough-and-ready West Texas. He went to a lot of movies whose plots did not unravel during car chases. Most suspicious of all, he formed opinions about contemporary artists. Then, he capped the climax by earning an MA in American civilization. When he returned to Amarillo, highly educated, he eagerly opened a bookshop.

"I wanted to do something of interest in the community," Marsh 3 maintains.

Protective of his "changeling" child's future, Marsh 3's father is said to have called him in and made him sign a document specifying that his brothers would inherit the business should the elder Marsh be killed.

After his father died in 1967, Marsh 3 left it to his younger brothers, Tom and Mike, to buy and sell stocks and hang out at the country club. He made no objection to their managing the inheritance. The younger brothers had inherited vast sums of money, and they liked to invest it and make it grow. They had no objection to Marsh 3 earning his money in different ways. As things turned out, he brought a certain cachet to the town.

Free to do as he wanted, Marsh 3 invested in things that interested him. His money allowed his quirky sense of humor full rein. His first purchase was the Amarillo ABC-TV affiliate, which his boundless imagination and energy turned into the station with the largest market share of any in Texas.

Bolstered by its own success, Marsh Media began to acquire television affiliates and cable franchises whenever and wherever they became available on the market.

Marsh 3 has said that he found the perfect business in broadcasting. He likes to talk about entertainment. He likes to discuss the news. He is more interested in the roles TV stars play in prime time shows than in the rise and fall of blue chip stocks. By choice, he would rather envision Sam Waterston as a good Abe Lincoln than as a spokesman for a brokerage firm.

He is most contemptuous of collectors like T. Cullen Davis and Priscilla, who buy art to match their color schemes, or ignorant people who buy because they get a good deal or an income tax write-off on a painting.

Marsh 3 and Wendy enjoy going to the theater, to art galleries, to concerts. For his own endeavors, he has this to say: "Art is a legalized form of insanity, and I do it very well." Whether he does art or insanity very well is open to speculation.

In their spare time, Marsh 3 and his brothers opened their own bank. However, he is a more or less silent partner. He understands that he is bad for his own business. People think outrageous television tycoons and eccentric bookstore owners are just fine. They do not look with favor on eccentric, outrageous bankers.

His wife, Wendy Bush O'Brien Marsh, part owner of the Frying Pan Ranch, contributes to their pretty much unlimited resources by being the daughter of cattle ranchers, whose grandmother's second husband made a fortune in pioneering machine-made barbed wire. Cattle with the Frying Pan brand graze on both her land and land that's part of the Marshes' Dripping Springs Cattle Company. The Frying Pan also raises wheat for human consumption as well as barley and milo grain for feedlots to fatten range-reared stock for slaughter.

Despite her ancestry, Wendy Marsh, like Marsh 3, educated herself for other things. An art history major at Smith, she took a master's in French at Cornell and a law degree from the University of Texas. For Wendy and Stanley, theirs was a marriage made in some happy, loopy Texas heaven. He created art of the kind never seen before in Texas, and relatively rarely in other places in the world. She encouraged him—even though it is outrageous art that begs the question, "Is it art, or it is a joke?"

At first, second, or third glance, Marsh 3 doesn't seem the type to be a brilliant entrepreneur, whose varied interests have made him an outrageous legend in his own time. For many years the citizens of Amarillo didn't know what to make of him—or his projects. As many of his neighbors consider him a buffoon and a failure as consider him a success. Yet today he is acknowledged as one of Amarillo's most important citizens.

He proudly declares that he has the interests of the town at heart with everything he creates and causes to be created. "What makes Amarillo a terrifically interesting town is that it has enough people that are so isolated that we create our own culture. It could be an island. We have to make our own fun. People in Austin make a lot of fun, but there's a lot of canned fun you can buy. In Wichita Falls or Waxahachie you're only an hour from Dallas. Those towns lack a certain luster because people go elsewhere to have their fun."

Besides the aforementioned Phantom Pool Table and Pigasus, Marsh 3 is behind the creation of one of the most famous attractions in the Southwest. Far and away his most outrageous project, this masterpiece can be seen today when I-40 tops an imperceptible rise eight miles west of the town—the Cadillac Ranch.

Highly original in concept, Marsh 3 commissioned its creation by Roger Dainton, Chip Lord, Hudson Marquez, and Doug Michels, an art group that called itself The Ant Farm (in honor of nature's great underground architects). The sight leaves most people speechless when they come upon it. And even those who have never seen the "ranch" are aware of it and the whole idea of such a brazen, misuse of the most sophisticated car America ever created. Interpret it how they may, people never forget it.

Constructed in 1974, the ranch consists of ten Cadillacs, all tailfin models as they evolved from 1949 to 1963. All face west toward Tucumcari, New Mexico, and are buried radiator down at exactly the same distance apart. Their frames are raised at exactly the same angle as the Great Pyramid of Giza. The Ant Farm made certain that the angles were exactly right before they drove or pushed the machines into their final resting place.

Art installations are primarily a twentieth-century phenomenon. People who admire them consider Cadillac Ranch to be the greatest of its kind in the world. Almost all other installations—such as swaths of yellow cloth around the trees in a park in New York City—are ephemeral, gone before even a small number of people can see them. A quick photograph in the daily paper, a thirty-second segment on the evening news, and they are gone, leaving nothing.

Not so Marsh 3's Cadillac Ranch. When the call went out for the Cadillacs, people rushed to be the first to offer their old vehicles. Most were acquired for between $200 and $300 apiece.

How did Marsh 3 come up with the idea? Where does any such outrageous idea from? From a creative mind constantly in action, thinking, dreaming, analyzing, flashing from object to subject and back again. And for what purpose is such art as ten Cadillacs half buried in the dry soil of the Panhandle? What is the purpose of any piece of art except to amaze, enlighten, and enrich? Some would say that it is something beautiful, but then beauty becomes difficult to define. One of its aspects, however, is something that is good because it pleases us. It engages our attention even when we have no desire to acquire it. It makes us glad we have seen it.

Most people are glad the Cadillac Ranch is there.

Marsh 3 claims that the ideology of art installations was what made the great cathedrals of Europe. They were built by people who worked a hundred years for something they believed in. He created his installations because he believed in them. For him the creation made a statement of something beyond America's predilection for "usage." A scarecrow representation of "beauty is its own excuse for being."

His brothers, Tom and Mike, have no problem with his Cadillac Ranch or any of his other quirky activities. For his birthday one year, they had a tomato red Volkswagen buried nose down in the yard in front of Toad Hall. We can presume that it too faces Tucumcari, New Mexico, at the exact angle of the Great Pyramid at Giza. Marsh was reportedly delighted. Though he kept the name Toad Hall for the house, he has now bestowed a more appropriate name on the estate: Cadillac Ranchette.

High falutin' as it sounds, no one can doubt that Cadillac Ranch is the people's art. Bruce Springsteen wrote a song featuring the old cars for a 1980 album: I'm gonna pack my pa and I'm gonna pack my aunt / I'm gonna take them down to the Cadillac Ranch . . . It was memorialized in the Walt Disney-Pixar film *Cars*. The full-length cartoon takes place primarily in the dying town of Radiator Springs beside old Route 66, one of America's most famous highways and the original site of the installation. In the movie the Cadillac Ranch tailfins tower high above the skyline of the little old town. True enough, they might be up-tilted layers of natural rock in colors of the Painted Desert, but anyone who has driven over the road or seen pictures of the installation recognizes the tailfins instantly. In case anyone is in doubt, a frequently seen on-screen map calls the mountains the Cadillac Range.

Interestingly, no one has ever been discouraged from using spray paint to decorate them with graffiti. Anyone may exit onto the I-40 frontage road and enter the cow pasture through an unlocked gate.

Visitors return to Cadillac Ranch again and again, never knowing what they'll find. Some stop every time they drive through to inspect what's new. From time to time, Marsh 3 has the venerable Caddies all repainted. Sometimes each is painted a different color. Once they were all painted blood red. In 2003, in memoriam for the death of Doug Michels, one of the four members of The Ant Farm, they were painted black. In 2005 they were all painted pink in tribute to breast cancer victims. The graffiti goes on over the new paint with seeming semi-religious zeal. After all, this is America's iconic car. Everyone who stops wants to leave his own version of an offering.

Just as people take pictures of themselves and their friends in front of, on top of, beside, under, and leaning against other national monuments, people have taken pictures of themselves with the Cadillacs. They have climbed inside them or sprawled half out of them as if they were victims of some bizarre car crash. They have stood beside, leaned against, and climbed over and around them. They are a source of great pleasure. People are gladdened when they stop by.

Jim McBride of the *Amarillo Globe-News* calls it an "American monument to the dream."

South of town on I-27 going toward Lubbock stands another Marsh 3 creation: "Ozymandias," a visualization of Romantic poet Percy Bysshe Shelley's sonnet, which begins,

> I met a traveller from an antique land
> Who said: Two vast and trunkless legs of stone
> Stand in the desert.

The sonnet was composed by the poet upon the arrival in England of a statue of Egyptian Pharoah Ramses II. Contrary to what most people believe, the "trunkless legs of stone" were not left behind somewhere in the desert. Indeed, they didn't exist nor had they ever existed. Marsh 3 was inspired to create in concrete the scene that Shelley himself had created out of his imagination. One leg appears broken off at the knee, perhaps twelve to fifteen feet into the air; the other is snapped off at the top of the thigh as much as twenty-five feet high. If such a statue had ever been, it would have been close to seventy-five feet tall, a colossus indeed.

Even broken, the sight is astonishing to say the least. Since the poem is one of Shelley's most popular, many people driving south see the installation and recognize the subject without having it explained. One wag even draped a pair of huge, huge, huge sports socks around the legs and took a picture, adding his own improvements to Marsh 3's roadside art. The number of yards of material and the hours to create the effect would have been substantial. Someone's idea of a joke became quite an undertaking.

Fortunately, Marsh 3 is "all right" with people "decorating" his monuments.

Eight miles northwest of Amarillo on the Tascosa Road, also named FM 1061, is the "Floating Mesa." Marsh 3 paid for hundreds of sheets of plywood to be painted sky blue and lined up horizontally across the mountainside. Unless the day is overcast—a rarity in the Panhandle, which has an annual rainfall of approximately twenty inches—the summit of the mountain appears to be floating above its own shoulders.

Almost any person would have to agree that the concept isn't one that he would have come up with—or one that anyone he knew personally would have envisioned. (So far no one has been ambitious enough to climb the side of the mountain with cans of paint to counteract the floating effect.)

And that is the nature of art of this type. It conceives and conceptualizes things that have never been from things that are. It is drawing together many objects and arranging them in patterns that form something entirely different. In the sense that it changes the familiar into the unique, who can doubt that it is art moderne?

Many have longed to see Shelley's "trunkless legs of stone." Tourists in Egypt actually ask where they are and want to know if they will be on the tour. Only the imaginative eye and creative impulse can envision them and make them rise out of the Great American Desert. Who but Marsh 3 would care enough about seeing "two trunkless legs of stone" to create them for all to see as Shelley himself saw them in his mind's eye? Who but a man with the imagination of Picasso, who took a bicycle seat and a pair of handlebars and created the skull of a longhorn steer?

And who would see the winged animal statue created eons ago by the ancient Assyrians, suddenly recognize a creative opportunity, and tattoo wings on a pet "Pigasus," hilariously mixing metaphors and historic periods with gleeful abandon?

By allowing himself to see beyond the mundane and to allow the common everyday shapes to tilt and twist in imaginative ways, Marsh 3 has in a sense set himself free. Detractors decry his work, saying things like, "If that's what it takes for Amarillo to be famous, God help us."

While the Cadillac Ranch is known nationwide, Marsh 3's efforts to create "affordable" art for the masses are well-known, mostly in his hometown. For three years he created his "Road Signs."

The idea began out of his quirky sense of humor. The Texas Highway Department installed a road sign adjacent to the private road onto Marsh 3's ranch property. It warned: "Road Ends." The prankster's immediate impulse was to contradict the state of Texas with his own philosophy of life, time, and metaphysical distance. He had the local sign painter produce another sign, which he put up beside the first: "Road Does Not End."

Within days he fell afoul of the highway department. Texas law forbids anyone from defacing, covering, or removing official road signs. Local law enforcement took that to mean that making philosophical jokes about them was illegal. "Those signs are to be taken seriously," they told him. "That could be dangerous. Suppose someone read that and kept on driving."

But many citizens of Amarillo saw the joke. Soon people wanted signs for their own yards. The signs were fun. They certainly helped personalize the property. They made their houses easy to find.

An art teacher wanted one that read "ART's exalted character clears my brain."

A former marine wanted to express his own attitude: "No Dishonor before Death Semper Fi."

Within days of the initial requests, Marsh 3 organized a group of artists he named the Dynamite Museum. They were strictly for the purpose of creating commissioned non-advertising art. If a person wanted a sign but didn't know what he wanted, the Dynamite Museum would help him to bring out his ideas or conceptualize an idea for him. They pulled ideas from books, television, and their own zany imaginations. The person who lived on Monroe Street got a picture of—who else?—the legendary Marilyn.

Some signs seem rather ordinary—as if the person were simply making a reflective statement. Some reflect a simple philosophy or a favorite joke. Some are simply op art. One reads, "My youth is spent and yet I am not old."

On the other hand, another announces, "When everyone goes to other planets I will stay in the abandoned city."

"I'll be right out Ma! For crying out loud," a third protested.

In one yard a black and sapphire-blue cat lounges in remarkable contentment on a bright red sign. His name is Tom Cat. The Bride of Frankenstein as portrayed by Elsa Lanchester is seen on one. Another features "The Naughty Lady of Shady Lane."

Quite priceless is the sign that reads, "What is a village without village idiots?"—a sign this writer wishes she had for her very own.

Because the signs cost relatively little, they are seen in front of mansions, middle-class homes, and trailers in mobile home parks. If people want the signs removed, all they have to do is call. The Dynamite Museum does it at no cost.

When some people sell their homes, they take their signs with them. They have been spotted in Austin, Lubbock, and on the New Mexico border.

So far the signs have neither lowered nor raised the property values of their owners' domiciles. They are exactly what Marsh 3 intended they should be—art in unexpected places. While no one agrees as to whether they are good or bad, everyone agrees they are conversation pieces.

Contrary to Marsh 3's attitude toward his Cadillac Ranch, he is very protective of his road signs. Back in August of 1995, Ben Whittenburg, a senior at Amarillo High School, was caught by Marsh 3 in the act of removing one of the signs from a yard.

The confrontation must have been exciting.

Eventually, Whittenburg and three accomplices brought suit against the entrepreneur. According to Whittenburg's testimony, Marsh 3 humiliated him by threatening him, driving him into a chicken coop, and using a hammer to nail him inside. Wittenburg further stated that Marsh 3 cussed him, took pictures of him in the pen, and ranted and raved about how he would run names and pictures over his television station.

Whittenburg also testified that he was not the only one involved in the incident. The law firm of the "coopee's" father—Whittenburg, Whittenburg, and Schacter—eventually sought to bring a class action suit involving the three other parties who participated in the vandalism and theft.

The strength of their combined testimony was diffused when the judge refused to let them bring one suit. Instead, he ruled that they should each make their suits separately.

In the course of the individual suits, various stories emerged, all followed with great interest by the citizens of

Amarillo and duly reported in the *Amarillo Globe-News*. According to Ben Whittenburg's sworn testimony, Marsh 3 called Whittenburg's mother "trash." In another trial, a teen claimed that Marsh 3 fired him from the television station after he had rebuffed Marsh 3's homosexual advances. In still another, one witness for the prosecution, Jodi Parker, accused Marsh 3 and some of his friends of coming to her family's home in clown wigs and Lone Ranger masks and terrorizing her while they were looking for one of her step-brothers.

The citizens of Amarillo had a wonderful time with the trials. Knowing high school seniors and their pranks, no one took them seriously, although one and all believed that Marsh 3 had nailed Ben Whittenburg inside a chicken coop. Some thought the humiliation good enough for the lawyer's son. Others deplored Marsh 3's high-handed manner.

In the end Marsh 3 pleaded no contest in 1998 to two misdemeanors—unlawful restraint and criminal trespass. In exchange the charges were dropped, including such major felonies as kidnapping, aggravated assault with a deadly weapon, and three counts of indecency with a child.

The judge ordered Marsh 3 to pay $4,000 (possibly $1,000 per child) and serve ten days in jail. Then he mitigated the sentence by allowing Marsh to perform ten days of community service without jail time.

The incident behind him, Marsh 3 made a public statement. Remembering the party for T. Cullen Davis, one can imagine the prankster and eccentric (who hates that word) tucking his tongue firmly into his cheek and smothering his grin as he made the following public apology: "Through this litigation it has been made clear to me that my conduct directed toward these young people was inappropriate, and I apologize for anything I said or did that may have caused them anguish."

End of story.

Furthermore, while the teens of Amarillo are relieved to hear Marsh 3's apology, one and all have learned not to bother his Road Signs.

In January 1999, Marsh 3 earned the enmity of the Weather Channel. Simon Ross, the field producer, had his live broadcast disrupted on Friday morning by an American Indian snow dance. The employees were getting live footage from the city when a sport utility vehicle sped up about 8 a.m.

Marsh 3, clad in an American Indian headdress, and three young people jumped out and began dancing around the camera. The theme song from "Star Wars" blasted over the radio.

Ross asked them to leave repeatedly, but the dancing went on. Finally, he canceled the broadcast and called the Amarillo Police Department. When they arrived, Marsh 3 agreed to leave. The sergeant in charge reported that Marsh was not cited for trespassing on a public street.

Ross was not amused. He had immediately recognized the owner of KVII, Channel 7. "It's not big deal," he said. "We just don't want to give Marsh any more publicity than he's already got. Usually people are really nice to us. One guy making a fool of himself gives everyone else in the city a bad name."

Marsh 3's story was that he and some friends were just driving around in the snow when they saw the camera. "I just did what people always do when they see a camera and danced around and made a show of it. I performed my Quanah Parker snow dance behind their news broadcast."

As for the noise of the "Star Wars" theme, he maintained that it was a perfect accompaniment for the dance. "I played it really loud. It was making the snow fall off the trees. It was really great."

Again, end of story.

Except that when people report the news and weather in Amarillo, it had better be local news and weather, preferably from Channel KVII.

Most recently, Stanley Marsh 3 has become the star of his own movie. *The Road Does Not End* is a short documentary made in 2007 and shown at the deadCENTER Film Festival at the Oklahoma City Museum of Art in Oklahoma City.

The idea occurred to Dallas filmmaker Todd Kent while he was filming roadside attractions for the travel series *North Texas Explorer*. Kent was in the Big Texan Steak Ranch, one of the town's main attractions. This Amarillo eatery is famous in the Panhandle and all along I-40 as the restaurant where a customer can get a free T-bone "if you're man enough." Anyone who can eat a seventy-two-ounce T-bone in an hour gets the meal for free. College football players love to come by to pile in the calories; few actually manage to polish off the monster, including baked potato and rolls.

As he was finishing a much smaller portion, Kent remarked that he had seen Marsh 3's art projects and installations. The owner made the introductions, and after an interview Kent set to work turning the Road Signs into a film.

Without too much trouble, he persuaded Marsh 3 to star in the movie if Kent would portray him as an artist and entrepreneur.

"I don't see myself as an eccentric," he insisted.

About the Cadillac Ranch Marsh 3 had plenty to say.

It's not an official place. There are no signs telling you you're five or two miles from it. There is no admission. We're not trying to sell anything. I think it's neat when people go out and graffiti them.

The reason for its popularity is a complete mystery to me. One thing though. It never takes a bad picture.

A lot of people like to shoot footage of road trips, and they come out to the Cadillac Ranch. I like to go out and see them and get their reaction. I'm accessible.

If I knew how to do it again, I'd do one a year. It's very gratifying that people react to it the way they do. They come to see it because it's mysterious to them.

And more mysterious hidden art awaits the adventurous. "Amarillo Ramp" is an earthwork fifty feet wide, curving four hundred feet around in a gradual upward spiral. The lonely mound surrounded by mesquite, sotol, and cholla looks like an Indian burial mound. The eerie story about the ramp is that the artist, Richard Smithson, died in a plane crash while inspecting it.

For the future, Marsh 3 is planning "The Great American Farmhand" to be created by planting a field of wheat and then cutting a section out of the center in the shape of a human hand.

He's also thinking that a soft, full-sized Statue of Liberty might be fun. He'd let her hold something different from the traditional torch and book.

Whatever he decides to do or not to do, rest assured that his fertile imagination will not shut down. If he had created only the Cadillac Ranch, his outrageousness would be spoken of with amusement and delight as people drive along the highway.

But Marsh 3 is constantly imagining, and he has the money to turn ideas into outrageous creations. He is an original and one of the best.

"TOO HOT FOR PARIS"

When scandalous Texas tornado Miss "Texas" Guinan tried to take her revue into Paris—France, not Texas—the censors refused her entry into the country. In 1931, "between the wars," France was as wild as ever. The "queen of the New York speakeasies" couldn't imagine such a thing. What was the problem? She and her troupe of "30 really ravishing blondes" whom she lovingly called "her kids" had performed their show for the entertainment of the passengers and crew of the steamship *Paris* in exchange for their passage across the Atlantic.

The outrageous dance that drew the most attention featured the girls dancing nude except for high heels and two large fans, one held behind the back and one held over the front. What was especially unsettling to a minister and several easily shocked women was that fans kept closing "accidentally," sometimes when the girls were facing front and sometimes when they turned their backs to the audience.

Guinan herself, ever the entrepreneur, had organized a tour through her manager, who had contacted Harry Pilcer, a French dancer and nightclub representative. The original plan had been for the show to land in England, perform, and move on to France for the summer.

To her consternation, the British would not let her off the ship. The risqué show with its shocking fan dance would probably have been too much for the staid, straight-laced nation, even though Queen Victoria had been dead for nearly thirty years. However, the show itself was not a "straw that broke the camel's back"; Guinan's reputation had preceded her.

She was met by Scotland Yard with a complete dossier of her antics, including her arrest record in New York. Scandalous! Outrageous! She was on the list of "barred aliens."

Though she was understandably upset, Guinan pretended to be much more upset than she really was. She called in the press and professed herself shocked—"shocked almost beyond words"—that the country would treat her so harshly, so uncharitably. "My parents were born in Great Britain," she loudly maintained.

In this she was absolutely truthful. Her parents were Irish immigrants who settled in Waco, Texas, before her birth in January 1884. Moreover, contrary to the stereotype, her parents were not poor, nor was her father an abusive drunk.

The British would not relent.

Determined to put on a show somewhere in Europe, she and her kids were forced to stay aboard the ship while it sailed across the channel to Le Havre. There she assumed she could land in France and make arrangements for the group to perform in Paris. To her horror, she was not allowed to go ashore for the second time. Because Guinan had planned to spend time in England before traveling onward, she had not applied for and received the visas required for entertainers.

Guinan and her girls did not have the proper documentation. Even so, armed with only their tourist authorization, she wouldn't have caused a problem for any red-blooded Frenchman. A Gallic shrug and a "c'est la vie" should have been the end of the problems—except that the French Entertainers and Musicians Association in Montmartre had petitioned the government to keep foreign employment out rather than bring the Guinan revue in to compete for a share of the audience. While French audiences would have undoubtedly cried, "Oui, oui, Madam!" the union bosses gave a resounding, "Non!"

Disappointed and angry, Texas chose to make the refusal personal and to "spin it to her advantage." Her revue would have a new name, with implications that would insure its success no matter on what stage it was shown. She had had excellent practice at excelling on her given "stage"; she had done it all her adventurous, exciting life.

She boasted that her show had become "Too Hot for Paris."

Mary Louise Cecilia Guinan was born in Waco, Texas, where she went to school and sang in the choir of the Loretta Convent. "Mamie" had a beautiful singing voice and won the scholarship offered by Marshall Field to the University of Chicago. For two years she studied music in the conservatory and in the School of Dramatic Arts. Her studies completed there, she returned home to graduate from the classy Hollins School for Girls.

Guinan was a smart, pretty girl with great opportunities ahead of her. She should have followed the safe and sedate life that her talents and her education had opened to her, but she wanted far more than "safe and sedate." In an initial fit of rebellion, she joined a Wild West rodeo-circus where she rode horses and twirled a lariat with the best of them. In December 1904, she married a newspaper artist named John J. Moynahan. By that time she had glamorized her name to Marie. As a "cowgirl" performer, she enjoyed the easy-does-it life of the rodeo as they toured the West.

Life with her husband soon deteriorated. He insisted that she quit the show and move to Boston, where he took over as executive of a newspaper. Boston! She shuddered at the very name of the town. It was a synonym for all that was staid and proper.

Despite her Catholic upbringing, Guinan left Moynahan and moved to New York, seeking any sort of job in the theater. For four years, though jobs were few and far between and she lived many times without a prospect of money coming in, she discovered that what she loved above everything else was to perform. Guinan lived to perform.

But New York was a hard town with few breaks for a little lady. The audition lines were full of beautiful stage-struck girls who tried and failed and went home.

First, she determined that Mary Louise or Marie Guinan attracted no attention on the "cattle call" lists. Swiftly, she adopted the name of her big, brawling home state. As Texas Guinan, she earned the right to boast that she had never met a town she couldn't tame. Her name was the first of her efforts to market herself and create a memorable persona. In 1908 she developed her own solo number imitating the Gibson Girl look based on Charles Dana Gibson's paintings. With her long, blonde hair lacquered stiffly and molded above her head, she portrayed a lovely blossom swinging in a basket above the audience and singing, "Pansies Bring Thoughts of You."

The act was a copy of the Evelyn Nesbit performance on the red velvet swing at the turn of the century. Sixteen-year-old Nesbit had been the centerpiece in a scandal that ended in tragedy when her lover shot the noted architect Stanford White. The city had pretended to be shocked by the goings-on.

In the case of Texas, who was known to have left her husband for the theater, New York reacted by flocking to see her. The city was always drawn to juicy scandals, particularly when they could watch the young women involved swinging above the heads of the audience with their bare legs kicking up to the chandeliers. Guinan's performance was a "must see," especially when it became known that she was seeking a divorce and had worked in a traveling show.

New York was that kind of city.

Eventually, Guinan met and was mentored by Lillian Russell, one of the reigning queens of the Broadway theater. With Russell's influence she began to work in musical comedies. As the protégé of an established star, she won better roles. She played a tomboy in *Miss Bob White* and *The Hoyden*. That wise-cracking, devil-may-care character added another dimension to her stage persona. Things were going swimmingly, even when she accidentally shot herself in the side in a farce called *The Gay Musician.*

Fortunately, Guinan's injuries weren't serious. "Spinning" the story, she was quoted by the New York papers as saying, "Nothing—not even a bullet—can stop Texas Guinan!"

From vaudeville, she moved up the scale of Broadway actresses. She was one of the stars performing in the Shubert Brothers revue, *The Passing Show* of 1913. She drew rave reviews from some critics. Only one critic, Julian Johnson, actually panned her performance. Perhaps by way of apology, he married her.

As if to prove the fickleness of fame and fortune, Texas allowed her name to be run in *Variety* to promote a weight-loss program, "Marvelous New Treatment for Fat Folks." The ad pictured her in a dazzling costume from the Shubert Brothers' show. The caption was "God's Masterpiece and the Most Fascinating Actress in America." Unfortunately, the compound that created the weight loss was a dangerous patent medicine. The U.S. Post Office prosecuted the maker who sent false advertising as well as the product itself through the mails.

Though no one believed her for a minute, Guinan refused to admit that she had been part of a false-advertising scam: "I was made a star of the *Passing Show* on account of my glorious figure." She insisted that before she took the treatments, she "tipped the scales at 204 pounds."

Guinan never weighed more than 136 pounds in her life.

Unfortunately, her career on Broadway couldn't bounce back from the adverse publicity. Too many people knew

Guinan was lying through her beautiful teeth, and singer-actresses were cheap and common. She was back in vaudeville almost before she realized what had happened to her. Still, her flaming self-confidence and joie de vivre never let her down. As several shows a day in vaudeville grew less and less appealing, she set her sites on a new medium, one capable of replacing vaudeville and even outdrawing touring Broadway entertainment throughout America.

Silent movies had come to theaters all over the country. *The Great Train Robbery*, produced in 1903, created a sensation everywhere it was shown. It had been made in Thomas Edison's New York studio with outdoor scenes shot in New Jersey beside the Lackawanna Railroad. Appearing in at least three roles was bulky Gilbert Anderson, who later became one of the first movie stars through his seminal role as "Broncho Billy."

In the final scene, an actor costumed as a gunfighter, who had never appeared in the story, pointed a six-shooter straight at the camera and pulled the trigger. The pianist hit a crashing chord. Smoke burst from the barrel of the pistol. Members of the audience screamed and ducked. They had never seen anything like it and didn't understand what they were seeing. Many thought that the actors with their guns drawn were somehow standing behind the screen.

Few realized that an entertainment revolution had occurred. The film was only ten minutes long. What a short amount of time to create such a radical change in the American way of life!

At first the old vaudeville theaters played the short silent movies between acts. But that was unsatisfactory because movies had to be viewed in almost total darkness. Clearly the familiar opera-house theater had too much light to create the proper effects. The result: All-movie houses were built with indecent speed all across the county, and the box office returns from them proved to be greater than vaudeville. The old acts were no longer booked. Live theater began to disappear all over America.

Vaudeville has never recovered as the "poor man's amusement," and live theater today falls into the category of elite entertainment to be viewed at irregular intervals by select groups.

The real essence of the change was that the movies drew in people once, twice, and three times a week. Almost in a single year, they swept the country. The desire to be entertained captured people's minds and changed their habits forever. Only television has reduced the movie audiences.

In the forefront of these new movie productions was Texas Guinan. In 1916 action adventures that could never be presented on any vaudeville stage were filling not only the old vaudeville theaters but also unused storerooms that could be darkened easily and quickly. The word *nickelodeon* was coined, a combination of the price of admission and *odeon*, the Greek word for theater.

Besides Broncho Billy Anderson, Tom Mix and William S. Hart became the first movie stars, in part because they were easily identifiable to moviegoers. They dressed as cowboys and rode galloping horses. (Actually, Broncho Billy rode very poorly, but nobody really cared. In later years, so did Gene Autry and John Wayne.)

Most of the movie audiences had never seen a man in a tuxedo or a woman in a sequined gown, but men in their own families or in families they knew rode horses and worked with herds of cattle. Moreover, cowboy movies were exciting. Horses galloped; men fought; cattle stampeded. Only occasionally did a caption flash on the screen. "Drawing room" movies contained too many black screens, too much reading, when many in the audience had only a third-grade education.

So phenomenal was their growth that by 1917, movies "occupied fifth place among the industries of the United States, being surpassed [only] by railroads, the clothing industry, iron and steel, and oil."

Texas Guinan set herself to become a star. She claimed she could "ride a horse, rope a steer, twirl a lariat—and shoot to beat any tobacco-chewin' cowpoke." She arranged for herself to be "discovered" by a talent scout for Balboa Amusements Producing Company, whose products were distributed by Famous Players–Lasky Brothers headquartered in Long Beach, California.

The night Guinan performed her big audition for movie stardom she asked permission to ride a "snow-white charger" down the theater runway. The only admonition from the theater manager was, "Don't kill too many customers."

Fortunately, the horse kept its footing. Nobody was killed, and absolutely nobody in the audience ducked and covered his eyes. Her costume consisted of a cowboy hat, a bandanna, a shirt, a belt, and black lace chaps with "possibly" nothing on underneath. Probably the chaps did the trick. She was hired to be a movie star.

Guinan's first effort, *The Wildcat*, was released May 3, 1917, a month after President Woodrow Wilson received a declaration of war from Congress. Almost instantaneously, nothing was as it had been. Prices skyrocketed. Food and materials of all kinds were short. Box office receipts fell disastrously. By June, American troops under the command of General "Blackjack" Pershing were in Paris.

Reassured that all would be well, audiences trooped back into the theaters. The slide had been only temporary, and suddenly, the demand for entertainment far exceeded the abilities of the movies to satisfy it. The box office took a big boost from government funds because the movies were wanted on the army bases for the Liberty Theatres, the forerunners of the USO. To the surprise of many, Texas Guinan was not around to star in any of those.

A truly good-hearted person, she had volunteered to entertain the troops in France. For her services south of Verdun in the heart of the fighting, she was awarded the Bronze Medal by none other than Field Marshal Joseph Jacques Joffre.

When she returned to the states, Guinan sought work with Harry Aitkin's Triangle Film Corporation in New York, but he hesitated to hire her. Aitkin already had under contract William S. Hart and Douglas Fairbanks. A gentleman and a conservative, he wondered if he really needed a woman who could ride, rope, and shoot. Was that really a woman's place?

Guinan was insistent. Of course it was a woman's place! Rodeos gave equal status to men and women. The rodeos were an outgrowth of Western tradition.

As a compromise, because she really wanted and needed the job, Guinan made another suggestion. If they didn't want her to be a blonde heroine, she would dye her hair black and create a new character, a bad girl—a villain-ess. The directors were intrigued with that idea. Who had ever heard of a lady gunslinger?

Aitkin decided that it might work. He signed her for a series of two-reel melodramas. Guinan was bound for Culver City, California. Her husband came along as a scenario writer.

The frail heroine might continue to faint and recover in the arms of the hero, but her stronger, more daring sister would have her moments too, and thousands of little girls all over America decided they would rather ride a horse than faint any day. Guinan created a new character, one that has continued to fascinate audiences. The scenery might change, the story might be tweaked a little to one side or the other, but Guinan always played the same character at heart.

She was the wronged woman out for revenge against the bad guys who took her daddy's ranch. She was the intrepid seeker after Klondike gold revealed only at the end as a woman. She was the wounded girl who recovered and taught herself to shoot to get her revenge. Or she was simply the mysterious woman in black, who confounded the hero until he finally fell in love with her. Her creation became a favorite dramatic ploy of romantic Western movies starring her as well as other daring young actresses who wanted to do more than faint.

Guinan made three melodramas in quick succession: *The Gun Woman*, *The Love Brokers*, and *The Hellcat*. The plot of the last movie involved a pair of twins, brother and sister. The movie was supposed to be shot on location in Big Bear country of Northwestern Canada, but Aitkin was already in deep financial difficulties. Guinan found she was supposed to make the movie on the Triangle lot with a few cedar trees and bags of salt to pass for snow. When she threw an inkwell at the director, she lost her job.

Landing on her feet, she signed with Frohman Amusement Corporation, which ran a two-page announcement in magazines coast to coast. Miss Texas Guinan would appear in twenty-six two-reel feature productions "typifying the rights, glories, and hazards of the women of the Great West." Her first four productions were *The She Wolf*, *South of Santa Fe*, *Malamute Meg*, and *Some Gal*.

Guinan was featured in the ad, staring intently out of the picture with the barrel of a six-shooter trained on the viewer. A gun-belt filled with what appeared to be rifle shells decorated her waist, and she wore silver-studded leather gauntlets.

Texas Guinan's career was off and running. She made so many movies in such a short time that she herself lost track of the number. Because they contained no dialogue, the script was often only a couple of pages describing the action. The black screen explanation or dialogue spliced between action segments was added later. The scenes were shot out of sequence, as they are today: the cabin, the prairie, the mountainside, the corral, the cattle stampede, the snowstorm, the Indian village, the town, and so forth. Guinan would break into a scene, defend some fainting heroine, gallop away, even struggle through blinding sand, snow, or rain storm to confront villains of all sorts and all persuasions.

Because she was always at home in the saddle, Guinan was in demand for all sorts of roles. No one else could do what she did, so she gained more and more control over her work. Eventually, she became a producer of her own movies within the company framework. As in so many things that Guinan did, she pioneered a genre without even meaning to do so. Outrageous she might be, but she was also an original.

The people who appeared in the two-reelers were part of an acting company, so the same people took the various roles every time. Jack Richardson was as often her leading man as her nemesis. Francis Ford was more frequently the hero, who might or might not end up with Guinan. Many times the same actress, Jean Carpenter, played some old rancher's motherless daughter, who spends much of the movie being kidnapped; swept away in a rushing flood; snatched up and carried off on horseback; or held captive in a cave, a bandit lair, or upstairs above the saloon, gamely resisting a "fate worse than death—marriage to the villain." After that point in the script had been established, the scene would cut to Guinan undergoing a change of heart and riding to rescue the shrinking violet or, at the very least, leading the hero to her side.

Guinan was especially valuable during the production because no forms of special effects or camera tricks existed in those days. The camera was a stationary object set up on a tripod. The director yelled, "Roll 'em," to cue the cameraman to turn a crank on the side of the camera as evenly as possible. The film moved behind the lens thereby recording frame after frame through reel after reel as the action progressed. The actors moved back and forth within its focus. That narrow focus made shooting action scenes particularly dangerous.

Any time a horse is spurred or whipped to run at top speed, the chances of its falling are always there. If a horse falls on the rider, the man's leg or his entire body may be crushed. If the rider is thrown headfirst, his neck may be broken when he hits the ground. Likewise, stunt men who gallop two horses along the edge of a cliff and dive off one to pretend to capture the other are in instant danger of breaking bones that will put them out of action and, more importantly—from the point of view of the director—delay production.

Guinan herself was injured when the script called for her to leap from a cliff—actually down the side of a hill. Instead of sliding gracefully down in perfect control, she was thrown headfirst down the slide when her horse threw a shoe at the crucial moment. Guinan escaped serious injury by a degree of luck and her own athletic ability.

According to the February 1921 *Motion Picture World*, the film company she was working for at that time, Victor Kremer Film Features, Inc., decided to insure Guinan for a record $500,000. The extraordinary amount covered her for the remainder of her contract, which called for eight more pictures. The policy insured her for $50,000 per picture with an additional $100,000 insurance to be paid if any accident caused the entire company to be delayed.

How much Texas Guinan was raking in at the box office for Kremer Films can perhaps be estimated by the unprecedented amount of the insurance. Possibly it was exaggerated for publicity purposes, but probably not by much. Texas Guinan movies were everywhere. Her productions graduated from two-reelers to five-reelers in response to the demands of the audiences.

The clichés invented by Guinan and her production company were used for the next fifty years while Western movies became talkies and then epics. Finally, these Westerns became too expensive to produce. The audiences that loved them grew up, and the kids of the younger generation identified with heroes who drove fast cars and favored vodka martinis "shaken not stirred."

At the end of her career, which she claimed produced more than three hundred movies, Guinan remarked, "We never changed plots—only the horses."

She was a clever businesswoman as well. She sold and resold her pictures all over the world. The American Western silent film was seen in South America, the Orient, and Europe. No translations were necessary except for the black screens that displayed a bit of dialogue or narrative.

So popular did they continue to be that Marcus Loew traveled the United States to open his string of movie theaters. Loew bought Texas Guinan films to headline in his chain, and he introduced her and promised to publicize her premieres. She traveled with him to put on a show with her horse Waco, sometimes on the street in front of the theater, sometimes on the stage itself.

Unfortunately, anything made so fast and so cheaply was quick to wane. In 1922 Prohibition changed the habits of the nation. Designed to eradicate the evils of the saloon and intemperance, it produced the opposite effect. Prohibition drove illegal, sometimes poisonous alcoholic brews into haphazard production on the back streets and in the American home. No longer a bastion of decency, the once sacrosanct home with the wife and family apart from the "doings of men" became the scene of illegal activities. Bathtub gin was no joke. While wives and husbands drank and smoked cigarettes together, their children looked on and more often than not were instructed to be on the lookout for the law.

Westerns had to compete with cops and robbers shows. The automobile became the vehicle of choice in daring chases instead of horses. And a new kind of culture flourished in road houses and speakeasies. Owners and customers alike flouted the law of the land. An underculture of illicit liquor traffic included rival gangs hijacking each other's booze, bloody gang wars with Tommy-gun retribution, and the very officials who should be maintaining order bribed to turn a blind eye to the whole mess.

In 1923 Texas Guinan went back to Broadway as a star with a national reputation, which she quickly turned into a musical revue at the Winter Garden Theater. Still, she felt that returning to the stage was somehow a step backward for her career. She had been in so many revues before.

According to Guinan, one night after the show everyone went over to Larry Fay's Beaux Arts Hotel lounge. Someone suggested that she sing. Always eager to go "on," she obliged. She sang everything in her repertoire and invited the audience to join in for the choruses. Then she invited various other members of the cast to come up and do their "shticks." Texas ran the show, telling jokes, introducing the entertainers, encouraging them to perform, and encouraging applause afterwards. As she remembered, "Everybody had a great time."

Guinan later said the hotel manager was so pleased with the way the party came to life and people behaved and had fun that he asked her to stay and accept a post as "mistress of ceremonies." Most nightclubs and speakeasies had "masters of ceremonies," but a glamorous woman in such a position was unheard of.

Would she have accepted that position based solely on the hotel manager's enthusiastic request? No one will ever know. What is known is that after the show she was approached by the slick entrepreneur Larry Fay himself

Larry Fay was an entrepreneur only if someone asked his profession. In truth he was a racketeer. He had his fingers in all sorts of pies—including the illegal distilling and selling of liquor. Racketeering covered a multitude of sins the federal government was now being called to crack down on.

Instead of creating a nation of sober, law-abiding citizens, the Prohibition Act of 1920 had created an ever-increasing population of petty and not-so-petty criminals who made and sold illegal alcohol to otherwise honest people. Gangsters hired out to these bosses and their suppliers. Huge criminal organizations were engaged in the distilling, transporting, and selling of an illegal product.

Unfortunately, for the morals of America, people who would never have entertained the idea of committing robbery or murder were perfectly happy to break the law in the purchase and consumption of illegal alcohol. All these men who created the booze, as well as the people who drank it, were criminals in the eyes of the law.

Larry Fay was a prominent one among them, with more than forty arrests. He had been hauled in for crimes as varied as offending the peace and dignity of the city, running a clip joint, threatening wholesale dairymen who didn't sell their milk to him at his prices, and operating a legitimate taxicab fleet whose drivers sold booze and carried people, mostly out-of-towners, to illegal speakeasies.

Fay saw Texas Guinan as a hostess who was also a performer. Her ready wit, her willingness to exchange insults with hecklers, and her vibrant personality would draw people into the club, especially when he publicized it through his organization. Thrill-seeking out-of-town buyers would beg to be driven to it, especially when they learned that they were going to be in the club of a movie star who almost all had seen numerous times on the silver screen.

Fay and Guinan talked the idea over.

It was the break she'd been looking for. Guinan was more than streetwise by that time. She'd been gone from the church choir in Waco, Texas, for more than half her life. She also recognized that she could no longer be the cowgirl and gallop horses at breakneck speed over all sorts of terrain. Eventually, she knew she'd be hurt. Moreover, Guinan had to admit to herself she didn't want to ride like that anymore. Though she was as beautiful as ever, Guinan had matured in both face and figure. At thirty-nine she needed to change professions.

She accepted his offer with enthusiasm. She'd gone from singer, to rodeo queen, to showgirl, to movie actress, and now to mistress of ceremonies. Her progression seemed like fate.

To her way of thinking, since she'd left Texas, her life had moved steadily along. Just as one career began to pale, another one appeared almost as if by magic.

No longer a neophyte, she was a serious businesswoman. These were the Roaring Twenties when women could do anything they were smart enough and brave enough to do. Guinan bargained with Fay and got a partnership. He would set her up at the El Fey Club, but she would run it. It would be hers to manage, and, most important, she would collect half the profits.

Self-assured as always, she had no doubt she could turn her "night club" into the most popular and prosperous on the Great White Way. The fact that it was an illegal enterprise bothered her not at all.

Night clubs were the new thing. Members paid stiff cover charges to get in. Once inside they could thumb their noses at Prohibition—dining, dancing, drinking, and enjoying lavish, more-than-slightly outrageous entertainments. Technically, they had been "invited"; Helen Morgan, a famous hostess to rival Guinan, even called her club Helen Morgan's Summer Home. Anyone could do anything so long as he could pay the cover charge with "long green folding money."

These were the clubs with shady reputations and an element of danger for everyone who entered. Larry Fay's taxicab drivers as well as other "entrepreneurs" knew the way. Sometimes customers walked hesitantly down a dark alley. Sometimes they entered through the basement of a luxurious mansion. Sometimes they crowded into the servants' elevators that carried them upward to a penthouse. Finally, they would arrive at a solid door. There they would knock twice. A little door at eye level would slide open.

The password for entertainment became the punchline of jokes, part of song lyrics, and a spectacular Broadway number: "Joe sent me."

Inside was almost every form of entertainment known at that time: chorus lines, gambling, drinking, jazz dancing, and emcees to conduct the evening's activities. The New York police turned their backs to ignore the vice in their midst. In most cases they ignored the steady stream of taxicabs cruising up to addresses on Forty-Fifth Street between Fifth and Sixth Avenues, "the wettest street in America."

Prohibition was a federal responsibility since the law was a federal amendment to the Constitution. But no one in Congress had counted on the hordes of Americans determined to break the law. Only two hundred dry agents were assigned to ferret out the thousands of clubs in the metropolis of six million people and a million visitors. The racketeers operated mostly unchecked. Everything was available for a price.

Those who came to the El Fey Club were greeted by a raucous voice. "Hello, Sucker!" Guinan would shout. "Come on in and leave your wallet on the bar."

The patrons already seated would laugh and applaud as newcomers froze in the doorways, no doubt wondering what they'd gotten themselves into. Their mistress of ceremonies habitually sat on a tall stool in the middle of the room. She was at her outrageous best as she dominated the bedlam that ensued among the dancing, drinking, and gambling patrons. She wielded a clapper noisemaker or blew on a police whistle to announce the chorus line.

People were scolded if they didn't turn and watch the dancers. As the girls pranced off the stage, Guinan would exhort the audience to "give these little girls a great big hand." If there was a chanteuse, the emcee quieted the place down, and then demanded at the end of her songs, "Let's give the little girl a great big hand."

Guinan encouraged hecklers, laughing uproariously when she embarrassed or insulted them. She was "never at a loss for a retort discourteous."

She wasn't the only hostess on the street, but she was the best known. Only Helen Morgan, the torch singer, could rival her. A tragic alcoholic, her voice sinking lower and huskier by the day, Morgan put on an act that was never as popular as Guinan's emceeing. Though it was a "classier" act than Guinan's, it was more likely to leave her audience crying in their beer than laughing until they had to hold their sides.

The gal from Texas was the "in" thing. She was "it." She was as big and wild and beautiful as the state of Texas that had produced her.

Guinan always denied that she sold liquor. What she sold were setups for her customers who brought in their own bottles. However, when she was reasonably sure that no federal agents had infiltrated her clubs, she did a brisk business in champagne and Scotch at $25 a bottle. The price was exorbitant when bread cost only a few cents, but it exemplified the type of clientele that came to see her. To say that Guinan was the toast of Broadway would be an overstatement, but for a certain element of the city and its constant stream of visitors, she was certainly one of the biggest draws.

According to legend, she was topped only once. She was encouraging the audience to applaud a singer with no real talent beyond a sweet voice. "Give the little girl a great big hand!" she called.

A federal agent supposedly stood up beside Guinan and put his hand on her shoulder. He called to a fellow agent, "Give this little girl a great big handcuff."

The incident was so memorable that it was recorded the next day in the tabloids. Guinan had no choice but to laugh with the crowd, who she then entertained with a commentary calculated to embarrass the men who raided the El Fey Club and smashed the fabulous liquor stock to smithereens, as well as all the chairs, tables, lights. Audience and employees alike were herded into paddy wagons and taken down to police headquarters. The premises were padlocked.

A few days later, Guinan was packing them in at the Del Fay Club just two blocks from the old place. With her arrests and the unsavory business she headlined, she was in some eyes the symbol of all that was mad and bad about the Jazz Age and Prohibition. Others considered her the symbol of all that was honest, brave, and beautiful.

Edmund Wilson was a much-respected New York writer and social commentator. He had served in France during World War I. He and Guinan were children of the Jazz Age when the whole scope and content of American entertainment changed forever.

Wilson reviewed theaters and nightclubs and ruthlessly voiced his anti-establishment bias. Like almost every sane moderate American, he had concluded that Prohibition was a stupid failure that had given organized crime a dangerous foothold in the country. Guinan and her clubs, opening and being closed, opening and being closed, but still forging stubbornly ahead, was one of his favorite topics. He described her in glowing, overflowing prose that can only make the reader believe he was half in love with her: "This prodigious woman, with her pearls, her glittering bosom, her abundant beautifully bleached coiffure, her formidable trap of shining white teeth, her broad bare back behind its grating of green velvet."

The object of such praise and good wishes, Guinan continued to move or be moved from club to club. Sometimes she entertained at the 300 Club, sometimes at the Melody Club. Unfortunately, her own popularity and the tremendous amounts of money she was bringing in nightly made her the object of a citywide attack. New York police commissioner George V. McLaughlin came up with a new law to wage war on nightclubs, particularly Guinan's.

With the help of the Bureau of Buildings, McLaughlin arranged to shut down all operations on premises that were not strictly zoned for such scandalous activities as *dancing*. Another tactic was to enforce the fire code to shut Guinan down if even one person more than the number permitted was present in her club. No less prestigious a newspaper than the *New York Times* kept audiences informed when Guinan's clubs were operating and when they were "closed for alterations." She was "the hot ticket in town."

One night in Guinan's 300 Club, the police raid caught two dozen members of the Georgia congressional delegation and its two U.S. Senators assembled to welcome golfer Bobby Jones home from winning the British golf championship. The police retreated in confusion and embarrassment. Later they held a press conference to complain that they knew nothing about the Bobby Jones night.

Always generous and good-hearted, Guinan had brought her brother Tommy up from Texas. While her brother was a mild success in his own hometown, she knew he could make more money in New York. She had a strong sense of family and longed to have Tommy with her. Together they opened Texas Tommy Guinan's Playground on the second and third floors of a building on West Fifty-Second Street. When it was raided, Tommy Guinan himself testified that "we do not have to sell liquor. We get $6 from every person who sits down at one of our tables. This is for the cover charges, and ginger ale is $1.50 a glass."

The police were whirling trying to shut down three Guinan clubs instead of two. Worse for their efforts, more clubs—Guinan imitations—were proliferating while law enforcement chased after Guinan.

Still enjoying her enormous popularity, in 1925, she took her club hopping from New York to Miami and then on to Chicago. Far from being unhappy about the federal raids, she capitalized on them, greeting the "boys" cordially, calling them by name whether they burst in with whistles blasting or tried to infiltrate the place unobtrusively. She would make jokes to keep the crowd laughing uproariously at the idea of climbing into the paddy wagon with their irrepressible hostess.

Customers actually complained to the management when they were not raided because everyone knew that Guinan conducted a party all the way to the jail. She was "something!" They couldn't wait to tell the folks back home in Indiana.

In 1926 while her clubs were being closed routinely, Guinan earned $700,000 in ten months. One night a group of federal agents led by a U.S. attorney disguised as a wealthy Englishman spent the evening. Another official posed as a Russian nobleman. Texas Guinan recognized them and blew each one a kiss as they started to stroll out. "Why are you leaving so early, boys?"

Though she was arrested later that evening, the club remained open. She was back before closing time and sang this ditty:

> The judge said, "Tex, do you sell booze?"
> I said, "Please don't be silly.
> I swear to you my cellar's filled
> With chocolate and vanilly."

On January 14, 1926, perhaps the crowning achievement of her entertainment career occurred. She entertained at "one of the most sumptuous and elaborate parties in . . . New York." The Lyre's Club held its twentieth annual party at the Ambassador Hotel. Magnates from Southern Pacific, New York Central, Long Island, and Nickel Plate Railroads were in attendance. The vice president of AT&T, the vice president of Consolidated Gas, and the president of Brooklyn Edison were all sitting in the audience, dressed to the nines. Guinan had ordered the ballroom decorated in Hawaiian style, with a sandy beach, palm trees, and fifteen girls dancing the hula in grass skirts. It was a night that no one present would ever forget.

That same year she came face to face and principle to principle with one of the other dynamic females of the Roaring Twenties.

Mrs. Aimee Semple McPherson arrived in New York as part of her cross-country tour taken to reassure her FourSquare Gospel Congregation that she was really back and as religious and sane as always. Dressed in white with a blue cape, rather like a nurse's uniform, she entered the 300 Club at midnight with a small group of the faithful. The year before she had gone for a swim in the Pacific and vanished. Everyone assumed she had drowned although her body had never been found. Months later McPherson appeared with the story that she had been held captive and had walked across the Sonoran Desert of Mexico to escape. Facts did not support her statements, so she was trying to reclaim her credibility.

The evangelist created a stir as she walked from table to table. Guinan, ever able to spin the unexpected into an unforgettable and outrageous evening, greeted McPherson cordially and introduced her from the dance floor.

McPherson announced that she was there to see a new side of New York, complimented Guinan on her clothes, and then addressed the audience, reminding them that there was "something else in life," and "calling them to attend church tomorrow afternoon," an hour at which she would conduct a special service for New York nightlife.

As she left, Guinan called out, "This is a woman I admire. She has the courage of her convictions. Give this little woman a great big hand!" At her command, the crowd cheered.

Guinan attended the service the next afternoon with a dozen entertainers from her show. She made her entrance in white furs and sat down front and center, keeping her countenance serious while the photographers snapped picture after picture until Sister Aimee asked them to stop.

Evidently, Sister Aimee's sermon had little or no lasting effect. Guinan went back to her nightclub the next evening for business as usual.

In February 1926, Guinan went to trial for operating a club that sold liquor. The whole case blew away when her lawyer announced that the evidence, a bottle of whiskey allegedly purchased at the 300 Club, had been taken from the Prohibition headquarters by the Prohibition agent as part of his disguise to establish himself as a good fellow.

The judge found the prosecution had not only failed to prove its case but was in serious danger of being prosecuted for manufacturing evidence. The case was dismissed, and Guinan became more famous than ever—if such a thing was possible.

Many of her expressions entered the language as the "*in things to say*" and stayed around for most of the twentieth century. For example, when a man with savoir faire and a roving eye entered the club, she dubbed him a "live one." If he passed around money, ordered expensive champagnes, and tipped well, he was "a big butter-and-egg man"—a big spender.

A story circulated that she spotted a man sitting at a ringside table, nursing his drink glumly. When she asked what was making him so glum, he supposedly replied in a choking voice, "I feel terrible—I lost $337,000 in the market today."

Patting him on the shoulder, Guinan turned to the audience and made a face. "These drunks will cry over any little thing."

Once when she was arrested and literally carried away by some federal officers, Guinan remarked to a reporter standing with pencil poised, "Where the hell would I be without Prohibition?" Behind her the band struck up "The Prisoner's Song."

Though Guinan was taken away to jail many times, she actually spent almost no time there. Charges were invariably dropped against her because no one could find any clear proof that she owned any of the establishments in which she worked.

In 1929, one of the most terrible years in American economic history, Guinan returned to Hollywood and starred in a talking picture, *Queen of the Nightclubs*, written for her and about her. It was not a big hit. Certainly the economic catastrophe that shook the country contributed to the failure, but her electric personality did not project from the film as well as it did in real life in an intimate club setting.

Returning to New York proved a disaster as well. The terrible economic conditions meant that the "big spenders," "the "live ones," the "butter-and-egg men" no longer had the disposable income to throw away in nightclubs. Many of them were back on their heels trying to scramble out of the difficulties in which the stock market's crash had left them. While suicides were never so common as myths portray them, times were hard all across the country.

With fewer and fewer clubs making money, she nevertheless opened one more—Texas Guinan's Salon Royale. Undoubtedly, she felt an obligation to her brother, to the men who had worked for her for so many years, and to her "girls," who had danced and sang and followed her from club to club. Almost without exception, they could have been her daughters, had she ever had children of her own.

Around the same time, Helen Morgan, the torch singer, had opened a new club as well.

Although it seemed as though both women and their club life could go on forever, the whole routine was getting tiresome, the country was growing up, and it was time for the famous mistresses of ceremonies to move on. Guinan was by that time forty-seven years old. She made one more movie, a Paramount production named *Glorifying the American Girl.*

Morgan was barely thirty when she took her smoky, whiskey-drenched contralto to Broadway to sing "Can't Help Lovin' That Man of Mine" and "Bill," two songs forever associated with her. Her role as Julie LaVerle in *Showboat* carried her to Hollywood and her untimely death in just ten short years.

In 1931 Guinan put her own show together and sailed for England determined to become the toast of Europe where audiences would appreciate her own brand of dancing-singing-laughing extravaganza. Sadly, they never got the chance. Both England and France barred her performances.

Landing on her feet for what would be the last time, Texas Guinan returned to New York and opened her show, *Too Hot for Paris*, for a limited run. On her way out of town, she posed for newsreel cameras saying that she would be taking it on the road "so's the city can get a good night's sleep."

As the show toured and Guinan continued to make fun of the French and their refusal to view the show, the French became embarrassed. No less a personage than Monsieur le Président de la Republique himself invited her to return as a guest of the government and let them entertain her. She graciously went for ten days and returned to change the name of her revue to *The Texas Guinan Revue*.

Guinan must have been shocked when, on January 2, 1933, her mentor and financier Larry Fay died on the floor of his own nightclub. Clinging to the only life he knew despite falling receipts, Fay had been forced to cut club salaries. A disgruntled doorman shot him.

He never saw it coming.

In the end, Guinan never saw "it" coming either. She and her girls were on tour in Vancouver, British Columbia, when on the night of October 30, 1933, she experience a severe pain in her belly. She was rushed to the hospital where the doctor diagnosed amoebic dysentery. He operated, but his skill was insufficient or her condition was too far advanced to be reversed. She died at 8 a.m., November 5, 1933, of a perforated bowel.

Her brother arrived too late to speak to her but accompanied the body back to New York for the funeral. She was viewed in her coffin in Campbell Funeral Church on Broadway in a white chiffon sequin gown with diamonds on her hand and at her throat. The crowd of nearly 12,000 passed to view her. The newsreel cameramen filmed it all.

How the woman called Texas would have loved it.

Among her pallbearers were Heywood Broun and Mark Hellinger, Broadway columnists who had often reviewed her shows, and Paul Whiteman, the orchestra leader.

She was buried in White Plains, New York, her hearse leading a funeral cortège of 500 cars. No one knows the amount of her estate. Her money, her jewelry, and her other possessions, their value undisclosed, went to her mother. Guinan's personal property was auctioned off and netted, according to the *Times*, $12,500.

On December 5, 1933, a month after Guinan's death, the Eighteenth Amendment to the Constitution was repealed as the Twenty-first Amendment was ratified.

Prohibition had made Texas Guinan a legend. No one can deny that it was somehow fitting that they went out together!

In later years whenever movies about the Roaring Twenties appeared, they almost invariably employed a scene inside a speakeasy with chorus lines and a female emcee in beads and fringe regaling the customers with bawdy humor and insults. Phyllis Diller played Guinan in *Splendor in the Grass*. Betty Hutton played her in a more romantic vein in *Incendiary Blonde*. Barbara Nichols sang her heart out as more of a chanteuse than an emcee in *The George Raft Story*.

Texas Guinan would be delighted to know that she returns from time to time to the milieu that she originated and loved.

THAT GOOD OL' TEXAS JEWBOY

In 1966 while he was a student at the University of Texas at Austin, Richard S. Friedman, known to his friends as Kinky, formed his first band of "merry pranksters" with musical instruments. The group called themselves King Arthur and the Carrots.

No one thought anything in particular about the silly name. Undoubtedly, it didn't mean anything. The group and the name were right in keeping with the sixties, when bands like Sam the Sham and the Pharaohs, Paul Revere and the Raiders, and Gerry and the Pacemakers were making the charts and entertaining people at concerts in clubs, auditoriums, and festivals all over the country. King Arthur's group poked fun at surf music like that supplied by the Beach Boys. To prove their musicality, the group recorded a pair of songs, which—when thrown into the sea of Texas's rich musical heritage—left nary a ripple. They really didn't care. It was just harmless fun. And above all, Richard S. Friedman was about having fun.

He was born in Chicago on Halloween in 1944. Although he has never wondered whether his birth on All Hallows Eve carried any special implications for him, he has twisted other facts from his life story because he could make jokes about them. For example, when he ran for Texas governor in 2006, Friedman falsely claimed that he was born in Palestine, Texas. Since he took care to announce that he was the "only middle-aged Jew in Texas that didn't own real estate," his audience laughed uproariously when he tagged that line with the outrageous lie that he was born in Palestine. The fact that his biographers in future generations might be confused by that misinformation troubles him not at all. It's all in the game.

Likewise, no matter what conclusions you may draw or racial slurs you might suppose, Kinky maintains that his nickname came from his mop of curly black hair—his Jew-fro, as he loves to refer to it. The fact that the name was given him by Nick "Chinga" Chavin, whose lyrics are famous in pornographic circles and notorious elsewhere, begs a different meaning. For the sake of propriety, close friends have always maintained it was because of the hair. He calls it a "Lyle Lovett starter kit."

Kinky's father, S. Thomas Friedman, lived with his wife and family in Chicago. Both were second generation Americans deeply grateful for the country that welcomed their parents. During World War II, the good doctor had been, at twenty-three, the oldest man and the navigator on a B-24 Liberator over Germany. The responsibility of bringing the plane, the "I've Had It," home safely was his and his alone, and he did so for thirty-five successful missions before he and his squad were sent back stateside, to the eternal gratitude of the crew.

Kinky was all set to be a Chicago Jew with all the trappings, but when he was only one year old, Dr. Friedman and his wife moved their family from the second largest city in America (at that time) to Houston, Texas—nowhere near the sprawling megalopolis it is today. In his onstage "autobiographical" routine, Kinky tells the audience he moved because he couldn't find work.

Kinky's life was perfectly normal, middle-class, and fairly idyllic. Dr. Friedman traveled throughout the Southwest doing community relations work. His wife was one of the first speech therapists in the state. Later they bought a four-hundred-acre ranch in one of the prettiest parts of the state—the Hill Country of central Texas. There they established Echo Hills. For the past fifty-five years, this beautiful summer camp has been a haven for Jewish children as well as those of other denominations. To this day, it is run by the members of the Friedman family, including Kinky's brother, Roger, a psychologist, assisted by his sister, Marcie, who now works for the State Department. Kinky currently lives and writes on a piece of land adjacent to Echo Hills in an old lodge he has decorated with old touring posters and photographs of his friends and family.

Growing up on a ranch outside Kerrville, Kinky displayed a talent for music and a love of chess. At age seven he was chosen to be one of fifty local players to challenge Samuel Reshevsky, the U.S. grand master. Kinky was by far the youngest competitor. He seemed destined for academic greatness during his public school and college years when he proved to be a brilliant student. He was accepted into the prestigious Plan II Honors Program at the University of Texas. Indeed, Kinky's first twenty years led everyone to believe that he would follow in his father's footsteps as an exceptional member of society.

But cracks in the yuppie façade were already beginning to appear. Nevertheless, King Arthur and the Carrots might have been a momentary aberration, a blip on the clean screen of life, had Kinky not taken a fateful detour. He volunteered to join the Peace Corps, which sent him to that part of eastern Malaysia on the world's third largest island—Borneo. Only five degrees north of the equator, he plunged into a dripping green hell of a jungle.

For two years, he gave his time and quite a bit of his future mental and physical health and well-being to the head-hunting Kayans of Sarawak. Fortunately, they no longer hunted heads, since civilization caught up with them during World War II. However, they still kept their trophies in hanging baskets on their porches. They also practiced intricate tattooing over all their bodies, which they kept mostly naked. Kinky was supposed to teach them how to plant crops, although he claims they were already successful farmers. How he would have changed them into twentieth-century farmers will never be known. The Peace Corps never got around to sending him any seeds.

What the new volunteer thought of both the society into which he had been thrust and the Peace Corps, who had seemingly deserted him, is unknown. After the initial shock, he ignored the baskets of heads and went about trying to teach them the joys of modern life. Kinky had come with a pile of Frisbees in his duffle, but the heat was too much for racing around after plastic flying saucers. He somehow escaped the tattooing. But he did join the Kayans in chewing betel nut and drinking tuak, a hallucinogenic wine, without which life beside the green river, where the natives go and "visit the fish," would have probably been unbearable. In accordance with adhering to native customs, he became entranced with chewing and drinking and going down to the river to "visit the fish" and watch the river flow.

When his parents came to visit him after nearly two years, they were advised to take a taxi from the airport to the "last outpost on the river." When they arrived, they quickly deduced that their son—half naked, bearded, unshorn, and barely able to communicate—had been out "too long where the busses don't run." On their return to civilization, they voiced their alarm to the Peace Corps in strong language.

Complaints voiced by two such respected members of the academic community got immediate results. The Peace Corps sent out a psychiatrist, who listened to Kinky's rambling story.

Kinky's seminal tale was memorable. He related how, since he was a Jew, he had not seen Jesus in the jungle. He had not seen God either. Instead, on a dark, primeval night he had seen a nine-hundred-foot Jack Ruby. Ruby kept appearing to Kinky over and over. Kinky was suitably impressed and inspired. He told how proud he felt to be a Texas Jew like the man who had gunned down Lee Harvey Oswald—who was arrested and in handcuffs, though not yet charged for the assassination of President John F. Kennedy—in the basement of the Dallas County Courthouse.

In lauding Jack Ruby's accomplishment, Kinky revealed his admiration to the psychiatrist. He talked about Oswald's firing the fatal shots from the "Texas Cookbook Suppository Building." The psychiatrist gaped and scratched his head, trying to figure out whether his subject was serious, when Kinky whispered, "Jesus! Ol' Jack must really have had some balls."

At length, concurring with Dr. and Mrs. Friedman's analyses of the situation, the psychiatrist concluded that Kinky needed to be returned to his own culture by the next plane out. Whether or not the Kinkster protested is unknown.

Later, Kinky swore in his autobiographical *'Scuse Me While I Whip This Out* that he was inspired to become a country-western singer by his life-changing experience in the Sarawak jungle. To that end, he announced that he was forming a new band with a name that his father called a "negative, hostile, peculiar thing"—Kinky Friedman and the Texas Jewboys. Of course, his father's disapproval was gasoline to the fire his son wanted to light in his corner of the world. When the rest of Texas and the world got over being shocked, they found the name hilarious.

In 1971 Kinky kept his "date with destiny." The Texas Jewboys were born. Their purpose was satire, and the lyrics that the group composed and sang were wildly insulting to all Texas cultures without fear or favoritism. In Kinky's own words, "If you ain't offending somebody, you ain't getting anything done."

They would proudly boast that they were "thrown off the stage in Dallas, chased off the stage in Buffalo, and threatened by both Jewish groups and anti-Semites in New York." A rumor has spread for years that Kinky and his group are the only artists to have taped an unaired episode of *Austin City Limits*. The CD *Last of the Jewish Cowboys: The Best of Kinky Friedman* includes his greatest hits and comes with the parenthetical warning in big, black capital letters: EXPLICIT LYRICS.

The seventies were the age of revolt against the materialistic, smug civilization that America had built for itself after World War II. However, many, including his own family and friends, thought "the Kinkster" had completely "wigged out." If he had been revolting against the materialistic establishment, that would have been perfectly acceptable. But what was with his revolting against the safe, wholesome personal life that he could step back into at any minute? What was there to revolt against in a summer camp—a world of happy children in a peaceful rural setting?

The group officially debuted in 1973 on the stage at Luckenbach, Texas. The town had been purchased by another Plan II graduate of the University of Texas named Hondo Crouch. It was home for the first "Outlaw" music festival under the sponsorship of Waylon Jennings and Willie Nelson.

The "Outlaw Movement" was so-called because it was different from the music being released month after month in Nashville, Tennessee. The singers were outlaws because they sounded different and sang, in part, about different things. When Willie Nelson won complete creative control over his work, he recorded the album *Red-Headed Stranger*, a huge popular hit. Singing along with Willie was Waylon Jennings, another successful country singer hoping to break out of the Nashville mold. Columbia Records argued against the simple piano and guitar accompaniment, but with such distinctive voices, Willie and Waylon didn't need anything else. The two then released the album that put the name to the entire movement. *Wanted: The Outlaws!* was country music's first platinum album.

The outlaws of Texas music and music festivals are reputed to have recognized Kinky as one of their own within a few minutes of hearing his lyrics. Kinky Friedman's subject matter did not fit with theirs, but it was certainly different from anything that was being sung.

In keeping with the name of the group, Kinky gleefully piled insult upon insult, managing to offend several sensitive ethnic groups in his first onstage introduction. The audience bristled, hissed, and probably booed as well as laughed uproariously when he introduced his musicians: Little Jewford, Big Nig, Panama Red, Rainbow Colors, and Snakebite Jacobs.

Their irreverence was what made them different from all the others who had blisters on their fingers from strumming their guitar strings and corns on their toes from tapping their cowboy boots. On the wave of outlaw music sweeping the country, Vanguard Records agreed with some trepidation to release Kinky's first recording in 1973. *Sold American* became a cult hit and remains a popular CD a quarter of a century later. Among its songs is "We Reserve the Right to Refuse Service to You," composed in the jungles of Sarawak. This satire of the restaurant business's mostly self-made problems offended many and elicited frowning faces from the first line.

Truth to tell, Kinky was delighted. Quickly, before the flames could die down, he assaulted religious sensitivity with "Top Ten Commandments."

When he wasn't singing about things religious, he was making offhand remarks such as, "The old testament tells us that the Lord created the heavens and all the earth in six days. There are those of us, of course, who think He might've taken just a little more time."

The women in the audience, especially those who had been espousing women's lib and burning their bras only a few years before, cringed and booed when he broke out with this less-than-romantic chorus:

> Get your biscuits in the oven and your buns in the bed
> That's what I to my baby said,
> Women's liberation is a-going to your head,
> Get your biscuits in the oven and your buns in the bed.

As the Texas Jewboys toured, they bragged that they were "closing clubs in their wake." Their drummer complained to their road manager that they didn't have any groupies. The answer was that the music was serio-comic satire, hard to write and hard to pull off. Instead of having pretty girls in short shorts and halter tops sneaking backstage and wanting to sleep with them, they were besieged backstage by "Jewish sociology professors taking notes!"

Of course, here and there, a "naysayer" would complain that they were all fakes. Kinky Friedman, from Chicago Jewish to Chess Club to University of Texas to Echo Hills Children's Camp, did not have the type of childhood that would give him the experience to become a country-western singer—in particular an outlaw country-western singer. He had not been born in poverty to an Arkansas sharecropper. Not only had he never been in Folsom Prison, he had not spent a single night in jail.

Kinky relished the criticism and nodded in agreement. As he often remarked onstage, "No one ever pointed at me and laughed and said, 'There goes the coal miner's daughter.'"

He had found his element. He loved touring and being part of the music world. He loved the applause. He loved the approbation. And mostly he loved his ability to anger and outrage the audience. His opportunity to poke fun at everything sacred and profane was a hoot and a delight.

Unfortunately, Kinky is hazy about this part of his life. He'd had a number of really bad experiences with drugs; "One of them lasted for several decades."

In one of his numerous satirical books, he writes about a doctor in Nashville people called Dr. Snap, who was well-known to people in the entertainment industry, which was about half of the town in those days. One of them would say something like, "Oh, I'm tired, really tired, Dr. Snap."

He'd prescribe something that would really pep them up. The audience knew the good doctor was prescribing "uppers" with a more than liberal hand. His medical business was taking care of the exhausted and oftentimes "strung out" singers, songwriters, musicians, and all those others who labored on and back stage at the Grand Ole Opry.

At that time, Kinky was claiming to be the only full-blooded Jew on the best-known stage in the United States. Not only was everyone else on the Opry stage down-home country boys and girls, but the town itself was regarded as the spiritual home of sentimental music that symbolized everything "waspish" in America. His oblique references to the rampant drug problems won him no friends in Nashville, a situation that he could live with.

When the Texas Jewboys finally drifted apart in the early eighties, Kinky moved to New York City, making his irreverent self into a headliner at the Lone Star Café with a following that included John Belushi, a guy that fit right into Kinky's life-style. Kinky was the darling of the antiestablishment celebrities. He was pulling down $6,000 a week, but he still couldn't afford a decent place to live. He freely admitted his cocaine habit was keeping him broke. The situation couldn't continue. He lost his record contract; his gig at the Lone Star ran out.

On March 5, 1982, at the Chateau Marmont on Sunset Boulevard in Los Angeles, John Belushi died of a drug over-dose at age thirty-three. The cause of death was a speedball—an injection of cocaine and heroin.

Kinky was brought up short by Belushi's death. He had recently lost one of his dearest friends, Tom Baker, to a heroin overdose. A girlfriend, Kacey Cohen, whom he referred to as the love of his life, had died in a car crash. His own mortality stared him in the face. Kinky remembers that his literary career began when he was at this very low point in his life. "Desperation drove me to those early books."

In 1984 on a typewriter borrowed from Mike McGovern, a former newspaper columnist, Kinky sat down to write a mystery novel *Greenwich Killing Time*, set in—where else?—Greenwich Village. A newspaper columnist became the police's prime suspect. No one can say Kinky doesn't pay his debts.

Vandam Press bought the book for enough money to get Kinky home. Since then, he has given up the drugs and left the wild life behind. What is wild about him now is his own irreverent commentary implemented by his lightning repartee and comic sense of timing.

In *Greenwich Killing Time*, Kinky Friedman's sleuth was a man he thought he knew better than anyone else in the world—sort of. In typical Kinkster style, he wrote himself in as the private investigator. Kinky claims he was stoned most of the time that the book was "becoming."

Some of his friends became the book's Village Irregulars, borrowing the name from Sherlock Holmes's Baker Street Irregulars. His friend Ratso Sloman developed into his Dr. Watson character, whom Holmes, played by Kinky, continuously insults. Sometimes in later novels, Ratso becomes Archie Goodwin when Kinky pretends to be Nero Wolfe.

Despite several obvious borrowings from famous mystery writers, the book sold very well and continues to do so. He had already made a name for himself, having been a touring entertainer for more than ten years and well-liked among reporters and entertainment critics. The *Chicago Tribune*, his hometown rag, so to speak, called it "A 24-carat American original." The *Boston Phoenix* managed a questionable left-handed compliment. "What's pleasantly surprising about [it] is that it's so damn good."

Kinky was probably as amazed as the book editors since he more or less "fell" into writing. He treats the idea of literary immortality a la Sir Arthur Conan Doyle as a joke and maintains that his single most important literary goal is to amuse Americans during their air travel.

Sadly, his mother died of a heart attack shortly after Kinky's return. She did not live to read Kinky's first published effort and read the excellent reviews. Kinky's first novel, published in 1986, is still in print. A modest literary success, the one-time singer settled down in a little green trailer on the ranch at Echo Hills to write his next book.

Besides writing books, Kinky is a regular contributor as well as sometime cover model for *Texas Monthly*. The cover that probably outraged the most people—after they stopped laughing—was the July 2004 cover. Kinky posed in drag, complete with mustache, goatee, and his favorite Montecristo No. 2 cigar, the kind Fidel Castro once smoked. He wore a bejeweled lace dress with a sweetheart neckline framing his hairy chest. A gold riband bedizened with rhinestone and pearl brooches slanted across his left shoulder. On his head he wore a dowdy white wig, a rhinestone tiara, and dangling rhinestone and pearl earrings.

He was Queen Elizabeth II with his right hand upraised, third finger pointing straight up. In order not to outrage too many people, *Texas Monthly* added a red "Censored!" sign covering half the finger.

The cover headlines an article entitled "Texas vs. the World!" with the subtitle "Yes, they hate us. Should we care?" It was not even written by Kinky Friedman, but it proved that the Kinkster would do anything for money. In this case he posed. The issue sold out shortly after it hit the stands, and copies disappeared under suspicious circumstances from subscribers' mailboxes.

All the attendant publicity did much to increase reader interest in Kinky's books. The first thing most readers notice when dipping into them is that the plot is decidedly secondary to the running commentary of the sleuth Kinky himself. He freely admits that many of the most important conversations in his early books are between him and his cat, Cuddles, who was a companion in New York for many years as well as a character in his books. As you might expect, neither real nor fictional cat answers back. The author's voice is everywhere in the book, commenting, reminiscing, riffing off into history, detective literature, personal observations. He spends dozens of pages talking to the reader, musing and pondering the "clues," carrying on a dialogue with Dr. Watson or Archie Goodwin. Where it's all going is a mystery to the readers, but the dirty words and the social commentary go on and on in brisk Rabelaisian style. Despite the reader's "shock and awe," he reads on because the book is so difficult to toss behind the couch, much less close on the coffee table.

The *New Yorker* called him a "somewhat addled cowboy-philosopher king." To which Kinky replied, "It's okay to think you're a cowboy, unless, of course, you happen to run into someone who thinks he's an Indian."

He never forgets his friends like McGovern, Rambam, Chinga, and Jewford. Tom Baker, his dear friend who had overdosed, appeared in the first pages of *Elvis, Jesus, and Coca-Cola*. Kacey Cohen, "the love of his life," killed herself as Downtown and Uptown Judy in the same book.

In 2006 he attained the age of sixty, although he will tell you with pardonable pride that he reads at a sixty-two-year-old level. Considering himself mature enough to move on to greater things, Kinky announced his candidacy for governor of Texas that year, although as he freely admits he has no political experience whatsoever. That lack, however, does not strike him as a handicap. The list of Texas governors that had no political experience is probably longer than the list of those that had. Over the years, the office has been sought and *won* by a flour salesman (W. Lee "Pass the Biscuits, Pappy"

O'Daniel), a housewife whose husband could not run again because he had been impeached (Ma Ferguson), a man named Beauford (pronounced Byewferd) Jester, and the owner of the Texas Rangers baseball team (George W. Bush).

Kinky ran in a field of five candidates. Many doubted the sincerity of his campaign. They felt that he was unqualified and making the run only to draw attention to himself and sell more of his CDs and books. On May 11, 2006, with 169,574 signatures, Kinky submitted his petition to get on the November ballot. He admitted with a smirk that the majority of the signatures came from bars and dance halls where he entertained.

One of the many successful events in his campaign happened in Houston, where he talked, told jokes, and sang a few songs to six or seven hundred people assembled. Since Kinky is a bachelor, someone asked who would act as first lady in the governor's mansion. Kinky immediately nodded toward his longtime friend and a member of the original Jewboys.

Jewford smiled and shrugged. "I need a gig."

Then Kinky unveiled his poster and his new t-shirt. Everyone laughed, signed his petition, and bought one or two of his campaign materials. His slogan read "Kinky 2006: Why the Hell Not?"

The candidate couldn't believe the crowd had actually signed his petition. He went back to his hotel room shaking his head. "Hell," he said to Jewford. "If I win, I'll demand a recount."

Certainly the national media took to his zany antics and gave him both air and print, and the cash royalty money kept flowing into his bank account. *60 Minutes* interviewed him while Texas watched, prepared to listen critically. He had them laughing within minutes. He traded one-liners with Jay Leno while the audience roared. He locked horns with Bill O'Reilly and came out the winner. He leaned back and puffed on his cigar with David Letterman.

He was an interviewer's dream. Texas and America were richly entertained.

All across the country, people stared at his costume and wondered if he indeed was a serious candidate or a joker. Kinky had adopted menacing black—a black bull-rider hat, black boots, and a black belt with a huge silver buckle. Over a black pearl-snap shirt, he usually wore a black leather vest. Sometimes he would walk into the interview in a black frock coat in the old style of a gambler in the Long Branch Saloon ready to slide an ace up his sleeve and be run out of town by Marshal Dillon.

Devotees of old Western movies might have recognized the outfit of a desperado concealing his pearl-handled pistols with which he planned to rob the stagecoach on the way to Deadwood. If his kinky hair were not enough of an attraction, he had grown sideburns and a thick moustache and carefully shaved a slim goatee arrowing down the center of his chin. Interviewing him proved to be more like feeding him one-liners for his comic act.

For *60 Minutes*, Morley Safer first asked if the candidate felt that Texas was ready for a Jewish governor.

Kinky fired right back. His answers proved to be less political and more part of a one-man show, calculated to make people laugh. "Absolutely. Listen, y'all can trust me. I'm a Jew. I'll hire good people."

When asked whether there was any truth to the stories that he had been a drug addict, he replied that he hadn't done drugs in twenty-five years or more. When he left New York, he came back to the Hill Country where his mother died, and it cleansed him.

When Safer asked him about his special relationships with various presidents, he told this story: "Bill Clinton was a fan of my books." While Kinky was at a book-signing in Barnes and Noble in Austin, this guy came up to him and said, "Sign one for the president." Now Kinky didn't believe him, and he signed it with one of his standard inscriptions, "Yours in Christ," and forgot all about it.

Then came a letter that the postman at Medina, Texas, thought was from the White Horse Saloon in Nashville "where they do the line dancing." It was really from the White House. In it was a letter from Bill Clinton with the last sentence, "I have now read all your books—more please—I really need the laughs."

In his autobiographical *'Scuse Me While I Whip This Out: Reflections on Country Singers, Presidents, and Other Troublemakers*, Kinky tells how his father and he were invited to the Clinton White House. In the time-honored tradition of country-western entertainers, he wore his black cowboy hat into the dining room. According to Kinky, two hundred people commented negatively on the hat. Then he found his place card.

People immediately stopped bitching. Instead, they asked, "Who is that interesting man from Texas sitting next to the president?"

As of this writing, Kinky has yet to use the former president in a cameo appearance in one of his books, but since he is still writing, the next book may have Bill Clinton slipping in for a few quick laughs.

Though Kinky didn't mention the following story in his interview with Safer, he likes to tell it as another example of his special relationships with various presidents. When George W. Bush was governor of Texas, he was also a friend and admirer of Kinky. According to the story, the governor was walking through the first Texas Book Festival sponsored by the governor's wife and former librarian Laura Bush. Larry McMurtry of *Lonesome Dove*, *Terms of Endearment*, and *The Evening Star* fame had not shown up. The governor saw Kinky palm McMurtry's nametag and clap it onto his vest. People soon began to stop by, to compliment him, and to discuss literature with him.

In typical Kinky style, he carried on the charade for a time—until he suddenly realized that the governor was listening and wasn't fooled for a minute. Kinky had the grace to look sheepish and say he was just helping Larry out. George W. made no comment, but Kinky noticed that he pulled his aides aside and whispered to them. Kinky was sure he was going to get kicked out. Instead, he learned that George W. wanted him for a campaign manager.

Kinky swears this is a true story.

Whether he sold and autographed any of Larry McMurtry's books is unknown.

Two years later, in July 2006, after he had announced his candidacy, *Texas Monthly* put him on the cover again, this time dressed as Uncle Sam with a stern expression and his index finger pointing toward the potential purchaser. The caption was "I Want You." What he wanted "you" for was pretty much obscured, but Kinky's publicity was infinite. Jesse Ventura, professional wrestler who amazingly was elected governor of Minnesota, came to Texas to lend his support to Kinky's campaign.

In *Texas Hold 'Em: How I Was Born in a Manger, Died in the Saddle, and Came Back as a Horny Toad*, Kinky recalled that people asked him if he hesitated before entering the race. He replied that he had no problem at all. In his inimitable style, he recounted how when a group of powerful Texans went hunting for Sam Houston to persuade him to be the governor, they found him drunk, sleeping under a bridge with the Indians. Kinky adds for good measure, "And he was the greatest governor this state has ever had."

His campaign provided plenty of laughs, but he seemed to be a bit short on viable ideas. When asked about his plans if he were to be elected governor, Kinky promised that he would put the Ten Commandments back in the public schools. "Maybe I'll change their name to the Ten Suggestions, you know." His reason was that schools seem to be less certain about what constitutes good behavior than they used to be. As for the atheist who was offended by them, "We all know what's gonna happen to him. His tombstone's gonna read, 'All dressed up and no place to go.'"

Kinky promised a "No Teacher Left Behind" program. He planned to finance public school improvements by video poker terminals in bars and dance halls, his "Slots for Tots" plan.

"I'm still a child, very immature," he told one interviewer. "I treat adults like children and children like adults." One of his favorite shticks when he spotted a child in the audience was to say, "The Kinkster never likes to say fuck in front of a c-h-i-l-d."

In front of a liberal crowd, Kinky threw in as many racist and sexist epithets as he could think of. If it was a country crowd, he used bigger words and made fun of rednecks. He promised that he planned to "get the moneychangers out of the temple. I'm a Judeo-Christian. Jesus and Moses are in my heart, two good Jewish boys who got in a little trouble with the government."

Away from the cameras, he was asked about eternal life. He replied by quoting Bob Dylan, "When you die they let you off the hook."

Only the *Weekly Standard* made a serious attempt to interview him in depth. Matt Labash reported that Kinky had a "shtick-Tommy gun" routine. He clarified that analysis by reporting that an eight-hour interview would get him seven hours of oft-told stories that have been around the world several times in several different versions told by several different comedians. Maybe one hour of the material would be original and somewhat pertinent.

Kinky cheerfully admits to being an entertainer who recycles his material. He's pro-recycling; it's like rotating the crops.

Since Texas is what Texas has always been, Kinky was making inroads with the electorate. Impressed by the polls, Chris Bell, the Democratic candidate, contacted Kinky and asked him to throw his votes to his campaign. Kinky, of course, refused.

Since only about 30 percent of the people in Texas bother to vote for the governor, Kinky figured he was running not against incumbent Rick Perry, but against apathy. He must have run well because he garnered 12 percent of the votes. He came in behind Perry, who had 36 percent; Bell; and Carole Keeton Strayhorn, who also ran as an independent. In Texas politics, the most votes wins no matter whether they constitute a majority or not.

Kinky maintains that he really won a victory for the intelligent, thoughtful members of the electorate. His poll numbers actually totaled around 550,000 votes. He attributes his loss to Perry's position as the handsome Republican incumbent. Perry garnered almost 2,000,000 votes. Strayhorn billed herself as "one tough grandma," easily winning many votes from sympathetic women and the occasional Texas gentleman. Still, she won fewer than 800,000 votes. Democratic candidate Chris Bell got 1,200,000. Even if Kinky had thrown his votes in with Bell, the Democrat would not have won.

Though he lost the election in November 2006, Kinky has consoled himself. He learned what W. Lee O'Daniel, the flour salesman of the 1940 election, came to know: winning isn't the most important thing to be gained out of running for governor. For O'Daniel, sales of his particular brand of flour went through the roof. Likewise, Kinky's CDs and books "flew off the shelves" in every edition, while he was making his run. He also has his own website, www.kinkyfriedman.com, which sells his t-shirts, caps, CDs, and some of his books.

Far from being upset by his defeat, Kinky was more troubled by the fact that so many people cast their vote for him. The number of people who will vote for just anyone astounded him. Moving past that sobering thought, he has decided to take this defeat as a mandate to continue to shock and outrage Texans, Americans, and the world insofar as his voice can be heard. He has many more strident songs, obscene observations, and pithy remarks to make before he retires in complete anonymity to the family spread in the Hill Country.

Now the world must decide whether or not Kinky is a serious artist—both musical and literary—or merely a poseur with a head full of offensive jokes and the wit and will to deliver them with all the purpose of a double-barreled shotgun.

Well, folks, you'll have to figure that out for yourselves.

By way of reporting "the facts, ma'am, just the facts," here's a last look at the black-garbed man with the huge cigar and the bottle of whiskey at his elbow. As he will tell you himself, he is a man who considers himself a serious soul whose fate remains never to be understood.

People have gotten him all wrong. When he sings an outrageous song like "They Ain't Makin' Jews like Jesus Anymore," people think he is serious in his sentiments. Likewise, everyone's anti-favorite, "Asshole from El Paso," is as yet unappreciated in Texas. The failure to achieve cult greatness with this particular song has wounded him deeply. He wrote it purposefully to give Texas a song at least as popular as Merle Haggard's "Okie from Muskogee."

On the other hand, Kinky is chagrined and retires in a blue funk when he croons, "Ride 'Em Jewboy," an elegy to the Holocaust, and no one seems to understand the horror in the lines,

Now the smokes from camps are rising
See the helpless creatures on their way

Perhaps the most puzzling of Kinky's songs is "The Ballad of Charles Whitman." Audiences simply do not know how to react. They stare at each other, the ceiling, their laps, the foam disappearing from their beers. The subject is a man who climbed to the top of the clock tower on the University of Texas campus with a high-powered Remington hunting rifle.

He killed five people on his way up. Then from his "sniper's post" he killed fourteen people and wounded thirty-one others. Later it was found that he had killed his own mother and his wife as the first acts of his rampage. Authorities have never come to agreement as to the reason for the ninety-six minutes of terror, which ended after Austin police officers were summoned; climbed, into certain danger and possible death, to the top of the tower; and, finally, shot Whitman rather than give him a chance to murder them.

The song shocked Texans and still resonates throughout America. It never fails to make any anthologies of Kinky's CDs as well as draw commentary from sociologists and psychologists who are unable to refrain from analyzing the composer while they analyze the murderer.

Kinky maintains that audiences take him seriously for the wrong things, but he makes no effort to clarify or separate the serious from the comic. Perhaps he sees no separation. Comedy is very close to tragedy. In fact, many comedians believe that in a perverse way the audience enjoys being uncomfortable, cringing in the face of horror. After a certain point, they can acknowledge its grotesque face no longer. At that point they begin to laugh to gain relief.

Kinky refers to several famous artists whom he admires: "You have your life and your work, and you *should* get the two as confused and as mixed up as possible. Make it all one fabric. Vincent van Gogh did that. Hank Williams did that, Allen Ginsberg, the poet Charles Bukowski, those kinds of people did it. Anne Frank, of necessity, did it."

Kinky classifies himself with a tilt of his chin. "I'm a writer of fiction who tells the truth," he insists, and then he winks. "A man who tells the truth should always have one foot in the stirrup."

Before his audience has time to consider the implications of the first statement, he leaps into the saddle and gallops away. And they laugh.

At home on the family ranch and camp, he probably allows his real nature to show more than just a glimpse. Among the many traditions and expressions of the love of nature that Kinky preserves are the hummingbird feeders that his mother hung from the trees and kept full of sugar water. He now takes the responsibility of keeping them filled. His father always told the boys at the camp that there were over two hundred species of hummingbirds, so that means there are many tiny beaks to fill.

On a fifty-acre tract down the road from the camp is Kinky's Utopia Animal Rescue Ranch. As he told Safer in his *60 Minutes* interview, he has saved to date almost 1,500 animals from euthanasia.

Why?

He replied in typical flippant Kinky style, "Money may buy you a fine dog, but only love can make him wag his tail."

In a more poignant moment at the end of his book *Jesus, Elvis, and Coca-Cola,* he wrote about the death of his cat: "They say that when you die and go to heaven all the dogs and cats you've ever had in your life come running to meet you. Until that day, rest in peace, Cuddles."

Lest we all get too serious, at that point in his book Kinky remembered the words of his longtime friend and mentor Willie Nelson. With regard to life and golf balls, "Fortunately, we're not in control."

He closed that section of the book with the ending for all his performances, real or unreal: "May the god of your choice bless you."

Kinky's latest book grew out of his run for governor. Since he had the opportunity to rub shoulders with many of the political class, he felt qualified to title it *You Can Lead a Politician to Water but You Can't Make Him Think.* It's subtitled is *Ten Commandments for Texas Politics.* Like all authors he writes about his own experiences. Besides the usual outrageous remarks about Texas, people, and God, he actually manages to talk briefly about some of the problems he saw as he traveled around Texas campaigning.

The many who have read the book believe that the real joke might have been on Texas. He would probably have made as good a governor as anybody.

No one will ever know.

THE HOLLYWOOD RANGER

Blackie, the bootlegger, thought he'd seen and heard it all until the day he was selling some of his cheap "grain" and one of Ranger's toughest town hooligans nudged him.

"Blackie, anybody botherin' you?"

"Well, no, I guess not," was his reply.

"Any law, any preachers," the voice at his shoulder whispered, "anybody you want to get rid of?"

"No."

"Come on." Again the nudge. "I guarantee the job. For a hundred dollars."

Even Blackie was shocked at the idea that any town had gotten so corrupt that a man could pay a hundred dollars to have another man killed. He shouldn't have been surprised. Robbery, murder, bootlegging, gambling, and prostitution were rampant in the oil boomtowns filled with strangers.

People were flat broke one minute. Then the well they'd sunk their life savings into would "blow in." They'd be rich the next. And the next, they'd spend it or lose it or have it stolen from them by the crooks who waited on every street corner.

Among the very worst was the town of Ranger, about fifty miles southeast of Fort Worth. In 1917, before the first well blew in, agricultural products—cotton, peanuts, and cattle—were

Ranger's only source of income, if drought did not intervene. As luck would have it, the drought broke the same fall that the first well blew in. Before long the streets were mud holes. Then heavy oil-field equipment turned them into swamps. The few automobiles in town sank to their axles in the mire. Drivers carried a chain and a shovel to dig themselves out or hired a mule team to pull them out of the oily, stinking filth.

As if by some evil trick, Congress passed Republican Andrew Volstead's Prohibition Act a couple of years later in 1919. It prohibited the making, transport, and sale of all alcoholic beverages, thereby creating an instant market for illegal liquor. At the same time, it created an instant underworld in Texas and the rest of the nation.

The men and women willing to break the law descended upon the little town of Ranger with its transient families, who mostly lived in tents, called "rag towns," on the edge of the fields where their men labored. As elsewhere throughout the country, oil-field workers and otherwise upstanding citizens regarded Volstead as a violation of their civil rights. They came to despise the lawmen sent to enforce it as much as they despised the moonshiners who made the illegal alcohol and the bootleggers who sold it. Indeed a heavy majority of American citizens recognized that the act indirectly put them in danger at the hands of the lawless.

For three years the intolerable situation continued, until finally R. C. Vandiver of Wichita Falls was robbed and shot at in broad daylight. When he returned fire, the criminals drove away. The intended victim reported the crime not to the county sheriff but to the citizens' Law and Order League. Vandiver's prominence as well as the general feeling roiling in the community led many members of the original townsfolk to stand up and demand justice. Enough was enough. The League requested assistance from Austin.

Three rangers rode into town on horseback, trotting smartly down the muddy main street. Along with H. P. Brady and Martin N. Koonsman came a man new to the service, but one who had already attracted attention. He had enlisted after five years as a special agent for the U.S. Treasury Department. His name was Manuel T. Gonzaullas, and he seldom worked with others. Undercover was his specialty, but the need to restore the rule of law had forced his superiors to send in the best they had.

Only a tiny percentage of the citizens was happy to see the three rangers. After the lawmen rounded up some of the most obvious lawbreakers, the Eastland County Chamber of Commerce, ever mindful of where their "pay" came from, ordered the sheriff to act. The rangers were surprised and outraged when the sheriff threw down his guns on them. Decent citizens stood by and watched as their own peace officer arrested and jailed Gonzaullas and Koonsman, charging them with assault with intent to kill.

The response from Austin was immediate. A company of ten rangers headed by a ranger captain and including the state assistant attorney general rushed to the town. Gonzaullas and his partner were released immediately on $1,500 bond each. Within a week a grand jury met and no-billed them. The Eastland County Chamber hastily withdrew the complaint.

So long as they were in the county in such numbers, the thirteen rangers began a retaliatory crackdown and roundup of the criminals. The chamber's actions had had exactly the opposite of the desired effect. Only the upstanding citizens, who were in the minority, were delighted and gratified.

Unfortunately, the roundup in Ranger did not provide much relief. Oil wells were blowing in not only in Eastland but in Stephens and Wichita Counties as well. The corruption was widespread, and the ranger troop had its hands full. In Wichita Falls, Ranger Gonzaullas had his first shoot-out with a pair of masked robbers who invaded a poker game in a newly rich citizen's home. Cursing, threatening, and waving their weapons— including a sawed-off shotgun—in the players' faces, they stole the money and jewelry on the table and fled into the night. One of the players had the presence of mind to dive for the phone and call the police station.

Gonzaullas volunteered to go with the local law. Quickly, he checked his guns and hurried out. Instead of walking down the street with the officers, he took the back alley, moving in the dark, pistol in hand. As luck would have it, he heard the men coming. Uncertain who was approaching, the ranger held his fire, but one of the excited robbers fired at him point blank. The shot missed, but the ranger had the blur of a white shirt as a target. He hit his man and heard the body fall.

The other man dragged his wounded companion to his feet and supported him as the two tried to run for it. They were quickly caught and arrested on the spot. The robbers were the first of many in the Eastland County jail.

The twenty-nine-year-old ranger had won his first gun battle. The Wichita Falls *Daily Times* praised Gonzaullas's cool courage. The soon-to-be-legendary lawman was a throwback Texans understood. He came to represent a simpler time when frontier justice was settled with a Colt Peacemaker. The man had walked alone down the back alley, facing the criminals and besting them in a fair fight. The editor gave him a signature nickname that stuck—"Lone Wolf." As more wells blew in and more and more people flooded into the formerly poor town, the rangers went about their business. Catching robbers was just a small part of it. Moonshiners and bootleggers were everywhere. Locating and chopping up stills, destroying the equipment, and smashing the bottles of illegal whiskey took days out of the week.

The rangers checked with storekeepers for the names of people who bought large amounts of "corn chop." They watched the skies for smoke from the stills. In the meantime they raided the gambling clubs, arrested the gamers, arrested the sellers (both men and women), and arrested the prostitutes that were everywhere. Gonzaullas saw the jails, both county and township, filling up faster than they could accommodate their inmates.

Using a tactic sure to outrage most of the townspeople as well as the shock the sensibilities of people today, Gonzaullas got rid of the jail overflow. What he did was illegal but time-honored and frequently practiced today by all sorts of lawmen. Rather than deal with the red tape, they escort the small-time crooks to the city limits and tell them, "Get out of town!"

Unneighborly this practice might have been to the state of Oklahoma, but Texas Rangers were pretty much laws unto themselves. In the cases of nonviolent types, Gonzaullas gave them two hours to make it to the Red River. Most of them made it in under an hour.

As Eastland County emptied out, the local law got a handle on the situation. Soon the daring Gonzaullas was operating pretty much on his own, for as the crime decreased, the company was assigned elsewhere. The good people of Eastland and the surrounding counties were left with the tall, thin ranger with the black hair and gray-green eyes. He was a godsend according to the "local buzz." The small-town newspapers headed their stories with "Lone Wolf."

He did nothing to discourage them. Gradually, the name became the man as it had for the great Texas lawmen of the nineteenth century—Big Foot Wallace; Samuel Walker, for whom the Walker Colt was named; and, of course, ranger captain John Coffee Hays. Possibly unconsciously at first, but later with cold dedication, Gonzaullas began to build himself into a legend that gave him particular pride in himself and his job. He worked with cool determination to grow into it and to let himself become it. Like some champion of justice, Gonzaullas's reputation attached itself to his name and preceded him into dangerous situations. It gave him an upper hand.

With a sense of personal satisfaction, he realized he was becoming famous and even dreaded. When he rode or drove into a new town, he could simply walk through the door of the sheriff's office and say, "I'm Gonzaullas."

Men within hearing would scramble to their feet, and someone would breathe, "My God. It's the Lone Wolf."

Manuel Trazazas Gonzaullas was born in Spain, the only Texas Ranger of such descent. His father was a Spaniard; his mother, a Canadian. They moved to America and became naturalized citizens. From the beginning he was drawn to law enforcement. He was a man with a sense of his own destiny. His life is carefully saved in scrapbooks assembled by him and his wife, perhaps with the idea of someday writing an autobiography. While he never got around to doing so, the materials—letters, clippings, commendations, and reports—constituted an exciting and valuable trove for biographers and historians as well as for himself in a later dramatic career that took him to Hollywood in the footsteps of Hayes and the legendary Wyatt Earp.

With his own legend growing, Gonzaullas carefully painted in the details of a dashing picture. He was a "flash" dresser, wearing perfectly tailored and pressed uniforms, black ties, hand-tooled boots, and white Stetsons. He bought himself a big diamond ring. He was famous for decorating his pistols and rifles with gold and silver chasing.

Despite General George S. Patton's stated preference for ivory handles since "mother-of-pearl handles belonged in cathouses," Lone Wolf's handles were mother-of-pearl and ebony. Unembarrassed by his fancy dressing, Gonzaullas paid jewelers to embed 14-carat-gold emblems in them—the symbols of the secret orders of the Masons and the Shriners, to which he belonged. He also had a set of his favorites decorated with cabochon semiprecious stones. Eventually, he had the captain's badge of the Texas Rangers set in as well.

As if his weapons were sacred like the sword of a medieval knight, Lone Wolf had cautionary orders inscribed on the holster of his service revolver: "Never Draw Me Without Cause or Sheathe Me With Dishonor." His favorite Colt .45 was inscribed with "God Created All Men Equal. Col. Colt Made Them All the Same Size."

From Eastland County, Lone Wolf was sent to the border region along the Rio Grande. He knew the area and was fluent in both Spanish and English. The flood of illegal traffic going in both directions was pretty much as it is today—a steady stream of liquor and narcotics carried by illegal traffickers. In this case most of the liquor was prime Canadian Club labeled as medicine. It was transported by ship from Canada to Mexico to be smuggled in across the southern border of the United States as it was being smuggled out across the northern border.

Cattle rustling was also a problem. Texas cattle were stolen and driven across the border to be sold in Mexico while tick-infested cattle were driven back across the border to supplement depleted Texas herds. Whole areas of the state had become infected. The cattle had to be dipped (run through concrete vats of water laced with arsenic) to get rid of the critters, only to be reinfected as the rustlers ran more illegal cattle into the country.

Lone Wolf became "El Solo Lobo" to both rustlers and smugglers south of the Rio Grande. After successful undercover work that led to numerous arrests, his growing reputation coupled with his ability to speak and understand both languages led him to be "hired out" to the federal government, who desperately wanted him back in their ranks.

Gonzaullas became one of the L-Men, the "Liquor-Men," in charge of one of their "flying squadrons." They operated all over the state in cars and on horseback, tailing, capturing, or shooting it out with the smugglers, after which they confiscated and destroyed the whiskey. Though their efforts were like a finger in a very leaky dike, the ranger squadron led by Lone Wolf made inroads that led to arrests all over Texas.

In one famous case, Lone Wolf caught up with two men in San Antonio whose sales of a lethal mixture of grape juice, soda water, and denatured alcohol had resulted in the deaths of at least eight citizens. For quite some time, the brew had escaped the regular L-Men. Because denatured alcohol was classified as a medicine, it did not constitute a violation of the Volstead Act, which listed intoxicants only.

Eight dead citizens led Lone Wolf to make the arrest and the Austin police agreed with him. Despite the jealousy of less-successful L-Men, "Austin's" Texas Ranger had caught the moonshiners with the "goods." Equally important was the fact that Gonzaullas had also collected the complaints from witnesses and survivors. He was always careful to be sure that he had sufficient evidence to arrest, to hold for trial, and, in most cases, to win a conviction. From San Antonio to Galveston to Mexia to Dallas, Lone Wolf's flying squadron moved. Sometimes they actually flew in small planes to get to the site in record time, but most often they drove. Their overall arrest record was good, but their effect negligible.

All lawmen were coming to recognize the incontrovertible fact that the Volstead Act was unenforceable. Texans were too addicted to alcohol and the ease with which they could obtain it. The relatively small prices they had to pay were a constant temptation. In addition to the high-grade stuff being smuggled into the state from across the border and in through the ports, illegal alcohol was being made on farms, in garages, and bathtubs everywhere. Lone Wolf remarked that he had seen enough copper tubing, a necessary part of the moonshiner's distillery, to make a complete arch over the nine-story Littlefield Building in downtown Austin, considered one of the most elegant and prestigious buildings in the nation.

The L-Men were, if anything, less popular than the Texas Rangers. Texas had always been wild. But now it was slipping into an outlaw state with a majority of the citizenry living outside the law. Hundreds of thousands of dollars were changing hands illegally almost daily, and the people who tried to stop it were in constant danger.

Moreover, they had very little cooperation from local law enforcement that accepted bribes on a daily basis to "look the other way." In July 1922 Lone Wolf killed a man who had drawn a gun with the intention of gunning down Federal Agent W. A. Nitzer. The man Gonzaullas killed was a local official.

In retaliation, a gang of thugs roughed up and threatened to lynch Lone Wolf and Nitzer. Lone Wolf was arrested again, refused bail, and placed in the county jail. Within hours a jury had returned an indictment of murder against him and also against Nitzer, who had not even drawn his gun. Fortunately, federal officers arrived on the scene and prevented what might have been two of the swiftest "all-done-legal" hangings in Texas history.

Though he resented his arrest and the lack of respect shown him by the citizens he was trying to help, Lone Wolf maintained a zeal for his calling and his oath to uphold the law remained strong. He loved the chase, the danger, the arrests, the successes, perhaps even the gun battles when men who had tried to kill him and had certainly killed others with poisonous products "bit the dust." So his reputation grew among law enforcement officers throughout Texas and among perpetrators.

On many raids, all he had to do was knock on the front door of the bootlegger's house and announce, "I'm Gonzaullas." The bootlegger generally would offer no protest, knowing that the Lone Wolf wouldn't be on the porch without sufficient evidence.

Always polite and considerate, when a woman answered the door with a child in her arms or in the room, he would caution his team to go quietly so as not to wake the baby. Gonzaullas was amused to learn that in addition to his well-known nickname, he was referred to as the "hooch sleuth." He had become an expert at studying behavior and picking up clues in the way of modern detectives rather than simply bullying and intimidating people into giving up the truth.

At the same time, the danger was everywhere and constant. Officers were shot and beaten up in the line of duty. They were abused and vilified by the people they were trying to help. The situation in Texas could hardly have been worse, as proclaimed by Governor Pat Neff in a fiery speech at the Houston Bar Association banquet at the Rice Hotel in 1923: "It is more dangerous for a Texas boy to be a prohibition enforcement officer in the State of Texas than it was to carry Old Glory on the battlefields of France."

The governor went on to state that some counties in Texas were so defiant of the Volstead Act that law enforcement was reluctant to cross county lines. The argument among these perpetrators ran that what a man did on his own land and drank in his own home was none of the government's damn business.

Equally dangerous and hostile were these counties toward the men of the flying squadrons. Using the new detection techniques that he had perfected, Lone Wolf continued to dare to do his job and cross the lines. He moved in under cover, disguising himself as an oil man seeking to purchase leases. When he had gathered the information and evidence that he needed for an arrest, indictment, prosecution, and hopefully a verdict of guilty, Gonzaullas would call in a squad of federal agents to make the arrests while he quietly disappeared, moving into other areas.

He even went out of the United States to the Bahamas for what he claimed was a short vacation. In reality he was sent to Nassau, the site of a gigantic smuggling operation. From there enormous quantities of rum sailed daily for ports on the Atlantic seaboard and the Gulf of Mexico. In deep cover he gathered information on perpetrators, sailing times, dates, ships, and shipments. When he returned to the states, men, including those in his own squadron, thought he'd actually been on a vacation.

His testimony in May 1924 in Mobile, Alabama, jailed most of the 326 people who had been arrested in previous raids and brought to trial. Two months later, he and Nitzer were acquitted of the charges of murder brought against them in Jefferson County two years before.

Abruptly thereafter, Gonzaullas resigned from the L-Men with the excuse that he was through with law enforcement. The Washington chief was dismayed at his agent's resignation. How could this good man, one of the very best, give up his job with pay superior to anything he could earn in Texas?

But Gonzaullas could and did. Within months he had been reinstated in his first love, the Texas Rangers. He gave his reasons for his actions in an interview, which is generally believed to have been given originally to the *Christian Courier*. In his opinion, Prohibition in America was doomed and would soon be repealed because an overwhelming number of people, drinkers and nondrinkers alike, had seen the harm it brought to the American family.

Whereas before, no woman took a drink or smoked a cigarette except in secret, now thousands did so in their homes and in public. He could see more were taking up the habits every day. The American home, once the bastion of honest, genteel behavior, was now the base of operations for every kind of vice. The making, drinking, and smuggling of alcohol, deemed a crime throughout the forty-eight states, had moved out of the bars and backrooms into the homes.

Still worse, Gonzaullas had seen the rise of organized crime and the citizenry's bland acceptance of criminals so violent and ruthless that no one was safe from them. He cited such people as Al Capone as an example of the result of the Prohibition law and the attempted enforcement of it.

He believed with all his heart that even unpopular laws should be enforced, *but* when a law was proved to be unwise, when ordinary citizens were driven by circumstances to defy and break it, then that law should be repealed.

The Texas Rangers were more than glad to have him back in their ranks. He headed back into the law enforcement aiding sheriffs who in turn moved across county lines to aid each other. After the unpleasant undercover work he'd done for the L-Men, it was good to be back among his own kind.

By Christmas of 1925, the L-Men were begging Lone Wolf to come back. He did so only with the understanding that he would be with them only a short time. Again he went in disguise, this time for three months. But then someone dropped his name in a chance remark, and the news spread like wildfire among the bootleggers of the Dallas–Fort Worth area. They lay low for several months, but Gonzaullas was too smart for them. In the spring he led a series of raids that smashed thousands of bottles of illegal beer, whiskey, and gin and the stills that made them.

In Wichita County he went after more stills, destroying them and the whiskey they were producing. Back in Dallas in a lightning-fast move, he netted "blue books" from various distributors. "Blue books" were prized by law enforcement as they contained the names, addresses, and car license numbers of the bootleggers' customers, along with the amounts of whiskey they had purchased and the prices they had paid. The books contained indisputable evidence that held up well in court and resulted in big fines and sometimes the confiscation of homes and businesses.

Still, for Gonzaullas, it was the same old dangerous routines that only slightly reduced the ranks of the perpetrators. He would be transferred from town to town and county to county to round up the very same men and women he had arrested several times before. He felt as if he were following them around the state. In a real sense, he was.

September 5, 1930, a well blew in that made all the other discoveries in Texas—including Spindletop, the first oil gusher in Texas, south of Beaumont—look like small potatoes. C. M. "Dad" Joiner's well, Daisy Bradford No. 3, spouted to the skies southeast of the tiny towns of Overton and Arp. No one knew that the well signaled the opening of the largest oil strike in the world at that time and one of the largest fields ever discovered.

Joiner's enterprise was a strictly penny-ante wildcat operation put together with scrap lumber and scrounged pipe. The crew spent a year and four months drilling a 3,500-foot well that should have taken about six weeks. Practically every citizen in the entire Rusk County had bought at least a couple of Dad's $25 leases to keep the project going.

Three days after Christmas and twelve miles almost due north, practically on the Rusk County line, another well blew in; the Lou Della Crim No. 1 had the town of Kilgore in ecstasies.

Then miracle of miracles! The town of Longview offered a $10,000 bonus to anyone who could bring in a well in Gregg County. A syndicate of local businessmen pooled their money and bought leases. Then they sold them again for the money to drill in a "hog pasture" belonging to F. K. Lathrop. The result was another well spouting to the skies on January 23, 1931.

A new oil field had been discovered, and by a fantastic bit of luck, the wells had been drilled at its edges. The Lathrop well lay 211 square miles north of the Daisy Bradford No. 3, with Lou Della Crim No. 1 approximately in the middle.

Of course, the usual robbers and murderers as well as the bootleggers, moonshiners, and prostitutes flocked to the new field, invading the small, relatively defenseless townships. Gonzaullas and the rangers followed as fast as they could to try to get the jump on their usual suspects. What they did not expect or even conceive was that entirely new problems would arise out of this gigantic flow of what would come to be known as "hot oil."

Since Lou Della Crim No. 1 was located in what was perceived to be the center of the field, Kilgore, with a population of 590, became the center of what is known to this day as the East Texas Oil Field. Before the discovery, the tiny town was too small to be listed in a census tabulation for an atlas. Three days after the well blew in, Kilgore swarmed with an estimated 10,000 people.

Two months later, Kilgore was an incorporated town with a newly elected mayor, J. Malcolm Crim, the son of Mrs. Lou Della Crim. Though he vowed to keep Kilgore law-abiding, he was pledging too late what had not been possible since his mother's well blew in. He had also hoped to keep the wells "in the family." This too proved to be beyond his control.

Spindletop had been a relatively small area. Major Texas oil producers had moved into Spindletop and controlled the amount that was pumped to keep the prices high enough to make production worthwhile. The various discoveries in central Texas around Ranger and Burkburnett had actually proved to be from separate pools, but East Texas was bigger than all the other fields put together.

East Texas was immediately overrun by wildcatters. Indeed, Dad Joiner, who brought in the Daisy Bradford No. 3, was a wildcatter. So was billionaire-in-the-making H. L. Hunt, who bought Joiner out and began to drill wells by the dozens. Soon Kilgore itself was a town floored with oil wells drilled so close together that people could and did walk from one platform to the next without putting a foot on the ground. Some wells had two horse-head pumps working in sequence to bring the oil up from the Woodbine sand twice as fast.

Like a creature consuming itself, East Texas was pumping more than the entire planet could use in 1930. The forest of derricks stretched forty miles long and three to twelve miles wide, from Gladewater nearly to Jacksonville. The price of "light, sweet crude" fell as low as two cents a barrel. Nobody was making any money at those prices.

To add to everyone's misery, the East Texas Oil Field is in a very wet part of the state. Its average rainfall is 45 to 48 inches, as compared to the central Texas oil fields, where the average is barely half that much. The streets in Ranger were relatively dry compared to Kilgore. Driving was already difficult, but the constant traffic with huge trucks bringing in heavy oilfield equipment made it even worse. The trucks gouged out deep ruts in the streets. Cars fell in and sank to their axles with no hope of moving until they were dragged out. Much equipment and goods were still moved by mule teams, adding to the stench and the filth.

Governor Ross Sterling, himself an oil man from the Spindletop field, reluctantly tried to exert martial law. Someone drove into the guard camp one night and shot the place up with the intent to kill young soldiers, all of whom were presumably Texas boys. The governor ordered in Lone Wolf and the rangers. At the same time, he attempted to put caps on the prices and close down the wells from their constant release of what had not yet come to be regarded as a limited resource.

With the streets in mind as well as the need to make a statement, Sergeant Lone Wolf Gonzaullas, accompanied by fellow ranger and long-time associate J. P. Huddleston, entered Kilgore on horseback. Lone Wolf rode his famous coal black gelding, Charcoal. Dressed to impress, he wore an olive drab suit cut in Western style over a khaki-colored shirt of finest serge. Beneath his black tie, his collar was pinned with a gold bar-pin. From the soles of his hand-tooled boots to the crown of his wide-brim Stetson, Gonzaullas certainly impressed the people on the streets.

Every knowledgeable person of that time knew that the traditional gun of the rangers was the single-action .45. As Gonzaullas intended, no one failed to notice the pair of ornate bone-handled Colt .45 *automatics* in their holsters on his hips or the rifle in his ornate saddle boot.

"Here comes 'The Law!'" one man yelled, and people hurried out of the stores on the main street to see the parade of two of Texas's finest.

As in every oil town the rangers had entered, the reaction to the two men was mixed. As their handsome horses trotted through the mud and filth, silence turned to jeers and catcalls. Ignoring the rabble, Gonzaullas and Huddleston made their way to the business section. There they greeted old friends from other strikes and undoubtedly caught sight of some crooks they had run out of towns in Eastland County. With the mayor and what passed for a town council assembled, Lone Wolf put out the word: bootleggers, robbers, and prostitutes should get out of town while they had the chance.

He delivered also a no-nonsense public statement to the local newspapers in Gregg and Rusk Counties: "Crime may expect no quarter in Kilgore. Gambling houses, slot machines, whiskey rings, and dope peddlers might as well save themselves the trouble of opening, because they will not be tolerated in any degree. Drifters and transients have their choice of three things: engaging in legitimate business, getting out of town, or going to jail!"

With no one in doubt what was about to happen, the rangers quickly organized an enforcement net utilizing local town and county lawmen and those they deputized. While the men were gathering, Lone Wolf put together what became famous as his "trotline."

The first sweep netted those who were obviously petty violators—the nonviolent criminals. In those days decent people had little sympathy for those who broke the obvious laws. Hardworking men had great contempt for the gamblers, the bootleggers, and the dope peddlers who preyed on their weaknesses and took their money.

Decent women despised prostitutes and their pimps and madams, who often worked in tandem with the robbers to steal hard-earned wages for the dirty, dangerous work honest husbands did. By robbing the menfolk, the outlaws stole the food from the children's mouths.

In the light of the twenty-first century human rights legislation and "rights of prisoners," Lone Wolf's trotline method is beyond outrageous, but since he never made a secret of what he was planning on doing, no one considered registering a complaint.

His trotline consisted of a long, heavy-duty chain with lighter trace chains attached to it at intervals. Each trace chain had a padlock that could be used to fasten the prisoner to the larger chain. Since women's lib and the ERA did not exist at the time, Lone Wolf felt free to treat the women differently from the men. The trace chains were attached to the necks of the male prisoners and an ankle of the females. Though tales are told of Lone Wolf attaching the main chain to the oak tree in the middle of town, he was more of a humanitarian than that, though no one would have blamed him if he hadn't been.

The First Baptist Church had been abandoned by the congregation after transients had taken to sleeping in it at night. Not only had they carried in mud and dirt on their unwashed bodies, but their clothing was infested with vermin, which had in turn infested the building. Their shoes had left the floor covered with filth. As it stood, the building was perfect for Lone Wolf's purpose.

He fastened the main chain to the floor at both ends of the sanctuary. From there the prisoners could sit or lie on the hard pews. Though the roof didn't leak, the building was miserably cold, wet, and drafty; March in east Texas usually is. Instead of being unlocked by guards and escorted to use the bathroom, the prisoners passed a bucket down from one end of the aisle to the other. While they were utterly miserable at night, during the day they were humiliated. Townspeople as well as a few of their own kind could look in the windows and through the open doors to jeer at them.

To discourage any attempted escapes, Lone Wolf enlisted the Kilgore policemen and temporary deputies as guards.

Carrying shotguns, they patrolled the streets and the area around the church twenty-four hours a day.

A few days of misery and embarrassment convinced many of these pitiful scavengers to beg for release. They were willing to promise anything for release. Most particularly they swore to leave town immediately and never return. Lone Wolf released them and let them make a "run for the Louisiana border" just fifty miles away. Thus there always seemed to be places open on the trotline for new criminals.

This sort of rough justice went on for nearly a month while Gonzaullas along with Huddleston investigated and gathered evidence on the "big fish." Lone Wolf had learned from long experience that without incontrovertible evidence sufficient to arrest, try, convict, and imprison, he was wasting his time, simply putting someone in jail for the night. When he had completed his investigations, he called in a ranger troop of eight under the command of Captain Tom Hickman.

At 1:30 on the afternoon of March 2, the sweep began. It was the second widespread cleanup in Kilgore, but this time the net spread wider and some seemingly solid citizens got caught. By supper time around four hundred men and women had been rounded up and arrested. They were marched down the main street lined with spectators who laughed, pointed, jeered, and called them by name.

No one among the respectable townspeople felt any sympathy or thought about whether the prisoners' civil rights were being violated. So awesome was the reputation of the Texas Rangers that no one murmured a protest. Indeed the prisoners themselves were silent. They had been caught red-handed in most cases. Technically, they were innocent until proven guilty, but very few townspeople doubted that Rangers Gonzaullas and Huddleston had the goods to send them to jail for the maximum time allowed.

Among the outlaws were the robbers who lurked in the dark near the rigs on the nights when men were paid their cash wages for the week. The payroll box was unlocked on the floor of the rig, and the money was counted out by the boss. As the roughnecks walked home with their money for their families, many of whom lived in the miserable rag towns outside of the field, they would be set upon by men who demanded a share of their earnings. If the workers refused, they were threatened with baseball bats and clubs. If they tried to fight back, they were beaten senseless and robbed of everything. Testimony against these gangs had been one of Lone Wolf's objectives in his evidence gathering.

In the church jail, the prisoners were fingerprinted and charged. A list of offenses as well as the names of witnesses and other hard evidence gathered by Lone Wolf was carefully recorded. This raid was only the first of many as the criminals were given speedy trials and hauled off to prison in Huntsville, less than a hundred miles down the road. Within a month, Kilgore was relatively crime free.

Sadly, Lone Wolf had seen this phenomenon before and recognized that he was merely making way for new elements of lawlessness to move in, and so it continued until January 1931 when the Wickersham Commission reported that the country was no longer able to enforce the Volstead Act. The liquor trade was making unbelievably high profits and paying no taxes of any sort on them. Likewise, public apathy and downright anger and resentment of the law were preventing even the most dedicated law officers from doing their jobs in most areas of the country. In fewer than two years, the Twenty-First Amendment to the Constitution repealing the Eighteenth Amendment became law.

Lone Wolf was glad to see it go. What he didn't know was that even as the ratification process was going on, a new type of thief was about to begin operations in the East Texas Oil Field, one that dealt in the new commodity—hot oil.

The people who resented the federal government's interference in the distilling and selling of liquor were nowhere near as angry as the oil men who were forced to stop drilling when Governor Sterling tried to limit the amount of oil that could be taken from the ground. His move was actually in the public good. Reasonable drilling would keep the prices up and at the same time prevent the wells from being exhausted.

The oil men didn't look at it that way. Oil was free for the taking, and according to the rules, the first person to "take it" or "capture it" as it ran from the ground was the person who owned it. Unless all the drillers obeyed the governor and stopped, none of the drillers would obey and stop because in a sense they were all drilling from this same huge lake of Woodbine sand that underlay more than two hundred square miles of the Piney Woods.

Governor Sterling, himself an oil man, had already seen the results of over-drilling and waste as the great discovery at Spindletop ran dry. When the oil was first discovered there, operators of wells would sometimes open them up and let the oil fly out through the top of the derrick for the entertainment of people on the trains riding through Beaumont.

The original Spindletop blew in and spouted for nine days before anyone thought to try to put a cap on it. Captain Anthony Lucas, the owner, never realized a tenth of what he might have done had he been able to control what was happening and conserve the oil that had been lost.

And now it was happening all over again, thirty years later. Nothing stood between East Texas and loss except Lone Wolf Gonzaullas and his new Texas Ranger partner, Bob Goss. In the mud and filth they operated while everyone else violated the law.

The price of oil had increased since Spindletop as more uses, in particular the general ownership of automobiles, increased the demand. Now with the overdrilling, its price fell to a dime a barrel. Chili con carne was thirty-five cents a bowl.

Within the city limits of Kilgore alone were seven hundred derricks. The sun was blotted out by the fires from the wells.

The very air smelled of oil. It spattered everywhere—on windowpanes, on porches, on clothing hung out to dry on the line. Clothes, towels, sheets, pillows smelled like it too. Tiny black spots, like pepper, appeared on the children's books when classroom windows were opened. The food set on the tables by the wives tasted like it. One man swore when he cut his arm, the first drops from the wound were oil.

In the dead of night, thieves drove trucks and wagons up to storage tanks, opened up the cocks, and hauled their loot away for sale. Though the drillers hired guards, they couldn't be everywhere. Sometimes the guards themselves would accept bribes. Robbers would tap into pipelines that ran from the well to a storage tank and steal it from under the noses of the men operating the rigs. Sometimes the roughnecks worked in collusion with the robbers, ignoring the thievery for a price.

Lone Wolf reported to Governor Sterling that there were not enough rangers in Texas to make a difference. Finally, the governor declared a state of martial law and sent in the National Guard. The citizens were more angry and defiant than ever at this "intrusion into their business," resulting in more lawlessness and anger against another phase of government. The men who drilled maintained it was their oil, and the government was keeping them from making a living. Their attitude was if they wanted to drink it, it was none of the government's "damned" business.

Any kind of lawman—ranger, sheriff, deputy, town constable—was in danger from angry men who were determined to defy the law. Sitting on a stakeout, lawmen were approached, "thrown down on," dragged from their cars, robbed, and beaten. The thieves would then drive away in the official patrol car and sometimes purposefully wreck it.

Lone Wolf was determined not to allow himself to be an object of such humiliation. In February 1932, he took delivery of a special Chrysler eight-cylinder coupe. Outrageous indeed. The glass in its windows was bulletproof. The windshield could be swung outward and up. Mounted on a swivel base behind it, next to the driver's seat, was a machine gun.

Lone Wolf was dangerous enough. Armed with a machine gun, he was too much for the men who might have otherwise tried to humiliate and even kill him. Fortunately, he never had to use it to dispel an angry crowd. Indeed, he was never bothered. Frequently, the sight of that car coming down the road with Lone Wolf behind the wheel was enough to send an unruly mob melting away into the shadows.

The answer to saving East Texas seemed to be proration drilling. Sterling placed the Texas Railroad Commission in charge of allocating the number of days a month a man could pump oil. No one liked proration drilling, and as a consequence the governor lost his race for a second term. In 1932 he was succeeded by Miriam "Ma" Ferguson, for her second term with her husband as her advisor. "Ma" had lost her bid for re-election against Sterling, but his unpopularity over East Texas had turned Texans back to her. With her return to the mansion, Texas had "two governors for the price of one." "Pa" had been impeached during his term and was thereby forbidden to hold public office again.

Sergeant Gonzaullas and Captain Hickman formed part of her guard to escort her to the platform to take the oath of office. The next day she fired them, as well as the Texas Ranger adjutant general and almost the entire force—payback for proration, for the trotline, for upholding the law, and for defending the decent citizenry.

The governor was also clearing the way for the Fergusons' special interests. Neither the governor nor her husband cared about oil and the problems of the oil men in maintaining its price. They were more interested in making legal the sale of liquor in which they had a vested interest. Volstead was due to be repealed that year by the Twenty-First Amendment to the Constitution. If getting rid of the rangers would keep both the oil and the liquor flowing without interruption, then Ma would disband the lawmen who many said placed no limits on their tactics. They were abusing private citizens. They needed to be taught a lesson by a higher authority.

Ma got rid of most of them completely and slid the rest into the newly created Department of Public Safety, which seemed redundant to many legislators.

One of the first rangers completely out of a job was Lone Wolf. He was immediately offered a better job with much better pay as chief special agent for the Atlas Pipe Line Company and Spartan Refining Company. Both operated primarily in east Texas. Both knew their pipelines would be in jeopardy without private help. Gonzaullas was able to bring eighteen of his fellow rangers into the business as pipeline guards.

For the two years of Ferguson's administration, Lone Wolf worked at various jobs in security as part of private law enforcement. When the Fergusons left Austin, the new governor rehired most of the ranger forces to be part of the Highway Patrol but separate from it.

Almost at the top of the list was Gonzaullas. He was brought in to be the head of the Intelligence Bureau and chief of detectives. It was a tribute to his lifelong practice of gathering information and securing the conviction before wasting the law's time with a trial the law couldn't win.

The years of exciting cases continued. Lone Wolf worked each one he was assigned and solved almost all his cases both in the laboratory and in the field.

He set his sights on being the best ranger of his time and perhaps to make a name for himself that would lift him into the ranks of fabled Texas lawmen before he would "hear the owl hoot." (According to tradition, the rangers say they hear the night bird call their name just before they die.)

In mid-1946 Lone Wolf, now a full-fledged captain, undertook one of the most sensational cases in the history of American law enforcement—the Case of the Phantom Murders. The mysterious assailant brutally murdered five people, beat and sexually abused two more, and critically shot and wounded one other in the vicinity of Texarkana. The town sits on the state line with Arkansas on the main east-west highway running between Dallas–Fort Worth and Little Rock and the north-south highway between Fort Smith and Shreveport. In other words, it was an easy place to escape from and a hard place to police.

The man and woman who survived the beatings and abuse of the first attack reported that the assailant wore a white handkerchief tied round his face with holes cut out for the eyes. Law enforcement in Arkansas was inclined to believe it was an isolated incident, but when the second attack occurred, both states knew they were searching for a serial rapist and murderer.

The news and the fear spread. Unfortunately, the site where the second victims were killed was quickly visited and walked over by the morbidly curious. When the Texas Rangers were called to the scene, Captain Gonzaullas seemed the logical one to head the investigation. Unfortunately, he was thwarted at first because, in modern technical terms, both crime scenes had been thoroughly contaminated.

Rather than wait for another pair of murders to occur, Lone Wolf set up decoy teams of two rangers each, one dressed as a woman, parking in secluded spots. The press, as often happened, did not cooperate in any way with Lone Wolf. They wrote the story over and over, describing the scenes, reporting on the ranger captain in great detail, speculating on what techniques he might use to trap the killer. Several stories reminded the public and the killer that it was almost three weeks to the day since the last murders.

The killer struck again two days before three weeks were up. He shot into a rural home, killing the husband with a shot to the head and shooting his wife twice in the jaw and the face when she tried to use the telephone. Somehow, she managed to run out the door and escape to her neighbors. Whether he figured he would lose her in the dark or simply thought he must have killed her, he didn't pursue. He entered the house and smeared his hands in her husband's blood before leaving the scene.

Lone Wolf much later reported that his team's investigations had turned up a suspect, but they were attempting to collect conclusive evidence before making an arrest. Whether the murderer suspected they were closing in on him and quit the area will never be known. No crime with that modus operandi was ever committed again. The murderer disappeared forever. Lone Wolf always regretted not catching that particular man.

In 1951 at the age of sixty, Lone Wolf resigned from the Texas Rangers. Though the force had kept his secret, *The Dallas Morning News* broke not only his retirement, but his future plan. He was going to Hollywood! He had been hired as a technical adviser for Western films. In 1952 he would be touring the country promoting a new motion picture, *The Lawless Breed*. The film starred Rock Hudson playing in a Hollywood version of the life of Texas's most murderous bandit, John Wesley Hardin.

Because the details of Lone Wolf's plans had been kept a secret, the paper failed to report that Gonzaullas and his boss Homer Garrison, director of the Texas Bureau of Public Safety and the Texas Rangers, had been quietly assembling cases for dramatization for a national radio and television series, *Tales of the Texas Rangers*.

Not only would the cases be authentic, but many of the scenes in the television series were to be filmed in Texas. All completed scripts were submitted to Gonzaullas and Garrison for review and correct authentication, if necessary. Gonzaullas would be on the set working as technical advisor to producer Stacy Keach Sr. The retired ranger considered that a bonus, since Keach owned half of both the radio and television series.

The radio version ran for two years, beginning in 1955. It starred Joel McCrea as Ranger Jace Pearson, who just happened to ride a horse named Charcoal. Audiences were told he had a horse trailer attached to the back of his car, so he could dash off across the desert or into the woods on horse-back in pursuit of a desperate criminal at a moment's notice. After each broadcast, McCrea returned with a bit of ranger lore and gave the disposition of the case, such as "sentenced to life imprisonment at Huntsville," where the Texas Department of Criminal Justice is located. Occasionally, McCrea would give the exact date that the convicted criminal had died in the electrocution chair.

The television series followed the same theme except it starred various actors. It ran for another two years. Each night the opening and closing of the show were particularly memorable. The camera trained on one ranger walking toward the camera, with a chorus singing "The Eyes of Texas" in the background. He was joined by another ranger and then another. Soon the screen was full of marching men. It closed in a reversed pattern. A screen full of men peeled off until only one man was left and he too faded as the marching music ended.

It was the visualization of the famous remark attributed to Captain Bill McDonald. When asked the whereabouts of the rest of the rangers the town had sent for, he is said to have answered, "Hell, ain't I enough? There's only one riot, ain't there?"

In 1960, after five years of commuting between Dallas and the West Coast, the Lone Wolf returned to Dallas where he kept busy and involved by serving on various boards and working for charities. He and Isabel, his wife of more than forty years, were charter members of the prestigious Lakewood Country Club.

The old ranger had all the windows in his home protected by a system of iron grilles. Too many men he had sent to prison might think an old man an easy target for retaliation. His wife always carried a gun in her purse. When he drove his car, Lone Wolf carried within easy reach his "hand machine gun," an automatic pistol capable of firing sixty-four rounds.

Though Lone Wolf did not live to see it, a 3-1/2 star motion picture was made in 1977, starring Ben Johnson as Ranger J. D. Morales, a thinly disguised portrayal of the old ranger himself. *The Town That Dreaded Sundown* was done in chilling documentary style with a World War II atmosphere. Liberties were taken with the plot for dramatic tension, but Johnson, who had been introduced to the man he was playing, gave a vivid portrayal.

Gonzaullas and his wife attended the dedication of the Texas Ranger statue that stands in the lobby of Dallas Love Field terminal. Fittingly a Dallas ranger, Captain Jay Banks, was a model for the statue, but the inscription "One Riot, One Ranger" might have applied to Lone Wolf, for certainly he went into many situations alone and came out the winner. Though he was forced to shoot and to kill in self-defense, he himself was never so much as grazed.

In 1976 at the age of eighty-four, he attended the dedication of the Texas Ranger Museum in Waco. Someone made a comment about his being enshrined there someday. He replied, "I would rather visit the Hall of Fame than be enshrined in it. I enjoy life!"

Nevertheless, old friends noted that day that he didn't look well. Though he had enjoyed vigorous health all of his life, he looked as if he had lost weight and his color wasn't good. He had cancer, though he didn't share any information. In the months that followed, he disposed of his weapons collection, giving 580 guns, knives, and clubs he had taken from various criminals to his friends. When a friend would ask why, he would say, "I just wanted you to have it."

Was he lucky to have taken that vast arsenal from other men who wanted, even attempted, to kill him? Certainly an element of luck is always present any time men draw guns with the intent to fire them at other men. But Lone Wolf was smart. He analyzed the situation and behaved in the safest manner possible to inflict the least harm to the guilty and, more important, the innocent bystanders who might be in the line of fire.

For thirty years he was the ultimate Texas Ranger, a legend in his own time and still today. Lone Wolf Gonzaullas died on February 13, 1977. Like the great ones who had gone before him, he had heard the owl hoot.

OIL, RAILROADS, AND "BOB-WIRE"

John Warne Gates wasn't born in Texas. He didn't live in Texas for most of his life. He didn't even die in Texas. But his visits to the state changed it and America forever.

Of all the men who ever set foot on Texas soil, he was one of the most outrageous. A "plunger," as more cautious gamblers called him, he once bet $70,000 on a horse named Royal Flush. The horse won and paid $600,000. Or was it $700,000? Or was it $900,000? Rumors circulated that Gates had won a million or two million that day. Who can say for certain?

No less a personage than August Belmont, owner of the track at which thousands were bet on every race, pleaded with him, "Why don't you limit your bets to $10,000?"

The answer came accompanied by a smirk that barely showed beneath Gates's thick handle-bar moustache. "I can lose ten thousand without being hurt. I think no man should bet unless he's . . . willing to bet every dollar he owns. For me there's no fun in betting just a few thousand. I want to lay down enough to hurt the other fellow if he loses and enough to hurt me if I lose."

Outrageous! Indeed. But the oft-quoted remark characterizes the man who never heard a dare he didn't take or a bet he wouldn't cover.

John Warne Gates was power and ambition personified. He was a steely nerved robber baron, a captain of industry, but, above all, an inveterate gambler at the turn of the nineteenth century when regulations were few and powerful men manipulated industries, put hundreds out of work with the buying or selling of enormous blocks of stock, and created industrial monopolies called trusts.

Gates's beginnings, however, were more than humble.

Born on a farm outside Winfield, Illinois, Johnny spent the first two decades of his life figuring out ways to escape his grumpy, plodding father and his whining mother. An entrepreneur almost from his youngest years, he loved nothing better than figuring out ways to make money—nothing better, that is, except gambling to turn what money he had into more. If he won, he looked around almost hungrily for something else to bet on. If his luck broke bad, he lost philosophically. Either way, the gambler's thrill swiftly became what he lived for.

At eighteen, young Johnny Gates was the bane of his father's existence. When the old man caught his son playing cards in the family barn, he flew into a rage. He chased the four railroad men out and shouted at his son, "An' you git too! You're no good! Never was, never will be!"

Johnny's mother made peace long enough for her son to get a five-month business course at Northwest College in Naperville, a suburb of Chicago. Equipped for the world, in 1874 he married the girl he would always love—Dellora Baker. Mindful thereafter that he was a man with responsibilities, he set out to make a life for them.

Times were hard, but the outskirts of Chicago were filled with enterprising people. It was the place to be—and Johnny Gates was there at the right time.

Barbed wire was a new development, an invention in the works that was drawing attention all across the northwestern United States. It promised to pen up herds of livestock cheaply and more efficiently than the traditional rail fences that rotted and had to be constantly replaced as cattle broke through them. So far, however, it was simply an interesting idea.

For forty years men had worked on that concept, experimenting with different patterns and methods of construction, but for something so simple, it had many problems early on. For starters, barbed wire was difficult to install properly because it had to be pulled tight between the posts and attached firmly. Even with heavy gloves, men got their hands cut up by the barbs.

Once attached, there seemed to be nothing permanent about it. If the wire was too thin, a frightened or angry steer could break through with one ferocious charge. In addition, it was metal; it would eventually "give." It might fall away in areas with blistering hot days, or it might rust and give way in pastures that got lots of rain, fog, and mist.

Thin wire also proved to be brittle, particularly during hard freezes. During a blizzard on the Great Plains, herds of range cattle tended to bunch together and move hind end before the wind. When they came to a fence, the ones against it were pushed by the ones coming behind. The brittle, frozen wire snapped and they moved on. Inventors tried versions with short barbs, but too short wouldn't stop determined cattle. On the other hand, barbs too long tore great wounds in the cattle's sides. The wounds would become infected or—worse— infested. The animal would have to be treated for screwworms.

Finally, Joseph H. Glidden, a farmer from outside De Kalb, Illinois, came up with the winning combination. Glidden fashioned barbs with an improvised coffee bean grinder, placed them at intervals along a smooth wire, and twisted another wire around the first to hold the barbs in a fixed position. It provided a doubly strong, flexible fence that kept the cattle in and eliminated the need for cowboys to ride herds all night and day.

For $60,000, Glidden sold his invention and lifetime royalties to Ike Ellwood, who began making the product in his factory. Steam engines turned the winches that twisted the strands and the barbs. He began turning out thousands of pounds every day, but because of incompetent salesmen, he wasn't able to sell it.

Johnny Gates saw his opportunity. Bluffing as seriously as he had ever played a winning hand in poker, he offered to buy an interest in the barbed-wire plant. He figured he could get $1,200 from his father-in-law.

Ellwood laughed in his face. His plant was worth millions, and he knew it. But what he didn't have was a fast-talking salesman. "I need a man in Texas," he opined. "You take the job and you get $25 a month with expenses on the road."

Like any good bargainer, Gates refused. "I'm worth more than that."

Ellwood sneered.

Gates waited.

In the end, Gates went to Texas for $30 a month. That night he won $60 off "Colonel" Ellwood in a poker game. The next morning he went back to the plant to learn all about his new product. The same day he wrote jubilantly to Dellora and his mother. He was traveling the next morning, and Ellwood was turning over the "whole state of Texas to him."

Once on the train south, he began to have doubts about the product he was selling. He realized that he had very little to offer except his brain and his nerve. Reading through his sales manual and other materials, Gates learned several carloads of barbed wire were still sitting in boxcars on the railroad sidings in Dallas and Sherman, Texas.

Apparently, the first sales had been made without instructing the ranchers and their cowboys how to string it, and thus word had spread that the wire was no good. It was considered by most a total bust, an idea that hadn't played out. Moreover, the cowboys whose livelihoods were herding and droving up the cattle trails to Kansas City immediately grasped the idea that barbed-wire fencing would put them out of business. They refused to unload the wire, and the dealers refused to pay for it.

Before he even set foot in Texas, he wired Ellwood in a panic, but Ellwood told him to go on to San Antonio and get the wire unloaded. "Trust me," he said. "You'll make big money." Whether Ellwood actually believed what he said will never be known. He knew the wire wouldn't be sold unless an enterprising salesman pitched it to the doubting public.

Johnny Gates was terrified. He had never been out of Illinois before. As he traveled south and west, fellow travelers told him that Indian wars were breaking out in Kansas and in West Texas. He was certain he had been tricked, bamboozled, hung out to dry. He would never see his wife and baby son, his whining mother, or even his grumpy father again.

The train was full of cowboys who sniggered and "hoorawed him" about his tight checked pants, his long black coat, and his green canvas bag that proclaimed him a traveling salesman. However, on a layover in St. Louis, somebody called, "Hey! How about a quiet little game?"

Gates's ears pricked up. He rolled into Dodge City feeling much better and $120 richer. The group grew friendlier and friendlier as they worked their way south toward Houston. The whiskey flowed as the cowboys told Gates what they thought of his "bob-wire." They'd had enough troubles with the "dang stuff." Bob-wire was no good. "Wouldn't hold a longhorn more'n a minute. A big ol' steer'd go right through it. It wouldn't even slow 'im down."

In Houston, Gates looked in the window of the warehouse that stored part of the wire he was supposed to sell. It was just as the cowboys had said. The barbs were three or four inches long and the whole mess was rusty. It would kill a steer. Moreover, it was already obsolete. The new Bessemer-processed steel, galvanized to withstand the elements, should have been used to make it.

How was he supposed to make money out of this mess?

In 1876 travelers rode from Houston to San Antonio by stagecoach; the Sunset Railroad was not completed until the next year. From the coach windows, Gates could see no fences. Only an occasional ranch house stood lonely and undoubtedly primitive in the middle of a huge sprawl of grazing land. Some few solitary riders on horseback watched over small herds of grazing cattle. The cowboys were doing their work. If he had his way, the day was coming when they would never work again.

The stagecoach deposited him in front of San Antonio's Menger Hotel in Military Plaza across from a forty-year-old ruin that people called the Alamo. Instead of going about his business, he headed directly for an establishment called the Silver King. Six hours later he had won a stack of chips worth $1,000. He was jubilant. The way these men threw money around, he was sure he could sell them bob-wire.

Moreover, he liked San Antonio. The dusty town with the ruin in the center turned into a different creature at night. No place was livelier than the Military Plaza. The San Antonio of today with the Riverwalk and the Mercado across from the Menger and the Alamo is a pale shade of the "hoo-rawing" town it was then. At its heart was a rowdy, vice-laden place like the French Quarter in New Orleans and the Barbary Coast in San Francisco. It was all bright colors, sizzling food, gamblers, cowboys, dance-hall girls, gunshots, shouts, howls, curses, pianos tinkling, guitars and trumpets playing, loud nasal music in Spanish that Gates couldn't understand, but instinctively liked. He liked the untamed world he'd stepped into as well. West of the Mississippi was a vast frontier where fortunes could be made if one had the luck and determination to make them.

Gates had plenty of determination, but he couldn't figure out how to make the first sale. When he tried to call on ranchers, they refused to let him in because, "Dad-burned stuff won't work." Nobody would even consider it. "We like you Gates," they said, "but your wire ain't any good."

Supposedly, while Gates was watching a medicine show selling Radway's famous Sarsaparillion Resolvent, the idea came to him to put on a show. Suddenly, he yelled to his friend that he would sell more damn wire than anyone ever thought of. He'd give them a show out in the street. And then they'd be all over him to buy.

He had dozens of hurdles to clear before he could put his idea into motion, but Gates was never afraid of work. He was a bulky man, not yet obese as he would be in later years, but filled with energy. When he had an idea that he believed in, he would put in long hours and sizable amounts of money to put it into action. In this case, like a medicine show salesman, he planned a demonstration. Of course, he kept the public informed of his efforts every step of the way.

The citizens of San Antonio laughed at him openly and began to place bets that Gates would fail, that the Yankee would go trotting back to Chicago with his tail between his legs. As busy as he was, Gates the gambler managed to place bets to cover $5,000 worth of the action. He stockpiled his materials in the plaza, and people walked round and round them, examining the mesquite posts and the rolls of wire and watching as he built the first barbed-wire corral.

People talked about it for miles around.

"Man! Them longhorns are gonna rip thet bob-wire t' pieces."

"Remember what happened in Kansas?"

"Say, what if there's a stampede?"

On the day of the show, cowboys as well as ranch bosses with their wives and families in buckboards and buggies pulled into the square to view the structure. The city of Houston even sent a newspaper reporter. Vendors sold food. Gamblers collected and placed bets. Music blared from the boardwalks of the saloons.

Gates had announced that the longhorns would be "the wildest damn cattle in Texas." In reality he had selected five dozen of the mildest, gentlest creatures he could find. But before he brought them out, he planned to stage an entire rodeo.

Some of the steers would be bulldogged, some would be ridden. Other acts would follow with cowboys demonstrating their skill at cutting some of the steers out of the herd by their brands. Trick riders on trained horses were hired to rear and pirouette and dance around the plaza to mariachi music.

Finally, a whole series of torches were lighted. Gates drove into the square dressed in cowboy gear, standing in a buckboard, and waving his hat to the crowds. "Ladies and gentlemen!" he shouted. "Now we're gonna prove to you, once and for all time to come, that bob-wire, good old bob-wire fence, will hold the longhorn and do him no damage."

With a sweep of his Stetson, he called. "Gents, bring on your cattle! Bring on your steers! We've got the wildest creatures on the plains! This is the best fencing in the world. It's light as air, stronger than whiskey, cheaper than dirt! No man can say John Gates don't make a fair and square test! Forty wild ones, wild steers, loco to get away!

"All right, boys, turn 'em loose!"

The longhorns saw the gate swing back in their wooden corral. The leader made a dash for the opening and through the chute into Gates's corral. While the noise of the crowd panicked the animals, they crowded into the back of the lead steer, who balked, then plunged forward.

Behind them came a Mexican vaquero howling and swinging his sombrero. Tossing his hat away, he seized two flaming torches Gates held out to him. Yelling curses in Spanish and waving the torches, he charged into the terrified herd. The steers scattered in ten different directions, stampeding for the fences. People fell back. Some screamed and dashed for safety.

Jostling in panic within the corral, the steers bawled as they thudded against the wire. A mesquite post snapped, but the eight tough strands of wire took the impact and held.

The herd began to circle, milling and trampling on the few that had fallen in the mêlée. Round and round, they milled until they finally came to a shivering stop. A few had cuts on their flanks. A horn or two had been broken. But the herd stood bunched in the center of the corral away from the barbs.

No one said a word. The entire assemblage stared open mouthed at the bewildered, silent cattle.

Then someone yelled, "Hurrah!"

And pandemonium let loose.

Gates called out from the top of the buckboard. "Thank you, ladies and gentlemen! Next week we'll give this same show. . . . I'll still be takin' bets. The steers that's been cut will stay here all week and . . . you won't see a screwworm in the whole lot of them.

"What'll y' bet?" someone yelled.

Gates's answer flashed back. "Betcha million!"

Another revolution occurred that day in Texas in 1876. It was bloodless, unless one counted the steers, but it was just as world-changing. As the show went on for week after week, ranchers from all parts of Texas poured into San Antonio to see the fabulous rodeo and to order the wire that would change the West forever. Incidentally, when they left, their money was in Gates's pockets. His only concern was how to fill the orders fast enough since his orders were far beyond the capacity of the De Kalb factory to fill. The plant went from selling 2,840,000 pounds of wire to 12,863,000 pounds. By the end of 1878, they would sell 26,644,000 pounds.

For the cattle industry, the bob-wire revolution had all the impact of the Industrial Revolution on manufacturing. Suddenly, the millions of acres of land that stood so far from the oceans and the centers of commerce were seen not as a great barrier to progress but as a vast new national resource. The longhorn was no longer the steer of choice because it could live off the land. Now purebred beeves could be kept within barbed wire fences and fattened on hay. The steer that could forage for itself and live on thistles during a drought was quickly sold off in favor of Herefords, whiteface, and black Angus.

Ranchers let most of their cowboys go and replaced them with wire. For a time some hands kept their jobs to dig the postholes and string "the Devil's rope." Eventually machines were invented that built the fences even more cheaply and efficiently than men. By and large from that time to the present, cowboys have hired out only for seasonal jobs such as the roundups and the branding.

With the money the owners expected to save, they bought blooded bulls and improved their herds. All sorts of exotic breeds from the East and Europe could be imported and raised not only on the boundless prairies of Texas but on the whole of the Great Plains as well.

Undeterred by the newspaper estimates that to fence off the average section of land would cost $3,840 and that wire was anywhere from 60 to 300 percent higher in Texas than in Illinois, the ranchers kept on buying. The price of wire was soon driven down by the increased speed with which the Sunset Railroad was finished. Where it had once hauled salesmen and a few passengers, it now hauled tons of bob-wire.

As the fences divided the boundless range into little boxes, range wars broke out over water holes and green grass. The price of cattle rose from $8 to $23 a head in Dodge City, Kansas, but fewer drives moved up the trail. And a way of life passed into legend as ranching became mechanized and much more profitable.

More and more, Gates came to realize that his talents as a salesman and promoter were being taken advantage of. Gates was resentful and ambitious. He made several trips back to Illinois to confer with Ellwood about making him a partner in the firm. He had no desire to work in the dust of the Military Plaza and depend on gambling earnings to buy luxuries for Dellora and their son Charlie.

Ellwood flatly told him to stay a salesman or quit.

"I quit," Gates snapped.

At this point Gates took a little time off to relax. Relaxing to Gates always meant going somewhere to gamble, so he and a friend went to a racetrack. According to the friend, Gates's first bet that day was a thousand dollars on a horse named Under the Wire. Gates laughed as he planked down his money. "Don't know anything about the nag," he joked, "but that 'wire' kinda appeals to me."

The horse won, paying $5,000.

With that and money he borrowed from Dellora's father, Gates stormed into St. Louis. Despite a Supreme Court decision giving all the patents to Ellwood and the Washburn-Moen Corporation, Gates opened his own bob-wire firm and from the first advertised his wire at "favorable prices." Without a single qualm he created an illegal but highly profitable business. He became a "moonshiner," no different from an illegal whiskey distiller hiding during the daylight hours and making his product by the light of the moon.

And just like the distiller, he was confident that his product was in demand. He had already established his market in Texas. Everyone in the state considered him a smart businessman and a heck of a good fellow. They trusted Johnny Gates, the man who had staged the rodeos in Military Plaza.

Missouri was several hundred miles closer to Texas than was Illinois. Distance in that case was money. Determined to undercut Ellwood's prices, Gates opened a new plant in St. Louis that he named the Southern Wire Company. He bragged he would sell his wire for only $100 a mile.

Big business in those days was largely a matter of control by various robber barons, who bought up or squeezed out small entrepreneurs by lowering their prices until the little guys went broke or were forced to sell. The Sherman Act of 1890 had declared such practices felonies, but the penalties were fines, relatively small in comparison to the millions the "titans of industry" raked in. They gathered all the competition into a single unit thereby creating a monopoly, but they called it a trust—as in "Trust me. I'll set prices for everybody as high as the traffic will bear."

The practice continued unabated as people like J. Pierpont Morgan came to control steel and John D. Rockefeller controlled every aspect of oil and its most important product— gasoline. By his retirement in 1890, Rockefeller was revealed to be the richest man in the world and its first billionaire.

Ellwood tried to emulate the "titans" when he tapped a Missouri judge for an injunction that sent process servers to shut his former salesman down. Unfortunately, they couldn't find him. Thanks to the spies Gates had hired back in Chicago, he had already moved his machinery and wire in the middle of the night. By ferryboat he transported it lock, stock, and barrel to the Illinois side of the Mississippi. In a different state he was out of reach of men with the Missouri-issued subpoenas that Ellwood had sent out against him.

Though his enterprise was illegal, Gates suffered no real penalties from the Supreme Court decision. The federal bench was not prepared in this case to punish those who did not cease and desist. Though Ellwood whined that his patents were being stolen, the big steel men like Andrew Carnegie, J. Pierpont Morgan, and Henry Clay Frick were in the process of buying patents of a different kind and reorganizing the steel industry into their own trust monopolies to control prices and make huge profits. They couldn't be bothered with Gates and his bob-wire, so long as he was a "little producer." They ignored Ellwood's complaints.

Rumors circulated that Gates was actually making wire on a barge in the middle of the river. The entire business community got a big laugh out of his moonshiner company making wire in hiding and underselling the bigger producers. The ranchers and cowboys who were his chief buyers had long been rebels against the big city businesses, whom they characterized—right or wrong—as a bunch of crooks. Gates's illegal doings merely added to their respect for him. Gates was a crook for sure, but he was their crook, and they gave him a new nickname—"Moonshine" Gates—which he disliked even more than the one pinned on him later: "Bet a Million."

If he had stayed small—under the titans' guns, so to speak—Gates would have probably been allowed to go on and make his millions with the "farm boys." However, he was too ambitious and much too daring to do so. With capital and a huge market, Gates began to play the same monopoly games the big boys did. Eventually, he owned or controlled four more steel companies: Consolidated Steel and Wire, Illinois Steel, American Steel and Wire, and Republic Steel Company. Though by millionaire's standards he was still a small producer, he was getting bigger.

A new opportunity presented itself in 1898. Arthur E. Stilwell, an ambitious St. Louis insurance dealer, was a devotee of spiritualism. He announced one day that he wanted to build a railroad from Kansas City south 778 miles to Sabine Lake in Texas.

How he came by this idea defies logic, but it is nevertheless a true story. In a stage whisper, Stilwell told several of his potential investors, among them Edward Harriman who had built the Union Pacific Railroad, that "Brownies," or "spiritual messengers," had told him to build a town, a canal, and port.

When the skeptical Harriman asked why, Stilwell explained that the Brownies had prophesied that Galveston, the largest port on the Gulf of Mexico after New Orleans, was due to be destroyed by a flood.

Though no one rushed forward with fists full of cash to invest, Stilwell was determined. He refused to abandon his great opportunity. He would first build the railroad, dredge the lake, construct docks, and then build a ship canal to the Gulf of Mexico. His new town would grow and be there to take advantage of the calamity that was sure to come.

In a last ditch effort, Stilwell turned to the gambler John Gates. It was a gamble of monumental proportions, just the sort of thing that set Gates's blood a-boil. Stilwell built the railroad using materials supplied by Gates's American Steel and Wire Corporation. Whenever Stilwell ran short of money, Gates kept the steel rails coming in exchange for stock in the Kansas City, Pittsburg (Kansas), and Gulf Railroad.

To demonstrate his faith in the project, Gates made a visit to the new town site Stilwell had created and named Port Arthur. Gates opened the First National Bank of Port Arthur and built a summer home for $50,000—a huge sum in those days. When Stilwell got into financial difficulties within a year, Gates stepped in and reorganized the property, eventually taking it over completely. All was in readiness for the great profits garnered from the trade that would be flowing through the port and up the rails into the heart of America. The railroad's name was changed to the Kansas City and Southern—eventually simplified to the Kansas City Southern—an operating corporation to this day with a million miles of rails through the central United States and deep into Mexico.

In the meantime, a wildcatter named Pattillo Higgins leased a thousand acres of land near Beaumont, about twenty miles northwest of Port Arthur. With Anthony F. Lucas, an engineer and former captain in the Austrian Navy, they began to drill on a salt dome just outside the town. It was called Big Hill because the top of it was fifteen feet higher than the surrounding area.

But the oil didn't flow out of the ground. They were down to two thousand feet, and their well looked as if it was a dry hole. Lucas was out of money. Higgins was out of money. Through Joseph S. Cullinan, a refinery magnate, they applied to John D. Rockefeller, whose Standard Oil Corporation was the richest in the world. The eastern millionaire turned down the project. He had no use for wildcat drillers in Texas. Oil was in Pennsylvania, where he controlled it then and for the future.

Cullinan was disappointed but undeterred. Shortly thereafter, he sent a representative to Gates, who was pursuing more millions in wire, steel, and now railroads from his headquarters in Chicago. The de facto owner of a railroad that had its terminus in Port Arthur would surely be interested in anything that would bring more people and money into the area. Gates's money had practically built the little town brick by brick.

Representing Lucas, Cullinan offered him 10 percent of the stock for $50,000. Gates all but laughed in Cullinan's face. Gates wasn't interested unless he could have a controlling interest in the well. "You go back and tell them I'll take 51 percent or nothing."

The others objected strenuously, but Gates held firm. "Suppose you do find oil? How're you going to sell it? I got the railroad and I got the docks. Cullinan, you'll need a big refinery in Port Arthur. You'll need a pipeline. You'll need docks, so you can load your oil on ships and send it any place it can be sold.

"You sell me 51 percent. If we get oil, I'll finance you to build the best pipeline and refinery in world. We'll build a fleet of oil boats."

Out of options but still fighting hard, Cullinan agreed to sell Gates 46 percent of any oil that came out of the salt dome. He retained 46 percent for himself and his associates. Gates's agent, George Craig, was sold the remaining 8 percent so that neither company would have the upper hand. Of course, Craig was Gates's man. Gates named his new firm the Texas Company.

On September 8, 1900, Arthur Stilwell's Brownies proved themselves to be purveyors of the truth, or at least of coincidence. A gigantic hurricane swept over Galveston Island, destroying the city and killing perhaps as many as eight thousand of its citizens. Shipping of all kinds immediately turned to Port Arthur fifty miles northeast and unscathed thanks to Sabine Lake. The large lake absorbed the fury of the hurricane's storm surge, so the little town sustained only superficial damage. At the same time, Galveston Bay, which sat directly behind the lowland of Galveston Island, kept Houston from being wiped out by the waves that destroyed almost the entire town.

If Gates was surprised when the predictions of Stilwell's Brownies came true, he gave no sign. Privately, he reasoned that hurricanes could happen at any place along the Gulf of Mexico. Still, the best was yet to come. On January 10, 1901, just four months later, the Lucas gusher blew in; the salt dome spouted oil. The hill on which the derrick had been erected had been referred to simply as Big Hill, but someone decided the spot needed a name that would at least identify it by a location. A popular picnic ground about a mile away on the banks of the Neches River was called Spindletop Springs. Thus, the first oil field in Texas became Spindletop.

So unprepared were Lucas and Cullinan for the enormity of their discovery that they worked nine days to cap the well. Lucas lost an estimated half a million barrels of oil before they could bring Spindletop under control.

The next problem, then, was what they were going to do with the oil.

Cullinan telegraphed Gates, urging the immediate construction of a pipeline and a refinery. Shifting his dollar cigar around his grin, the gambler sent $500,000 to do the job. Within a year, 138 oil-producing wells were pumping on Spindletop and in the surrounding areas. Thousands of hopefuls flocked to the area around Beaumont, only to lose their investments and return home in despair. A few like John Gates made more money than he had ever dreamed.

He controlled Port Arthur, the docks, the shipping, the refinery.

Hell! He controlled the whole countryside!

He turned down a $25,000,000 offer for his holdings from no less than John D. Rockefeller himself. It was a fair price, but Gates enjoyed turning away the great man. The way he looked at it, no wager was attached to it. No game was to be played, and to Gates, it was all about the game. He saw himself as one of the "titans of industry." He was in the same league with Morgan, Frick, and Carnegie; he had spotted a good deal that Rockefeller himself had turned down. Gates had played the greatest gamble and won.

In the meantime, Andrew Carnegie had announced that he wanted out of the industrial world completely to devote his time to endowing his various charities. In May 1899, he had let it be known that what he had was for sale—at top prices. Excited speculation stirred on the floor of the stock exchange—the United States Steel Corporation was for sale.

Gates attempted to buy it and other companies from the aristocratic moneymen who controlled the entire country. He failed again and again. They were too entrenched, and, more to the point, they despised him. Reluctantly, he looked for games to be played with others in the next generation who were eager to be his friends. Meanwhile, he dined at Delmonico's and gambled at Canfield's decorated with Chippendale furniture, Chinese porcelains, and teakwood floors. The casino catered to Senator Edward Wolcott of Colorado; Phil Dwyer, "king of the race tracks"; and Reginald Vanderbilt.

The waiters fought to serve these people, for they were all heavy tippers. Gates was the most generous. The man who served Gates frequently had to wait on him for long hours in order to collect his fabulous tips. Gates had unusual stamina and would often play three days and nights without sleep.

In the end, it was Gates's outrageous reputation for huge bets that made him a public figure. "Bet a Million," the man with all the luck, caught the imagination of the country. Gates was the builder, the entrepreneur, the man of ambition with the intelligence and drive to acquire a great fortune and spend it in ways that benefited less fortunate groups of people.

Stories grew more and more outrageous, and they were believed because no one like him had ever been seen. He was said to bet $1,000 to $10,000 on the speed of raindrops trickling down a window pane. He flipped coins for $10,000 a toss. He had once made an outrageous bet with the multimillionaire founder of Bethlehem Steel of Pennsylvania, Charles Schwab, who demanded the $30,000 that Gates's American Steel and Wire owed him.

"Tell you what I'll do," Gates said, "I'll flip you. Double or nothing. If I lose, I'll owe you $60,000. If I win, I owe you nothing." After some "hemming and hawing," Schwab agreed. Gates flipped the coin. It spun high and dropped with a soft plunk on the plush carpet.

Gates won.

September 6, 1901, President William McKinley, a friend to big business, was assassinated by an anarchist. His vice president was the former governor of New York, a young buckaroo named Theodore Roosevelt, known to one and all as "T. R." He had been a great vote getter for the dour McKinley, who had conducted his campaign from his "front porch."

Big business breathed a sigh of relief at the assumption of T. R., who was known to be more a Progressive than a Republican. He was also known to believe in capitalism and had nothing against wealthy businessmen so long as their practices were open and aboveboard. However, he was deeply concerned about the way some of them manipulated the stock market to cause panics.

If J. Pierpont Morgan or John D. Rockefeller sold a large block of stock in some profitable concern, other investors would immediately sell theirs, believing that Morgan or Rockefeller had insider information and the company was going bankrupt. The result would be a run on the stock, which would lose significant value within hours. The company would be prime for a takeover by one of the financiers or become worthless so it could be bought for very little.

These manipulations resulted in the richest men acquiring more businesses for their monopolistic trusts or simply buying them to shut them up tight, putting thousands of working men out of jobs and causing their families to starve, all in the name of reducing competition.

T. R. quickly put about that he would be a "trustbuster." It was a nickname he loved as well as the political cartoons that showed him as a little muscular fellow wearing glasses and boxing gloves taking on the "big guys."

Because Gates was making money and in many cases beating Morgan, Rockefeller, and the others at their own games, they hated him. As he made more and more money, not only from Spindletop and the Kansas City Southern, but also from steel and other metals, Gates was snubbed by the men he wished to associate with. He was a gross, uncouth Westerner. The manager of the Waldorf-Astoria, where Gates often ate lunch, found it politic to criticize his customer's manners to everyone he felt would be interested. Meanwhile, Gates ordered full course dinners, paid in cash, and tipped lavishly. The manager might turn up his nose, but the bellhops, waiters, and cigar clerks all but fell over their feet to see to his every wish.

Just how deep was Morgan's hatred Gates discovered when he suggested to several of his friends that they put up his and his son Charlie's names for membership in the New York Yacht Club. The answer from the board, a group New York businessmen who found it politic not to irritate the great Morgan, was a thunderous "No." While Gates cared nothing about yachting, he was angered because Charlie, his scion and the light of his life, was denied something he wanted.

Morgan regarded Gates as an uncouth westerner who had merely had a streak of luck. He despised such types, particularly when they dared to challenge his own acquisitions. Morgan's attitude did much to set Gates on the prowl for ways to hurt the people who had revealed their snobbishness. With malicious intent he began to acquire shares in Colorado Fuel and Iron, Sloss-Sheffield, and Tennessee Coal and Iron, three independent but valuable steel producers that were "off the map" so far as United States Steel Corporation was concerned.

But Morgan was on the prowl as well. Gates discovered that every word he uttered with regard to good business interests caused that business's stock to be unloaded quickly. The brokers believed that if Gates was interested in those companies, they would soon be destroyed by Morgan.

To Gates's disgust, the value of Colorado Fuel and Iron fell sharply. Gates confronted Osgood, the company president, and threatened him with court action for stock manipulation. Then, showing his usual philosophical farsightedness, Gates dropped out and sold his shares to George J. Gould, son of the railroad magnate of the previous century. The stock price fell even farther. No one would touch it, and in the end Rockefeller got it. Ten years later it had still earned not one penny in dividends.

Because of these battles, 1902 was a time of the "rich man's panics" as the wealthy men manipulated their trusts and monopolies to defeat Gates and send him back west where he came from.

He went.

Back in Chicago, he fell ill. He complained of severe headaches and digestive pains. Dellora took him to Saratoga for a few quiet weeks. He came back refreshed, but still not returned to his old fighting form. He was only forty-seven years old, but badly overweight. He smoked or chewed on cigars from morning till night, and sometimes the nights went on until dawn and beyond.

Still he plunged on, determined to make one great push that would drive Morgan from the position of sole power in steel and force him to recognize Gates as an equal. Gates envisioned himself the head of a great iron and steel trust in the

South. Three or four good companies would do the trick. Together they would rival U.S. Steel's holdings. To give himself time to acquire the steel and iron ore properties, Gates resorted to misdirection.

Morgan was at work building and acquiring the various transportation systems that carried people back and forth and in and around New York City. Gates let it be known that he was also interested in transportation, but then began to buy heavily in railroads, wheat, and copper.

What was going on? Where was he going with this? Wall Street reacted with alarm. Rumors flashed back and forth on the Stock Exchange floor. Morgan moved to thwart Gates's plans.

August Belmont, Morgan's stooge by that time, pressured the New York City fathers to refuse Gates a right-of-way for a line from the Bowery in the south to North Harlem. The goal was to keep the line from running through Manhattan, either by elevated rail or by subway tunnel. Unfortunately for Belmont, groups of citizens appeared to stage a "spontaneous demonstration" in front of Tammany Hall. Frustrated, Belmont still refused to talk to Gates or to compromise. Then Gates attacked Belmont's Interborough Rapid Transit Company stock on the open market. Prices fell.

With the pressure and protests growing in intensity and the price of the stock declining into nothing, Belmont resigned from Republic Steel. John Gates became its president and immediately began to implement plans to establish his own southern steel trust. He was playing for keeps.

The next jewel in the crown was Tennessee Coal and Iron, or TCI as it was familiarly called. As the market slid downward, helped by disgruntled financiers who had long hidden their distaste and downright hatred for Morgan, Gates accumulated shares of TCI.

In January 1903, in control of blocks of shares in three southern companies, Gates sent invitations out to the heads of the firms to meet with him. After he outlined his plans, several hours of dickering drove him frantic. The men were obviously scared almost witless of J. Pierpont Morgan. In the end someone whined that he wanted consultations with the major stockholders.

Gates lost his famous temper. "The hell with that!" he shouted. "We've got control and I can prove it!"

But their fear was too great. They continued to block his scheme. "The deal is off," he said unhappily to Dellora. "But it may be reopened in the future."

Unfortunately, the scheme was blown. Morgan figured out what was afoot, if he hadn't known all along. Still he didn't consider Gates a threat. Indeed Gates had suffered a well-publicized financial loss amounting to $2,000,000 in wheat futures, one of the most highly speculative areas of finance.

The loss was a clever misdirection. Gates could well afford to lose the two million and the wheat futures as well. He had come to recognize that his son had no stomach for the rough-and-tumble world of Wall Street. He told friends he intended to close the brokerage firm and get out of the business entirely. He already planned retire to Port Arthur and live out his days in peace and tranquility.

Except for one last gamble.

He trained his guns on J. Pierpont Morgan.

Ruthlessly shuffling and firing executives left and right, Gates prepared to merge Republic and TCI. The companies fit perfectly together. Each had raw materials the other did not have. Each had plants and mills that when united would make them an independent unit. They would be an impregnable combination—the ideal monopoly, a trust to be reckoned with.

Gates rolled into Birmingham, Alabama, in his private railroad car. He gave its citizens his glimpse of the future—prosperity for everyone. It was Port Arthur on a huge scale. He handed out pamphlets to the members of the Commercial Club entitled "Why Birmingham Will Have a Million

Population in 1920." He predicted he would change TCI into TCI and Railway Company. He guaranteed that shares would be worth $500 each. So excited and so spirited was he that he might have raised his fist and shouted as he had in San Antonio so long ago, "Betcha Million!"

He went back to Wall Street with the intention of liquidating his brokerage and going to Alabama. But the word was out. Instigated by Morgan, the "silent panic" struck. A few small banks collapsed, but Roosevelt was able to hold the center together with gold bullion.

In May 1903 Gates moved from the Waldorf-Astoria, his home for so long; the new Plaza Hotel on Fifth Avenue was now his address. As one of the privileged stockholders in the United States Realty Company, he was permitted to design his own sixteen-room apartment. One feature was an enormous bathtub, custom-sized for his obese body. There he bathed twice daily.

He considered himself safe now that he owned the controlling interests in TCI and Republic. He, Charlie, and Dellora sailed for Europe on July 7. Gates was unreachable.

And so he would have been if Grant Schley, the broker for TCI, had not been in major financial difficulties through his own incompetence. Illegally, he used $6,000,000 of TCI shares as security for a $40,000,000 note.

It blew the door open.

The panic grew wilder. Morgan left the city with instructions that his bank was not to take the checks of the Knickerbocker Trust. The millionaire planned to be unavailable for the request that was sure to come. He was incognito in Richmond, Virginia, as a lay delegate to a retreat for Episcopal clergymen.

Because of Schely's incompetence and sheer panic, the banks would no longer accept TCI stock.

Gates was rushing home by ocean liner with $7,000,000 in gold bullion in hold, but the Atlantic was wide.

Morgan then proved to his constituency that he was the wiliest pirate on Wall Street. Of course, he had to remain behind the scenes. Roosevelt would be instantly suspicious of him. Instead, the millionaire sent Henry Clay Frick, one of the most respected men in America, along with Elbert H. Gary, a shrewd lawyer with whom Gates had a long and unpleasant history, to explain the U.S. Steel version of what was happening during Roosevelt's administration. To save the country, they offered magnanimously to buy TCI for half the value of the stock and avert a complete financial collapse. But the president of the United States had to agree to it.

Frick and silver-tongued Gary boarded a special train to travel through the night from New York to Washington—a locomotive, a tender, and a single Pullman coach.

They found the president at breakfast and persuaded the trustbuster to allow the creation of the greatest trust of all. T. R. sent a note to his attorney general giving approval, but in such a way that he did not appear to know which companies were actually involved in this salvation. With the president's signed approval, the panic disappeared as if by magic.

By the time Gates arrived at his offices, he had heard the whole story. Then Schley called from Morgan's offices asking Gates to speak to Morgan. "I'm putting Mr. Morgan on the wire," Schley said.

"I'll see you in Hell first," Gates roared and slammed the receiver on the hook.

But in the end, his dream of a steel empire was gone. The southern trust would never be. Although there were outcries in legislative and public halls, Morgan had won and Gates knew it.

When toasts were made at a dinner in the Waldorf-Astoria some nights later, the tribute to President Theodore Roosevelt was greeted with polite silence. Then someone proposed a toast to J. Pierpont Morgan, "the uncrowned king of finance who has saved us all." Loud cheers rang out through the ornate dining room.

Though the financial world counted him out, Gates was still richer than most of the men in that dining room. He was still head of Republic Steel, among his first acquisitions. He still had Texas with her railroads, her bob-wire, and her oil. Texas was where he belonged—Houston, Beaumont, San Antonio, and Port Arthur. Wherever men maintained their businesses because of his support, he was welcomed.

Later in 1906 he had given the ship channel to the federal government to maintain on the condition that Congress designated Port Arthur an international port of entry. He had established the town's first bank; built the rice mill; built the Port Arthur Light, Power, and Ice Company; and constructed new docks. He could gamble as he wished. He created a boom as more and more people followed him there, drawn by the sure presence of his money.

When his mother died, Gates built the Mary Warne Gates Memorial Hospital in Port Arthur.

On the night of November 15, 1909, millionaires from New York, Chicago, and Houston came for the "billion dollar banquet" in the Plaza Hotel in Port Arthur. Cullinan was there. Orson Welles, who was a longtime friend of the Gateses, came as well as Hopkins, of the Diamond Match Company, and Hill, the railroad builder. Port Arthur was more impressed than ever, if such a thing were possible. Forgotten was poor Arthur Stilwell, whose idea Port Arthur had been in the first place.

Back in Washington, things were not going smoothly. A hue and cry arose as other powerful people called for investigation of this flagrant violation of the Sherman Antitrust Act. Too late the trust-busting president realized he had been lied to, and he had actually enabled the building of the most monstrous trust of all. He did not like being taken advantage of, nor did he like the part Morgan had tricked him into playing.

Moreover, the president's political foes, led by Charles Culberson of Texas, introduced a resolution ordering the attorney general to deliver the reports of TCI and U.S. Steel for their investigations.

Furious, T. R. bellowed like the bull moose that he likened himself to. The legislature had no right to question the president. But he realized that, then as now, in politics timing is everything. The president was ending his second term. He wanted to be remembered as a great president, not a toady to J. Pierpont Morgan as the papers had begun to paint him.

Talk of censure was in the air. Although the papers played it down, reporters were fairly certain that T. R. had enabled the delivery of TCI to Morgan, but they liked the president. He had always made good copy. They thought with a little publicity, the public would be ready to forgive and forget.

Roosevelt's friend William Howard Taft ran for president and won with Roosevelt's blessing. Surely everything would settle down now. But it did not.

Congress was not satisfied at the huge monster U.S. Steel dictating prices throughout the American economy. The Senate wanted answers. John Gates received a subpoena to appear before that august body to answer their questions. On May 27, 1911, Gates faced the solemn men.

Perhaps a clean breast would have created new legislation, new rules, but despite Morgan's conniving, Gates chose to live by the businessman's motto: "Never squeal, never squawk." He circumvented the incriminating questions even when he had a chance to lambaste his hated enemy. Time and again to Senate questions regarding what was done to him, Gates would answer with great certainty that business was "survival of the fittest." In the end, the Senate hearings droned on and on; and, as Senate hearings do today, proved nothing to anybody's satisfaction.

Theodore Roosevelt lost his bid to be elected for an unprecedented third term as much as anything for his failure to curb the monopolies in his previous administration. He was labeled a "friend of big business."

To escape the furor, John and Dellora Gates set sail for France. While in Paris, Gates consulted doctors about the abscesses that had developed in his throat. Four specialists advised an instant operation to remove the lesions that were indeed cancerous. They then treated the area with radiation.

In his weakened state he had no voice. He lay listless in the oppressive Paris heat despite the open windows. Dellora sent for Charlie. The doctors gave stimulants, but the results were only temporary. On August 9, John Warne Gates died at age fifty-six.

In defeating the upstart from Texas, Morgan had let loose the hounds that bayed and attacked his mighty empire. In October 1911, the U.S. government brought suit against the massive trust, ordering that it be dissolved. The trial dragged on and on for the next ten years.

J. Pierpont Morgan never found out whether U.S. Steel survived. He died in 1913.

Dellora and Charlie were very, very wealthy indeed. In addition to Republic Steel, Kansas City Southern, and the Texas Company, which became Texaco, "Bet a Million" had acquired Kentland Copper Company, Furnace Valley Copper Company, Manufacturer's Coal and Coke Company, and Missouri Railway Construction Company as well as numerous other securities.

Charlie died of natural causes probably related to his obesity the year after Morgan died. Dellora lived on for another four years, making the people of Port Arthur very happy by donating money for the Gates Memorial Library, which became the foundation for Lamar University.

John Warne Gates's Bet a Million legend lives on despite his dislike for the name. His shocking behavior pleased him almost as much as it pleased the people around him. It is a legacy that adds to the reputation of Texas.

Was it truly outrageous?

Bet a Million!

EVERY STATE NEEDS A CHICKEN RANCH

If a whiskey drummer had pulled up to the hitching post of the small pine-board hotel in La Grange, Texas, in 1844, in at least one room he'd have been greeted with open arms. And open thighs.

Literally.

Although the establishment mostly consisted of rented rooms, its most popular and lucrative business was to sell a modicum of pleasure to the gentlemen who came by. To tell the plain, unvarnished truth, it was a whorehouse. Prices were cheap. The two girls were probably as clean as they could be after servicing the traveling salesmen, cowboys, farmers, townsmen, and others who enjoyed their wares.

The local law in the person of William Nabors, who was absolutely no relation to the television star of Gomer Pyle fame, was the sheriff of Fayette County. Undoubtedly, he took his cut of the profits of the place. In exchange, he kept order and protected the girls in case one of the customers got rough.

The relationship between lawmen and prostitutes is one of the ill-kept secrets of most western states. The Earp brothers of OK Corral fame were arrested more than once for keeping a "house of ill fame." Very few in central Texas looked down on Nabors's status as brothel keeper. Many men with lesser opportunities for a profitable sideline probably envied him.

Perhaps some circuit-riding preachers might cast a look askance, but in those days, Texas was a man's world populated by rough, tough, and sometimes mean-spirited males with notably fewer females available.

The Alamo had fallen only eight years before. Any man who lived here was most likely a survivor of the Runaway Scrape. Chances are he'd high-tailed it when General Sam Houston led a frantic retreat before the advancing army of Generalissimo Antonio López de Santa Anna, whose army was by far the largest on the North American continent. When Sam turned to face the heavily armed, uniformed *soldados* at San Jacinto, most Texans with any sense kept one eye on the escape route across the Buffalo Bayou. Each man was pretty sure he was in the fight of his life, and he was probably going to lose it. Louisiana in the good old United States would sure be preferable to Heaven.

No one could believe what happened next, but General Sam had called it right, 'cause he'd sure caught 'em with their pants down. They were taking their siesta, and we stormed through the bivouac and captured old "SantyAnna hisself."

And tarnation! We won!

With the Spanish and the Mexican governments gone, the victors took full advantage of the spoils. Texas was a sovereign nation—not yet annexed by the United States of America. The country had many fewer women than men. And when a man's worked hard all day at farming behind a mule-drawn plow, keeping the cattle herded together, maybe prospecting for something that might be valuable, minding the few stores, or operating a saloon, a man needs recreation.

Derned if he don't!

As for the working girls that plied their trade in the whorehouse in La Grange, no stereotype fits them. As they came and went, they were "from every social, racial, religious, and economic group in North America." Some were there to escape poverty. Some were brought by their "loving" families. A dark Texas secret is that some of the girls, who appeared to be lacking in good sense or were crippled or disabled in some way from birth, were brought by their own kin, who didn't want to be bothered with rearing them past a certain age. Some came, though not many, through ignorance of what the job entailed.

Sad to say, some escaped abusive husbands, fathers, stepfathers, uncles, brothers, and even farm hands. Rather than remain crouched on a miserable pallet in a corner or huddled in a haystack in a cold and lonely dark field, for some, the decision to walk into a brothel brought blessed relief and a life of relative comfort and safety. There at least they'd be paid rather than despised and often beaten by the men who claimed them as their right.

And who among us can blame them? Easy enough to say "death before dishonor," but death is terribly permanent while dishonor may—just may—lead to something better. According to Jan Hutson, biographer and historian of the Chicken Ranch brothel, "Many a frontier floozy is remembered today as 'a great-great grandmother, a charmin' little lady. Charter member of The Daughters of the Confederacy, you know.'"

Most, although not all, shared one common characteristic: they had a very poor education or no education at all. Without training, how could any female live alone and earn a living? Prostitution was the only life open to them. They walked in and found it was not so bad as they had been led to believe.

The actual life of a prostitute was generally not glamorous or filled with erotic experiences. People expecting to find licentious descriptions in this chapter should read no further.

Of course, then as now, in most circles it's still an outrageous profession. What is more outrageous is that people choose to give it a bad name and push it outside the law. When it is conducted in a professional manner with proper safeguards, prostitution performs a service that far more citizens take advantage of than they would be willing to admit. A woman can work in reasonable security rather than live in poverty and want. Nevertheless, the sheriff of the county is a good man for the madam to have on her side. If he's on her payroll, both of them can work together in perfect harmony.

The focus of this chapter is on one house in one county with a succession of interesting women keeping their shoulders back and chins up despite a difficult life. In the cases of the women of La Grange, they had the help of a succession of tolerant lawmen, who also profited in ways that they didn't suspect when they entered into the clandestine "partnership."

To the law-abiding and prudish reader—for you what follows is outrageous! Be warned!

The nation's oldest continually operating whorehouse opened for business in 1844, sixty years after America was born and just five years after La Grange became a town. Its location changed from time to time. Its name changed depending on the name of the madam who conducted the business for the girls.

But no one can say that it didn't "rise" in the estimation of farmboys, cowboys, and their educated equivalents—Aggies from Texas Agricultural and Mechanical College, flyboys from Bergstrom Air Force Base, the traveling salesmen that found a haven in their town, and probably the county's solid citizens from time to time. Moreover, when the visitors came to enjoy the brothel's growing reputation, they contributed to the town's wealth by patronizing gas stations, liquor stores, and cafés. Generally speaking, if you were tolerant and had your eye on your bank account, you didn't mind the fact that "Texas has a whorehouse in it!"

If you weren't tolerant, you prayed, "Lord, have mercy on our souls!"

Its first madam was a dwarfish woman of incredible ugliness. She had a short, squat body; little sausage-like arms and legs; a wide-nostril nose; and a horrible overbite. Her tiny black eyes peered out from under a low brow over fat pink cheeks. No one ever knew her real name, but, of course, she was called Mrs. Swine.

She wore black wool dresses that never saw soap and water. Nor was she ever once known to bathe her corpulent body. In a word, she stank. Her hats were black as well and sat atop a huge bun of oily black hair.

On her pudgy, stumpy-fingered hand, she wore a large diamond ring, mute testimony to the fact that she must have been someone's favorite "something" at one time or another. She started her business with a miserable pair of girls the town came to refer to as "the Piglets." At least one was retarded and both were illiterate.

Mrs. Swine would have been unusually lucky if over the course of her years of managing the brothel, she never employed some girl who had syphilis, which is not an easily recognizable disease until it reached its contagious and subsequently deadly stages. Likewise, since tuberculosis was rampant among the lower classes of society in those days, undoubtedly, some girls were carriers if not sufferers from full-blown cases.

If there was a bright side, Mrs. Swine did provide these girls with a roof over their heads that eventually became a home of sorts, food to eat, and beds to sleep in until their unfortunate deaths. Most prostitutes did not live past twenty-five in those days. In that respect, their sisters who had married farmers were more fortunate. Their average age of mortality was thirty-five.

The brothel was a stopping place for all single males, a majority of whom were cowboys who ceaselessly herded the thousands of wild cattle left by the Spaniards to whom Texas had belonged. Barbed wire had not yet been invented to keep one man's herd separate from another. Brands could be and were often changed with a running iron, so herds needed many cowboys to keep watch. Generally, the cowboys that stopped at Mrs. Swine's were as young as or even younger than the girls. Their education was probably less than that of the prostitutes. Most of them had had to climb hand over hand up the stirrups to throw a leg over the saddle. "The West was won" by very young men with vocabularies of about 300 words.

Old cowhands "from the Rio Grande" were rarities. The cowboy life was much, much harder than the movies portray it. Accidents involving horses and steers, both of which outweighed cowboys by several hundred pounds, were almost certain to be crippling if not fatal. The untimely death of "Little Joe, the Wrangler" beneath the hooves of stampeding longhorns was a song based on fact.

To begin her business, Mrs. Swine was able to rent one room in the hotel that eventually became the Chicken Ranch. When not actually at work, her girls sat in the hotel lobby doing needlework and perhaps hoping that a good man would come in and want to marry them. If a single client arrived, he could have his pick. If two clients arrived together, both girls would lead them upstairs.

The single room contained two beds with straw ticks resting on bed-cords. On a washstand was a chipped bowl, a pitcher, and infrequently changed towels. The daunting Mrs. Swine sat in one chair, facing the beds. Another chair was provided for an extra cowboy who could wait eagerly for one of his friends to "finish."

The only position was woman on top, man on the bottom. The girl usually faced away from her client, and, to preserve their modesty, neither man nor woman undressed. It took only a few minutes to complete the act. Since watching and hearing was arousing, many a man, after watching his pals, barely "made it through the gate" himself. Mrs. Swine collected their money. They buttoned up and went on their way.

Given these circumstances, the number of men a girl could service during an evening, if a trail-herd was bedded down close by, was truly outrageous.

Men of that era considered the whorehouse coupling extremely erotic because in this position, they didn't have to do all the work. Those who had wives at home were especially excited because "normal" decency required that a woman wear her nightgown, close her eyes, spread her legs, and lie on her back stiff as a post while he "did his business." This man-on-top position was known round the world as the "missionary."

Some girls actually did find husbands among the men who came to have intercourse with them. A whore was not accepted into society under any circumstances. However, if she married, society was tolerant. If some good-hearted man "made an honest woman out of her," more often than not she was accepted into the community because she had "seen the light, come to Jesus, and returned to the fold."

Then the Civil War exploded, referred to in many parts of the South as "the War of Northern Aggression." The rumor spread that Mrs. Swine was a Yankee sympathizer and possibly a spy. Who knows what she would have learned worth selling to the North in a brothel that catered to ignorant trail hands, farm boys, and Confederate privates and noncommissioned officers? She left town while the "gettin' was good," taking with her a steamer trunk that was rumored to have all her considerable goods and money stored in it. No one mourned except that her storied wealth had disappeared with her.

The years following the Civil War were hard for everyone, including whores. They no longer had the protection of a county sheriff or town marshal who could be counted on to take care of them. More often than not they were exploited rather than protected. While no one missed Mrs. Swine, possibly everyone would have been better off if she had remained and made the arrangements. Her intimidating reputation would have spared her girls much.

Instead, Southern sheriffs lost their authority because federal martial law—especially harsh during Reconstruction—disarmed them. For that period the saloons employed the girls and cared little for how they were treated. Alcohol, and the violence and debauchery that accompanied it, made the situation downright dangerous for prostitutes. For the girls that had been taken care of by Mrs. Swine, the situation got so bad and sad that they migrated from the saloons and hotels to a shack alongside the Colorado River of Texas. It was a fortuitous location because the girls could include river traffic as well as town and countrymen among their clientele.

At about that time, a farm girl who had had diphtheria as a child appeared "just up the road a ways" in Waco. The debilitating disease left her too weak to work on a farm. Though she tried honest work in town, she was not strong enough to sustain that either. In the end, she went into a brothel where she was greeted with open arms by the madam. She was prettier, smarter, healthier, and much more refined than any other female who had darkened their door. Her real name was Faye Stewart.

For her new profession, Faye changed her hair style, her dress, her habits, and her name. Shortly after she learned her trade, she took over her own house as Miss Jessie Williams. Though it became successful and profitable, she left Waco and moved to the weathered shanty on the banks of the Colorado.

Why?

Miss Jessie never chose to say.

Instead, she immediately established herself as the madam to be reckoned with by making a deal with the local law enforcement officers, the Loessin brothers. August Loessin was sheriff of Fayette County. His brother, Will, was his chief deputy doubling as town marshal of La Grange. Together they formed a law enforcement team that outlaws feared to tackle.

August in particular was famous throughout the center of the state for driving the vicious Ku Klux Klan out of the county completely. The girls at Miss Jessie's loved him for his determination. One act that Klan members loved to commit was to drag whores out in the public square and whip them.

Though many other Texas law enforcement officials across the state tried to drive the Klan away, Fayette County was the only place that could actually boast that no members there threatened and terrified citizens with their midnight rides in their white sheets and hoods.

As a matter of fact, the Klan was not run out of Texas until 1925 when Miriam Amanda Ferguson became the first woman governor in the world. As one of her first acts of office, she signed the anti-mask bill, which effectively destroyed the Klan's power of intimidation. When they could no longer hide their faces, the membership simply melted away.

Meanwhile, Miss Jessie was solidifying her status with the important members of the community of La Grange. Her house offered gracious hospitality to lawmen and politicians. With the law behind her, she bought eleven acres and a two-room house outside the city limits and two blocks from the Houston highway, with convenient connections to Austin, San Antonio, and Bryan–College Station, home of Texas Agricultural and Mechanical College. Another one-room house on the property was quickly moved and connected to give her three rooms. She had a kitchen and two bedrooms with plans to build more rooms as soon as needed.

In a whorehouse, the number of rooms usually corresponds to the number of women at work there. From the oil fields Miss Jessie recruited two young, freckle-faced women who had developed a style that was "wicked but cute." They were probably sisters, but no one knows for sure. From the oil field workers, they had learned lots of tricks that the farm girls didn't know.

Moreover, they had learned that "sweet and concerned" demeanors worked wonders with their clientele, from farm boys to old men. When the farm boys went off to World War I, the girls became their favorite pen pals. They baked cookies, knitted socks, and sent "love and xxxxx's." Shortly after the war, one of the young ladies fell in love with an older gentleman, who "took her away from all that" to San Antonio, where she became a wealthy widow thirty years later and a great benefactress and patroness of the arts.

The older girl eventually replaced Miss Jessie, and she too became known as a benefactress of the community, but all that was years in the future and much later in the story.

World War I brought a flood of vehicles onto America's highways. Henry Ford's Model T enabled men and boys to drive miles to the country whorehouse to enjoy themselves with the girls who now catered to everything fashionable. They bobbed their hair, rolled their stockings, painted cute faces on their knees, drank gin (although not on the premises), and smoked cigarettes and occasional cigars.

Miss Jessie herself retained her decorum even though she allowed her house to succumb to the siren call of velvet cushions and horsehair sofas, tassels on the draperies, plush carpets patterned with cabbage roses. She even bought a Victrola with a stack of records and allowed the boys and girls to roll back the carpets, "wind 'er up," and dance. The "best little whorehouse in Texas" was more like a home away from home.

Moreover, the girls were making money, so much money that they could afford roadsters to drive themselves into Houston, just slightly over a hundred miles away, for shopping excursions on days when they couldn't work.

The only drawback to all this money and all this mobility was that the criminal elements flowed back and forth as well. Small towns often fell prey to criminals of the Bonnie-and-Clyde variety, who robbed and hijacked and then stopped at Miss Jessie's for respite. They were men who were not in a position to have a home and family, but they could buy female relationships. Their lives were lonely, and pillow talk with a whore was their only chance to brag.

From 1920 to 1933, Miss Jessie was especially helpful to Sheriff Loessin and his minions, who were trying to nab bootleggers as well as moonshiners and other lawbreakers who were in business to circumvent the Eighteenth Amendment. The sheriff's day wasn't over until he'd paid his evening visit to Miss Jessie's, where the girls were eagerly helpful in reporting pillow talk. When their clients boasted about how much money they were making and how they could bring some "real good stuff" over for the girls, Sheriff Loessin was on the spot to intercept and arrest them.

Since Miss Jessie allowed no liquor on the premises at all, the bootleggers' attempts at bribes were meaningless. Her information allowed the sheriff to gain a reputation as a brilliant detective, the envy of every lawman in that part of the state, including the Texas Rangers. With that sort of intelligence, Miss Jessie had a gold-plated guarantee to keep herself in business.

After the boys returned from World War I, they rolled into Miss Jessie's eager to teach what they'd learned in "Gay Paree," but the madam was having none of that. Though arthritis had confined her to a wheelchair, she was determined to keep her house "decent." She had to double her duty of rolling down the hallways from room to room, listening at the doors when some particularly frisky customers came in. If she detected noises that indicated that something else was going on besides the usual, modest position, she would burst in with a long iron rod and send the culprit flying with at least one red mark across his buttocks.

One client recalled that he "didn't go back for a week. Then she wouldn't let me in. Not till I'd showed her I could be right happy with just your ordinary piece of tail."

When the Depression hit in 1929, the effect on Miss Jessie's was especially devastating. Not only were there fewer customers, but more girls came seeking employment. Still, prostitution continued to flourish during the thirties.

Nobody had any money, and Miss Jessie had many mouths to feed. Swiftly, she hit on the perfect solution. She converted to the "poultry standard": she charged "one chicken for one screw."

It was the perfect solution. Farm boys could always find chickens. Moreover, the birds were a self-renewing resource. Every farm had at least one rooster, who serviced the hens. They reproduced themselves by laying eggs. At night they were kept in coops and little houses with simple latches on the doors and, although they did make a terrible racket if they were awakened, a careful man could "grab and go." Men who didn't keep chickens could also count on "finding" them the same places the farm boys did.

Soon the whole parking lot was full of chickens, and the girls ate eggs and chickens until they were practically squawking themselves. Hence, the name—the Chicken Ranch— became famous throughout central Texas and beyond. And no one went hungry, and every girl had plenty of customers.

The Depression began to ease only after the election of Franklin Delano Roosevelt to the presidency. At Roosevelt's insistence, Congress passed a bill authorizing the building of labor camps throughout the country for jobless young men. Many were needed to provide jobs of all different kinds. At the same time, Tennessee Valley Authority built a magnificent dam over the Tennessee River and created enough electric power to take care of most of the towns east of the Mississippi. The Rural Electrical Administration brought lights to the farms. Miss Jessie's girls could now have electric lights and ceiling fans.

Another program especially dear to Jessie and her girls was the CCC camp—Civilian Conservation Corporation. A whole campful of young men went to work as forest rangers at jobs dedicated to improving the national, state, and county parks and to contributing to the general beautification of the environment, as well as conservation enterprises in central Texas.

Thus, one might find the following inscription in autograph books that young girls of that time filled with the epigrams and signatures of their friends: "When you get married, don't marry a tramp. Just marry a boy from the CCC camp."

Camp Swift was built just a few miles down the road from La Grange, and it proved a boon to Miss Jessie and the girls. The men from the camp literally piled into their trucks and rode over to the Chicken Ranch night after night, bringing money and incidental improvements in the girls' menu with the occasional side of beef.

When World War II exploded, the girls even got gasoline for their roadsters because the farm boys got unlimited ration coupons since raising crops was an essential industry. Unfortunately, when Miss Jessie tried to teach the girls how to take care of a "victory garden," she ran into trouble. Though the customers might be rural, the girls had ceased to be. No longer were they pitiful creatures like Mrs. Swine's two original "Piglets." Nor did they know how to plant, tend, and harvest vegetables. Though their diets suffered in that respect, the GIs from military encampments in the vicinity brought some staples.

Of course, the girls were bringing in so much money that Miss Jessie generally bought their food, despite the rationing of certain items like meat and butter for the war effort. Though the famous Chicken Ranch name persisted, the chickens had been eaten long ago.

Mechanization of farm machinery allowed larger crops to be harvested, and food became cheaper, more plentiful, and generally available to all. Thanks to the bounteous, fertile acres of America's heartland, no one went hungry. Because the machines did the work of many hands, the children were no longer needed to plant, cultivate, and harvest crops. Across the country the level of mandatory education rose from third grade to the eighth grade.

As a result these girls were prettier, healthier, and better educated. Moreover, they had very little or no guilt about their chosen professions. They went about in public, and no one complained. In most cases because the population was in flux, no one even noticed them. More than one worked at the Chicken Ranch to put her Aggie husband through college.

The girls might be better educated, but they were not geniuses by any means. Very few had high school diplomas. Of course, every whorehouse claimed to have at least one girl who had a degree.

Miss Jessie loved to tell the story of the girl who put herself through the University of Texas and became a concert pianist on her summer earnings from the Chicken Ranch. During the semesters, she worked nights at the house of Miss Hattie Valdez in Austin, where the madam taught her to walk, talk, eat, sit, stand, and dress. Miss Hattie boasted that she always "graduated" ladies.

The musician married very well and became a patroness of the arts. Both madams told that particular story many times. It was a symbol of respectability and a story of hope for all the girls who worked for them without hopes of going anywhere when their working days were done. Both women were also careful never to reveal or even drop hints of the name of the girl who turned out so very well.

By 1946, at least a part of the town's economy depended on the Chicken Ranch. The only voiced complaint from several merchants was that the ranch didn't have enough girls to make a real impression. "If they'd hired more whores, they'd have spent more money."

Only occasionally would all the girls traipse down to the automobile dealership to help one of their number pick out a car. What a gaggle that was!

Miss Jessie ordained that each week they would shop at a different group of merchants, so each establishment would get a fair share of the earnings of the Chicken Ranch. To say the merchants in town admired Miss Jessie would be an understatement. The general consensus of opinion was that she was "one smart gal."

When the last Loessin brother finally retired from the sheriff's office, the county elected former Texas Ranger Jim Flournoy. Six-foot-four topped by a high-crowned white

Stetson, crisp white shirt, string tie, high-heeled cowboy boots, Flournoy had been a lawman since the age of twenty.

One of his first improvements was to have a direct phone line installed between his office and the table beside Miss Jessie's wheelchair. That way he no longer had to make the walk down to the Chicken Ranch as the Loessins had done since the beginning, but he had another reason for his improvement. Since Miss Jessie could no longer patrol the halls because of her arthritis, she had only to pick up the phone if one of her girls had a problem.

One night thieves broke in and demanded money. Pretending to grovel before their threats, Miss Jessie revealed that the money would be found in the closet at the end of the hall. It wasn't all in one place, she told them. They'd have to look because she'd forgotten where she'd put it from one time to the next. While the thieves were rummaging through old hat boxes, old shoe boxes, the linings of old coats—the general detritus of fifty years—she made the call. "I'm being robbed!" she exclaimed.

In a matter of minutes, Sheriff Jim walked in, caught the thieves in the act, and arrested them on the spot.

Only a short time later, Miss Jessie got out of the business. Realizing that she could no longer protect her girls with her iron rod, she gave up the house and went to live in San Antonio with a girl who had left her house to move into the best society circles. "Old friends are the best friends after all."

Miss Jessie turned the house over to a smart, pretty redhead named Edna Milton, who had come to the Chicken Ranch when she was twenty-three years old. Miss Edna left Oklahoma at sixteen after she got pregnant and her family turned her out. The baby died, and she was left to make her living as she could.

After six years of hard times that made her even smarter, Edna arrived at the front door of one of Texas's most important "underground" tourist attractions. The year was 1952, and for those who lived in La Grange, Texas, the next ten years were the best decade of this or any other century. The number one tourist attraction brought visitors—and, more importantly, their money—to the town. Many of them stopped at the old filling station to ask directions in voices that occasionally trembled with nervousness and sometimes even cracked. Many a red-faced kid would then gas up his car, drink a Pepsi or a big RC Cola, and eat a moon pie.

While the college boys from Bryan, Houston, and Austin came in cars, the airmen from Bergstrom Air Force Base came in helicopters. The pilot would radio the small airfield in La Grange to give the time of arrival and the number of passengers. The airport would phone the rancher/manager of the Cottonwood Café, who would then arrive at the airport with his cattle truck to drive the men to the ranch. While the airmen completed their business, the café manager would drink beer in the kitchen with Miss Edna.

In 1961 Miss Jessie died at the age of eighty. Miss Edna made arrangements to buy the house and land from Faye Stewart's heirs. She paid more than the place was worth, but she was buying the town's good will, and she knew that didn't come cheap. Though she paid more than $30,000, the property was assayed on the tax records for a mere $8,000. Of course, county assessors take many things into consideration when judging the worth of property.

Miss Edna saw the investment as her chance to live as comfortably as Miss Jessie had; and though the work was hard and beyond the pales of polite society, it was her big chance to have more than she had thought possible in the beginning.

Far from being ignorant, Miss Edna read widely and could discuss philosophy, history, and theology. She was noted for carrying on deep conversations with men who knew her and came to visit her rather than to take their pleasure with one of her girls. In another place and another time, she might have been a treasured mistress of an important man. In Europe she would have been some "continental gentleman's" valued hostess.

As part of running a clean, popular establishment, Miss Edna wrote a handbook titled *Rules and Regulations*. She insisted that the girls read it regularly once a month, so they were thoroughly familiar with rules and could quote them to any client who might try to persuade one of them to do something Miss Edna didn't allow. She kept copies lying around on the tables in the living room, so the clients could read for themselves as they waited their turns. She had copies made to pass out to lawmen who happened by. It was published in 1976 by the Hunt Company, although in a very limited edition.

First on her list was the announcement to the law officers: "This place nor I have any connection what so ever with any other place mob or syndicate of any type." The book was printed exactly as she wrote it. Though Miss Edna might have had a problem with some bits and pieces of structure, style, and punctuation, every rule is crystal clear.

Her friends and lovers were never customers. Miss Edna was never known to "turn a trick." Like Mrs. Swine and Miss Jessie before her, Miss Edna was a madam and her business was not to entertain. A brothel keeper's business was business.

Though she was operating now in the 1960s, she never "spruced the place up." Miss Edna bought no red velvet cushions, swags, or draperies. Every room had a bed, a bureau, and a sink. She did not employ attendants. The girls still had to clean up after their customers and themselves. She never bought a piano. Instead, she installed a jukebox that cost a quarter to play one record and a Coke box that sold drinks for a dollar apiece, about ten times what they would cost at a service station. Her cigarette sales were a big hit too even though a package sold for seventy-five cents at the Chicken Ranch as opposed to thirty-five cents at the local grocery store.

After each girl finished with her customer, she was supposed to take him by the Coke box and reach in for a drink for herself and one for him. She would open them and they would drink together. An attendant would come forward to take his money and offer him a package of cigarettes. The place would never have survived in a big city. It didn't have any class, but the prices were low enough that rural males could afford their pleasure.

Miss Edna did add on a dining room, so the girls could eat supper together sitting at a table. Strict rules forbade "guests" being invited for dinner. She also installed window-unit air conditioners in the bedrooms. Again these were not for the convenience of the "guests," but for the comfort of the girls. Even with the window open and the ceiling fan turning, prostitution on a hot, humid night in August was sweaty work.

Women today, engaged in intercourse of any kind, including prostitution as a group, take the well-known pill as well as a wide range of devices to prevent contraception. Though the pill was available when Miss Edna took over, it was by doctor's prescription only.

However, pregnancy was not a problem among most women who worked in the whorehouse. Doctors have wondered for years why pregnancy was not an occupational hazard. Putting the axiom that "heaven will protect the working girl" aside, the best scientific theory is that extensive sexual activity causes fatigue of the sphincter muscles, which in turn causes a malfunction of the mucous plug at the mouth of the uterus. If the muscles are exhausted, the uterus does not descend far enough for the sperm to reach the plug, which in turn enables the sperm to "swim up" to meet the ovum. If the sperm can't reach the ovum, no pregnancy can occur. The position of woman on top also probably contributed to the failure to conceive.

Miss Jessie had already had a high fence built around the property to prevent voyeurism by the passing "peeping Tom." Miss Edna kept that fence painted white. She also installed a floodlight over the front porch steps, which clearly illuminated anyone standing there. A black or sometimes Mexican attendant, who also doubled as the cook more often than not, had orders to turn away anyone who didn't look honest, anyone who wasn't white, or anyone who was visibly drunk.

Miss Edna had no illusions about the racial attitudes that prevailed in La Grange. The rest of the United States might be going through a civil rights movement, but allowing it to reach her house would be committing professional suicide.

The Chicken Ranch charged $15 for its service or $1 a minute. Miss Edna's cut for providing the facilities was 75 percent, or $11.25. The girl received $3.75. One might think that since the girl did all the work, she should get more, but $3.75 for fifteen minutes' work amounted to a minimum wage of $15 an hour, which was higher than most people made in the United States in the sixties. Usually, a girl would have between five and twenty "dates" a day. She wouldn't even have to work hard to make $300 per week, and $14,400 a year was more than the La Grange schoolteachers made.

By that time the house had fourteen bedrooms, one of which was Miss Edna's. Usually at least a dozen of them were occupied by girls. The furniture was cheap early American, the Sears, Roebuck special of the sixties. The bedspreads were all the same, all washable chenille, another Sears, Roebuck special. They started out in magenta, gold, turquoise, and other vibrant colors that gradually, after repeated washings, faded to muted tones—until they finally would be discarded and replaced.

The house had six bathrooms, which the girls were encouraged to use and to point out to the customers. When the date began, the girl was supposed to take down the man's pants and bathe his penis in warm soapy water. All this was included in the fifteen minutes. A condom was never offered to a customer, a more-or-less standard practice in all houses of prostitution. The client should never be reminded that he might contract a venereal disease. However, if the man requests one, the girl will oblige him by putting it on for him. This service was free of charge although it was included in the fifteen minutes. (A less experienced, younger man might never get beyond the washing and the condom.)

No local bankers ever complained about the Chicken Ranch ruining their business. While the girls didn't spend all that much, they opened up savings accounts to which they regularly contributed a high percentage of their weekly earnings.

No one could say that the girls didn't do their fair share to help the economy. They were required to make a weekly trek to the County Medical Examiner, an officer hired by the Fayette County Grand Jury specifically for their use. With that business behind them, the girls would go shopping all over town. From the drug stores they bought cosmetics, candy, and magazines. From the grocery store they bought snacks to take back to the ranch in addition to Miss Edna's weekly grocery purchases. From the dress shops they bought clothes. In the sixties when gold shoes came in style, every girl had to have a pair with high stiletto heels and pointed toes. They thought they were the "cutest" things, and their customers loved them too.

Though Miss Edna was always generous in her charitable giving to the town, she kept a very low profile. She gave $10,000 for the building of the new hospital and $1,000 for the new community swimming pool. She donated all the balls, bats, and gloves for the Little League team. A reporter found out about the baseball donation and suggested that the team be renamed the La Grange Chicks. When his joking suggestion got a few people riled up, it was quickly withdrawn.

When Hurricane Carla hit the Gulf Coast in 1961, refugees from Houston and Galveston poured into La Grange, seeking shelter in the buildings at the fair grounds, the American Legion Hall, and the courthouse. They wouldn't have been as comfortable as they were if Miss Edna's husband hadn't trucked in his entire inventory of mattresses from his second-hand furniture store in Austin. Whether the people of La Grange were sufficiently grateful or more than a little resentful of the couple's efforts will never be known.

The Chicken Ranch finally became up-to-date. Sexual mores were changing in the age of the pill. High school girls and boys were having protected sex—and sometimes unprotected—so the missionary position, which was commonly used nowadays, was considered really boring—certainly not worth fifteen dollars. Miss Edna's girls added oral sex to their repertoires and group sex by request. Both of these "specials" cost the customer extra.

It also behooved an enterprising girl to leave the bureau drawer open to display an assortment of interesting erotic paraphernalia for the discriminating man or for the boy who thought he'd like to try "something new." The "package" cost $40.

When Sheriff Jim Flournoy was interviewed about the Chicken Ranch, from which he gained so much information about illegal goings on in the community and county, he was quoted as saying, "It's a clean place to go to. Ain't got no pimps, no narcotics, no alcohol, no trouble.

"I've been Sheriff all these years and there's nevah been no rapes. And we ain't got a bunch of pregnant gals in the schools. It just don't have no ill effects."

Sheriff Jim had one of the best arrest records in the state and invariably produced evidence that led to conviction and incarceration. Certainly, the girls of the Chicken Ranch must have been one of his most valuable undercover sources.

Only Larry Connors, a Houston newsman, remarked rather cynically that "he makes the whorehouse sound like a damn county non-profit recreational facility."

At the same time, an Austin artist who grew up in La Grange remarked, "Any trouble at the Chicken Ranch and Jim would go out and womp the guy of the head with a pistol butt; no trouble, no publicity."

In 1973 after nearly 130 years of uninterrupted operation, the Chicken Ranch came under the eye of a publicity seeker from Houston. Marvin Zindler had worked hard to create the look of a crusading, crime-busting television reporter. He had donned a blonde toupee and padded his suits over the shoulders and buttocks. He'd had his nose bobbed and his chin sculpted until he bore no resemblance to Ma Zindler's little boy.

Now all he needed was an infamous criminal organization to bust. Failing to find such a thing easily, he turned to manufacturing his own plots. Ultimately, Zindler's eye lit on the Chicken Ranch. There were whorehouses a-plenty in Houston, but they were more of the "what-else-is-news" variety. They were not newsworthy, much less famous.

He maintained that he had nothing against the ranch per se, but he had learned through channels—channels that only he had possessed the intellectual acumen to discover—that it was a headquarters and focal point for those twin devils: "political corruption and organized crime." He claimed on television that he had intelligence compiled by the Department of Public Safety that the Chicken Ranch was grossing in excess of $3,000,000 a year. To counter pictures that revealed a building that looked like it might clear more in the neighborhood of low thousands, he revealed that his investigations had discovered the vast majority of the profits were going into Mexican bank accounts that belonged to corrupt state and local officials who were receiving fortunes in payoffs.

He maintained that the state capital was where the real headquarters was. In January 1973, no less a law enforcement body than the Texas Rangers asked him not to do anything about it because they planned to "move in." For five months Marvin waited, his camera crew ready at his beck and call. Then he learned that the whole thing had been shelved.

Furious but determined, he took his cameraman to the Chicken Ranch and hid out in the mosquito-, chigger-, and tick-infested woods outside the house, counting cars and taking license numbers and photographs. The cameraman Larry Connors volunteered to go in "undercover" and came out with the pronouncement, "There was whoring going on in there!"

Three more months of "inside investigations," and Marvin said they had enough evidence to prove conclusively that indeed there was a whorehouse in La Grange. By that time all pretense of Mafia connections, political corruption, and Mexican bank accounts had vanished. In order to keep the story alive, Marvin needed action.

The fact was that nothing about the Chicken Ranch was news. Every goat roper and cedar chopper, not to speak of college kids from the half dozen or more institutions of higher learning in central Texas, knew exactly where and what it was. The Chicken Ranch had marked itself for destruction because its public relations had worked too well.

On August 1, 1973, Marvin met with Governor Dolph Briscoe, Attorney General John Hill, and Department of Public Safety Chief Wilson Speir. Behind closed doors they heard Marvin's allegations and came forth spouting righteous wrath and vowing to uproot and destroy the corruption bred by this foul institution.

Sheriff Flournoy had no choice. If he didn't close the house down, the Texas Rangers would. He made one stab at saving the place by going to the governor himself with a petition in his hand signed by a majority of the citizens in the town, including housewives and schoolteachers. Governor Briscoe would not see him.

The *Austin American-Statesman* quoted Sheriff Flournoy as saying, "It's been there all my life and all my daddy's life and never caused anybody any trouble. Every large city in Texas has things 1,000 times worse."

He returned with the bad news, and in a single night the girls were gone from La Grange. Almost to a girl, they moved to Houston, where they were quite right in believing that

Marvin would never notice them among too many of their profession. The only person who remained at the ranch for a time was Lilly, the maid, who accepted sympathy from men who dropped by, unable to believe it had happened and sincerely sorry to see it go.

The next day Marvin was on his way to Jamaica for a "well-deserved" vacation from his arduous efforts in decency's behalf.

Miss Edna, who had divorced her first husband, the second-hand furniture salesman, got married to a man who owned a couple of restaurants in an east Texas town.

Sheriff Flournoy went back to his office an angry man, spoiling for revenge.

A year later Marvin Zindler returned to do a documentary on the improvements seen in the town since that house of depravity had been removed. He interviewed several people, whose responses ranged from cool to downright surly. He saved the afternoon, and the best photo-taking light, to call out the sheriff.

The argument that ensued was the most fun the town had seen since the girls stopped coming in from the ranch to shop. The sheriff told Marvin what he thought of him and his crusading, expletives included. When Marvin tried to lead the sheriff to admit that things were better, the sheriff shoved him, grabbed the camera, and ripped out the film. Marvin's wig fell off, and Flournoy stomped on it with his cowboy boots.

Marvin later filed a $3,000,000 lawsuit charging that the camera had been broken and his ribs had been fractured.

The folks in La Grange staged a barbecue to help the sheriff pay his lawsuit. His first choice for lawyer was Racehorse Haynes, but Haynes was in the midst of a case defending a corrupt Houston politico.

In September the sheriff abruptly asked that soliciting of funds stop. He even asked that the selling of t-shirts and other souvenirs of the Chicken Ranch cease (though they could still be bought from under the counter at several local establishments for years). People nodded wisely to each other and opined that the sheriff no longer feared that it would come to trial.

And as a matter of fact, it didn't. The suit was settled out of court, and the amount of the settlement never revealed. Rumor was that Marvin received $10,000 from an unknown source.

No one has ever speculated aloud that if Miss Edna could give $10,000 to the hospital, she could easily afford to spend a like amount to help the friend who had protected her and her girls for so long.

Miss Edna wanted to remain in the friendly little town where she and her girls had generated so much money. Since she knew practically everyone, she expected that there would be no objections; but when she tried to buy a nice home in the neighborhood where Sheriff Jim Flournoy and his wife Gladys lived, the "nice" folks returned her down payment. It was a sad slap in the face for the woman who had brought so much commerce, not to speak of fame, to their town.

The ranch's last hurrah was on Broadway on June 19, 1978, when *The Best Little Whorehouse in Texas* opened. Though the Chicken Ranch had been closed for five years, a very-mini-renaissance occurred when curious men came to visit the place. There was nothing there to see. The house had been torn down before it fell down. The play insulted Marvin Zindler through the buffoon of the show, a character named Melvin P. Thorpe.

Miss Edna Milton was delighted to be given a small role in the original Broadway cast. She played Miss Wulla Jean, a portrayal of Miss Jessie in a wheelchair. She had no lines to speak, no entrances to make in the role. She was wheeled on and off the stage in Act I, Scene 1. However, she did appear later in a different costume as one of the townspeople.

In 1979, *The Best Little Whorehouse in Texas* swept the Tony Awards: Best Musical, Best Book, Best Actor, Best Actress.

Texas's own Tommy Tune was nominated for best choreography. Though he did not win the Tony, he won the Drama Desk Award for his inventive dances. The show ran for 1,584 performances over nearly four years, with shows touring all over the United States.

In 1982, an equally successful movie was made with Dom DeLuise playing Melvin P. Thorpe, the Marvin Zindler of the "watchdogs." Burt Reynolds played the sheriff named Ed Earl Dodd, and Dolly Parton played the madam named Miss Mona. Charles Durning, playing the befuddled and beset governor of Texas, was nominated for an Academy Award by the Motion Picture Academy.

Sadly, Edna Milton was not in that cast. She had probably put her past behind her and had no wish to be more than a quiet housewife somewhere in east Texas.

Marvin Zindler's death was reported on local news stations throughout Texas on August 1, 2007. Ironically, his only claim to fame was that he had shut down the "best little whorehouse in Texas." People sniggered or shook their heads, depending on their attitudes.

Today, although La Grange is the Fayette County seat, its population has fallen to barely four thousand people. Like so many towns off the major interstates in Texas, the traffic doesn't drive within fifteen miles of its "historic courthouse," especially since its number one tourist attraction has been closed for as long as anyone can remember. Apart from a historical monument to a small group of martyred heroes of the Texas Revolution, there is no longer reason for any man to go to La Grange.

JAZZ BABY TO *BABY JANE*

That magical night in 1945 when Joan Crawford won the best actress Academy Award for *Mildred Pierce*, she had been acting for more than half her life. The lingering image of her as a "jazz baby" dancing the Charleston on a tabletop was dispelled forever. Her work had been recognized by her peers as that of a serious actress. She should have been over the moon.

But for months she had worked in the grip of terrible fear that her career might be over very shortly. *Mildred Pierce* was the first of three pictures contracted for by Warner Brothers, without much enthusiasm. The resulting paranoia had convinced Crawford that she would not win. She would be forced to sit in the audience smiling graciously until her face ached while Ingrid Bergman, Greer Garson, or Jennifer Jones walked up to receive the coveted Oscar. They were respected women and fine actresses. All had been nominated before, and all three had won. One of them was sure to win, or perhaps the last nominee, newcomer Gene Tierney, would strike the fancy of the academy and pull off a surprise upset.

Crawford was sure most members of the academy would not vote for her. No one liked her. She had a reputation for being impossible to work with, and they all resented her despite her efforts to fit into their "group." She was very much aware of her humble beginnings, of her made-up name, and of her fading star.

She couldn't face them. Spurred by a full-blown case of paranoia, Crawford "developed" a case of pneumonia. Her friends, publicity people, and members of the cast and crew called all day long to find out if she was planning to attend. She told them no. To later biographers, she claimed that her Christian Science abilities to keep herself well also allowed her to control her breathing and body temperature. She created a fever of 104. She was too, too ill.

Then the call came. She had won! Against all odds, her name had been called to glide gracefully across the stage to receive the award that meant so much to her. But her own fear had denied her the greatest moment in her life.

Though her producer, Jerry Wald, had instructed that the picture be hyped as an Oscar contender from the first day she walked onto the set, no one had believed it had a chance. The Warner Brothers publicity department was caught flat-footed. The movie was in their typical film noir style, just another dark, passion-driven picture—a "woman's picture" intended for the thousands of women who sat in dark theaters in the afternoons before their children got home from school. Until World War II was over and the men began to come home, *Mildred Pierce* was just one of an undistinguished string of such films—except that Crawford suffered so beautifully. Even she could scarcely believe it. After so many years in the business, where had this sudden recognition come from?

Swiftly the studio put together a camera crew to accompany director Michael Curtiz, whom she had personally requested, to hurry to her bedside. Frantically, she put on an elegant gown and negligee and full makeup. Filming her at home against a satin-tufted headboard garnered interest and publicity, so everyone was satisfied. Perhaps—

To the elegant, gorgeous, thrice-married Joan Crawford, born Lucille LeSueur in San Antonio, Texas, the Oscar was as much as anything a symbol of her absolute determination to succeed. And no one was more determined than Joan Crawford. She had had so much to overcome from an early age.

Her mother, Anna Bell Johnson, married Thomas LeSueur in San Antonio, Texas. Lucille LeSueur was born March 23, 1904, or 1906, or 1908—whichever date served her best. Since no birth certificate was required in those days, none was ever issued. When her father discovered he couldn't support his wife and two children, he did what many men did: he "caught the westbound freight."

Her mother then married a man who managed a vaudeville theater. Henry Cassin soon moved the little family to Lawton, Oklahoma. The surrounding farm land grew cotton, and oil had been discovered in the vicinity. The town seemed to be headed toward prosperity.

Lucille, who Henry Cassin called Billie, loved the man she thought was her father. He allowed her to stand in the wings backstage where she could watch the acts and dance along with them. She didn't realize she was imitating the dregs of show business, nor did she care. She was determined to learn. She loved to dance.

The same determination brought Crawford back on her feet to dance again after she cut a tendon and an artery in her foot when she was only six. The doctor who sewed her up predicted that she'd never walk without a limp. She proved him wrong. When Crawford wanted something, she would walk through fire or blood to get it.

Eventually, Henry Cassin moved his family back to San Antonio where he and Anna managed a hotel for transients. The work was especially hard on Anna, but they made enough money for Crawford to study at St. Agnes, a convent school for girls. Then Henry Cassin embezzled some money, and he too caught the westbound freight.

The only way Crawford could stay in school was to work for her room, board, and tuition. Rather than give up the education she was determined to have, she waited tables and worked in the kitchen at St. Agnes. She discovered she was quite satisfied there even though the work was hard. She had a clean room and bed of her own and plenty to eat. Her mother and brother, Hal, lived in three drab rooms behind a laundry where her mother worked long hours. Their food was skimpy and the place stank of lye and dirty clothes.

Crawford could see that the drudgery of washing and ironing was killing her mother's spirit and making her old before her time. Anna Cassin became remote and embittered. From the age of 7, 9, or 11—depending on which served her purposes best—Crawford started earning her secondary education. Eventually she managed to attend prestigious Stephens College in Columbia, Missouri, famous nationwide for its fine arts program.

Unfortunately, the St. Agnes education she had slaved for proved to be substandard. She was told she just couldn't do the college work. Moreover, she believed the girls there were rude and snubbed her because she was working in their dining hall. Before the year was out, Crawford went back to Kansas City even though, according to her biographer, the college president himself begged her to stay.

On all her résumés and biographies, Crawford listed Stephens College as her alma mater without going into details. The only time she ever heard from her former classmates was when one sent a note backstage: "Remember me. We used to be friends at Stephens."

By that time, she never "knew" them.

In Kansas City Crawford auditioned and got a job in the chorus line. The agent offered her twenty bucks a week and asked what name she was going to use. When she told him "Lucille LeSueur," he grinned. "Honey, you sure picked a fancy one." The show was headlined by Katherine Emerine, who sang and performed the latest operetta tunes from New York.

The show folded after only two weeks. Crawford later wrote in an autobiography for a fan magazine that she took the train to Chicago, desperately trying to find Emerine to ask for help, but the singer/actress had already joined another tour. Fortunately, Crawford remembered the name of the star's casting agent and producer in Chicago—Ernie Young.

According to her account, Crawford dodged his secretary and burst into his office exclaiming, "I may not be as beautiful as those girls out there, but I've only got two dollars and I've some experience. . . . Please don't kick me out."

Though Crawford was short and a bit on the plump side for a chorine, the agent gave her a break. He sent her to Oklahoma City and then to Detroit to entertain convention-eers. One of the troupe showed her how to apply makeup, especially to her fabulous mouth, and, more important, how to save her highest kick for the last. She got promoted to the end of the line, so she was the last girl to leave the stage.

Crawford also learned how to look directly into the eyes of the men in the audiences and smile as if she were enjoying her-self while entertaining them. Then she knocked J. J. Schubert's drink off his table one evening. No one will ever know if she did it on purpose, but he came back and offered her an audi-tion for a new show.

She started out in the back row of *Innocent Eyes* because she had never had a formal dance lesson in her life. With steely determination and not a little outrageous behavior, Crawford quickly moved to the front row. When the show ended in New York, she stayed and managed to see and be seen in the show business world there.

According to her biographers, Crawford was all very prim and proper. Some of her try-outs for other shows consisted simply of smiling and showing her legs. Whether or not that was the full extent of the audition, she was hired for another chorus line in *The Passing Show*.

Eventually, Crawford hit the right agent who offered her a chance to get into the movie business. The year was 1925. In only twenty years, motion pictures had taken over America's theaters and replaced vaudeville as the people's entertainment all across America.

Louis B. Mayer, preparing to effect a merger with Samuel Goldwyn and Metro Studio Productions, was offering five-year contracts at $75 a week to those girls who passed his screen test. When Crawford stepped off the Sunset Limited train in Hollywood, California, to her disappointment, she was met by a flunky, who escorted her to the "fleabag" hotel arranged for the "contract" girls. He explained it was only six blocks from the Metro-Goldwyn-Mayer (MGM) studio, so she could walk to work.

Then the flunky took her around the studio to see shows being filmed with people she had heard of: Lon Chaney, John Gilbert, Norma Shearer, and Lillian Gish. Because the moviemakers were filming silents and were not concerned about sound, different motion pictures were being filmed quite close together, many times in the different parts of the same studio. Likewise, movies were much shorter, mostly only two reels, because black screens with dialogue had to be spliced between the scenes.

Crawford was disappointed that no movies were being filmed with dancing in them. Then her contract was explained to her, and she learned that the studio could release her from her contract after six months if she couldn't perform as they wanted.

Crawford told her biographer the charming story of her first screen test. She was asked to cry, so she conjured up pictures of her childhood when Daddy Cassin left. The tears flowed, but when she tried to stop, she couldn't. Her fear that she was blowing the screen test made the tears worse. She couldn't stop.

An Irish electrician knelt before her. "You're a dancer, aren't you?" asked Tommy Shagrue. He pulled her to her feet and challenged her to repeat his steps. Within minutes, she had danced her memories away. And the dancing electrician found employment on every Joan Crawford movie until his death.

She was disappointed when she heard nothing more about the screen test, but the experience taught her the importance of crew members. Beyond that lesson, she was on her own. She had no one to teach her what she needed to know. The business was too new, and everyone was experimenting and learning as she went along.

With no books to read, she bought movie magazines and read that movie stars had to get up at dawn to be in their makeup to start shooting early in the day. The light for outdoor shots was best in the morning. Moreover, before air conditioning, the studio lights heated the studios to exhausting temperatures.

Determined to make a full-length contract happen, Crawford set her alarm, got up every morning at six-thirty, dressed and made her face up, and hurried to the studio to be on hand to learn the business and—hopefully—be noticed. One of the people she sought out was the director of publicity, the gifted Pete Smith, who also wrote, directed, and produced short subjects for the studio under the name of "A Smith Named Pete."

He took a good look at her and decided that he could do something for her and, more important for himself, "with her." He sent her down to the Ocean Park beach with a newspaper photographer from the *Times* to take pictures of her and other girls tossing balls around, bicycling, and being generally at play. Her face and figure in bathing suits, in shorts, and in sports outfits ran in newspapers all over the country, usually with her name and the word "starlet" under the picture.

In the meantime, she continued to hang around the sets. Sometimes she'd be part of crowd scene. Her first time on camera, Crawford stood in for Norma Shearer. Only the back of her head was shown. Finally, she went to the agent who'd gotten her the contract. Gritting her teeth, she flashed her eyes at him and told him she wanted work—or else. Fortunately, he didn't ask what the alternative might have been. Perhaps in his estimation she had proved herself.

Thus, in 1925—the same year she began her attempts to break into the movie business—Crawford landed her first role. After *Pretty Ladies*, she followed with two other movies the same year—all as Lucille LeSueur. Each role was more important than the last, and her contract was renewed. At that time, the studio started to manage her career. Their first move was to change her name. LeSueur sounded too stagy and too foreign, like a silent-screen star. And Sueur sounded like "sewer." Obviously, anything would be better than what she had.

For her fourth movie, the name Joan Crawford was selected after a nationwide campaign that won a New York woman $500. The studio released a story about how the woman had been so grateful because she needed the money to help pay her medical bills. Joan's adopted daughter, Christina Crawford, later revealed in her tell-all book *Mommie Dearest* how much her mother hated the name. She thought it sounded like "moan" and made people think of "crawfish."

But Joan Crawford she became—for better or for worse—for the rest of her life.

While filming this fourth movie, a cameraman named Johnny Arnold gave her the most important advice of her life: "Your face is built," he said. "It isn't like any other actress's. The bones are made just right. . . . There's only one trouble."

"What's that?"

"The camera can't see them. You have to lose weight."

Immediately, she gave up starches and sweets. She ate steak and grapefruit for breakfast, steak and tomatoes for lunch and dinner. She drank only water and lots of it. She lost twenty pounds off her five-foot-four frame. And suddenly she radiated "mega-watt" star power. The camera loved her with her enormous eyes and her high cheekbones.

At the same time, her past caught up with her. Her mother and brother moved from Kansas City to "be with her." Both resented her success. Hal in particular sniped at her endlessly about what he wanted her to believe were her shortcomings. Her mother was simply happy to be able to use a new idea in merchandising—department store charge accounts.

The advent of her family caused Crawford to try to buy some place for them all to live without annoying each other. To do so, she exerted her feminine wiles for the first time. She had heard Louis B. Mayer liked to play the paternal role to young actresses. She told him she needed his advice. She had found a bungalow she could buy for only $18,000, but she didn't have enough money yet. (In the 1920s most ordinary houses sold for low four-figure numbers.) When she smiled so prettily, he was delighted to help his little starlet. He loaned her the money for the down payment.

From three movies in 1926, Crawford was cast in six movies in 1927. Only one could be called important—*The Unknown*—starring Lon Chaney. Tod Browning, who would later create *Frankenstein* for Boris Karloff, directed the film. Crawford had little to do but pantomime screams, but she looked better scared to death than any other woman either Chaney or Browning had ever seen. The experience of working with the "Man of a Thousand Faces" gave her valuable tips about pantomime. Since the movies were still silent, projecting her emotions was exceptionally important.

Even as Crawford learned from Chaney, change was on the way. The first motion picture with talking sequences was released in 1927. With the enormous popularity of *The Jazz Singer*, moviemakers and producers quickly came to realize the handwriting on the wall. The whole technique of making movies would have to change. However, it came slowly. They could not immediately adapt to the new, expensive technology and equip the old vaudeville theaters to show it. The problems were multiple and the popular starring actors and actresses were in many cases unsuited and unsuitable for sound.

Joan Crawford was already slated for *Our Dancing Daughters*. Her frenetic dancing required only music, which the theaters could supply with musicians and phonographs. The next year she made a sort of sequel, *Our Modern Maidens*, her last silent film. Again she danced as only she could, projecting energy and verve, sparkling like a diamond, demanding that the audience like her. In both films, she was the star with top billing. In the second film she acted with the man she was soon to marry, Douglas Fairbanks Jr.

And the "fun" began.

The little girl from San Antonio had met and fascinated "Hollywood royalty." He was hers. Douglas Fairbanks Jr. was the son of "Zorro" and "America's Sweetheart," Mary Pickford. Though in the movie, Joan ends up in the arms of Rod LaRocque, a lacquered heartthrob whose career began to wane as more "homegrown-looking" male stars came into fashion, Fairbanks was the one she was out to capture. And capture she did.

Douglas Fairbanks Sr. hated the idea that his son was four inches taller, starring in movies, and planning to marry an upstart actress. His second wife—the fabulous Mary Pickford—kept staring at her daughter-in-law's waistline, dreading the announcement that she was going to be a step-grandmother. In this area Crawford was disappointed again. She had miscarriage after miscarriage throughout the course of their marriage.

At this point, Crawford's outrageous paranoia began to assert itself. Fairbanks spoke deep-voiced cultured English that the sound booms and mikes picked up easily. How was she going to lose her Texas twang and make the shift to sound films?

The studio was also concerned, so they arranged diction lessons for her. Her coach had once instructed Enrico Caruso. Unfortunately, Crawford thought the coach was trying train her to her speak unnaturally. (The reader might recall the scenes from *Singin' in the Rain*, when Jean Hagen as actress Lina Lamont is being taught to pronounce words with a broad "a" and to enunciate every syllable.)

Crawford took only one lesson. Thereafter she locked herself in her room to read magazines, newspapers, and books aloud and listen to herself. Her own husband had taught her how cultured people sounded. She deepened her voice because the microphone distorted high-pitched voices. She slowed her words and enunciated each syllable clearly because now she was speaking to the audience; they could no longer read her words on a black screen. Crawford kept a dictionary with her. When she came to a word she didn't understand, she looked it up and said it fifteen times correctly.

She was terrified the first time she heard her voice from the screen. It was so husky, so low. She shuddered, waiting for the director to tell her she was through. But everyone was fascinated, women in the audiences in particular. She sounded exactly like she looked—sultry. Her first talking movie *Untamed*, made at the end of 1929, was a revelation to everyone.

That next year after two empty-headed flapper movies, Crawford begged the studio head Irving Thalberg to let her replace the pregnant Norma Shearer in a dramatic role in a movie called *Paid*. He didn't want to do it, but she kept after him until he finally agreed to let her "shatter her patented screen image."

Once he agreed, she was terrified. What had she done to herself? Again, Crawford experienced paranoia. No one would ever like her again. She had ruined her career. During her early scenes in a prison smock without a trace of makeup, her hair unkempt, she got no encouragement from the director, from the camera man, from the soundmen. She was ready to collapse.

She looked upward. "Her" electrician Tommy Shagrue was handling the lights on the parallel overheads. He nodded down at her. "Good girl, Joan."

The movie was a tremendous critical success, and her status rose in all studio eyes. Only her husband was less than pleased. While her career was moving steadily upward, his was declining because of his own personality. Fairbanks was charming, but too easygoing. He lacked his father's dash. The films that he chose or was offered were trivial. Even a superb war movie, *The Dawn Patrol*, directed by Howard Hawks, did nothing for him. He was simply the pilot who didn't get killed.

Joan considered his greatest sin that he didn't "work at it" all the time as she did. He never even campaigned for a part. They came his way because of his name, and he was satisfied with himself. In 1931 she made $146,000; he made $73,000. After four years and no children, they agreed to divorce.

A new leading man appeared on the horizon, one that she fell in love with as Fairbanks was on the way out. For years the actors she had known had been less exciting than she was. Clark Gable was a different kind of man—a man Joan Crawford could appreciate. Rather than suave sophistication, he radiated masculine sexuality. They were instantly attracted to each other. The director of *Possessed*, Clarence Brown, made full use of the heat they generated.

Their spouses appeared not to care, but Louis B. Mayer did. He was furious and wanted the affair stopped. Gable backed down. His star status was not yet assured as was Crawford's. Though they were reunited in several films, the studio head prevailed. Two divorces would besmirch the reputation of the studio.

In 1930 the Motion Picture Association of America had formed. Censorship was ironclad, and promiscuous behavior on the part of motion picture stars would create adverse publicity. They devised a code that would be enforced for every picture beginning in 1934. Its lengthy list of "don'ts" was not abandoned until 1967.

Aware that Crawford was sulking, Irving Thalberg assembled an all-star cast for *Grand Hotel*, including Greta Garbo, Lionel and John Barrymore, Wallace Beery, and Lewis Stone. When Crawford was signed as well, she was at first excited, then frightened. How was she going to be noticed in a group like that? Thalberg was unmoved by her protest. The movie was destined to become one of the great motion pictures of the thirties.

Unfortunately, its troubled set increased Crawford's fears. Garbo was aloof. John Barrymore was constantly drunk. Beery was rudely inconsiderate. All three stars knew they were on the way out. The two men treated her badly—as if she were indeed the "compliant" stenographer Flaemmchen from the film. It was just another movie to them. To Joan it was a great opportunity for her to be considered an artist as well as a star.

The girl from Texas was outraged that they did not give her the respect her sex and her profession demanded. She was also frightened. Her love affair with Douglas Fairbanks and their divorce had created problems for her at MGM. Her parts were less important and more formulaic. For the first time, she became "the girl in the picture." She was cast in a Howard Hawks World War I drama *Today We Live*. Her part was cobbled into the William Faulkner script as Robert Young's younger sister, the love interest of Gary Cooper and Franchot Tone. The picture did badly at the box office and helped no one's career.

Crawford considered *Today We Live* a turning point in her life because she met Tone. Her next movie, the famous *Dancing Lady*, cast her again with Clark Gable as her rough, tough leading man and Tone as the rich debonair playboy, who nevertheless wants to marry her. Crawford played a "hard-bitten flapper." For a whole series of movies thereafter, her scripts were the same. She played a character who thought she wanted the wealth and soft life the playboy offered her until Clark Gable or Robert Montgomery or Spencer Tracy convinced her otherwise. She was the darling of matinee audiences, but she was getting no more important parts.

Dancing Lady also utilized the performances of people who would later be recognized as geniuses of their particular genres: the Three Stooges, Robert Benchley, Nelson Eddy, and Fred Astaire. Crawford was ecstatic about getting a dance number with Astaire. Later she told biographers that she broke her ankle and feared she would be unable do the specialty number. But like the trouper she was, she soldiered through. A still picture shows their costumes. Astaire wore Alpine lederhosen and hat; Crawford wore a blonde wig and long full skirt. The story made great theater. Perhaps her ankle really was broken . . .

Previously, Gilbert Adrian, the famous costume designer, had created the "Crawford look." It was totally different from anything other "feminine stars" were wearing. The "look" announced that she was a woman and a star to be reckoned with. The padded shoulders became her trademark.

The formidable suit look became the rage of the post-Depression era when women couldn't afford new clothes. They took their husband's old suits and nipped the waistlines in. They cut off the trouser legs, turned them cuff-side up, and made skirts with kick pleats in the back. Thanks to Adrian and Crawford, American women carried the fashion into World War II when materials were rationed. The padded military look became the rage.

At the end of 1934, Crawford was teamed twice more with Gable. Audiences were thrilled, but the time for them to resume their love affair was past. The next year Tone and Crawford fell in love and married. He was fascinated by her steely determination, her ambition, and her willingness to constantly look at her career with unblinking realism. Perhaps she was fascinated by his sophistication and gentleness. He moved without complaint into her house, the one she had shared with Fairbanks. She earned $242,000 that year. He earned $1,000 a week. For the first time, she began to avoid the press because reporters wrote such unflattering things about Tone.

Irving Thalberg, the talented head of MGM, died in 1936. Suddenly, his wife, Norma Shearer, who had gotten plumb roles that Crawford had envied for several years, was unprotected. Crawford's first break came when Louis B. Mayer cast her in *Idiot's Delight*, a play she had wanted to do because the leading man was Clark Gable, whom she always secretly loved.

In 1937 *Life* magazine proclaimed Joan Crawford the "First Queen of the Movies." The title was based on a poll of theater owners who listed her as their number one actress.

That same year while the widowed Shearer was doing some stills in a nearby studio, she sent a messenger to the stage where Crawford and costar Spencer Tracy were being directed by Joe Mankiewicz. Their cameraman, William Daniels, was "the best in the business." Imperiously, Shearer requested that he be sent over to photograph simple publicity stills. Crawford lost her temper in public for the first and possibly the only time in her history.

She dropped her prevailing pose of gracious lady and exploded in outrage. Wearing only her bra and panties, she flung open the door of her dressing room behind the retreating messenger and planted her feet wide apart in the doorway. Everyone gaped.

"And you can tell Miss Shearer that *I* didn't get where I am on my ass!" she screamed.

In 1939, Crawford divorced Franchot Tone. His personal dissatisfaction with her success and his own lack of progress had boiled over into verbal and physical abuse. She blamed herself because she had suffered two more miscarriages. Children would make everything all right, she reasoned. She began to look around for a way to adopt a child without a husband in the household.

She also began to concentrate on her body, maintaining it through diet and exercise with the discipline of a drill sergeant. She joined the Christian Science church and adhered strictly to its principles to avoid illness. Though Crawford would never admit her age, she was probably thirty-five; the time was now to start protecting her most important asset.

In May 1940 she made arrangements to adopt a baby girl, and she brought Christina home from Nevada. Many people thought her outrageous to adopt a child without a father figure to support her. People actually disapproved of the idea of a single woman rearing a child, although all over the country single women, whose husbands had died, divorced them, or simply taken the westbound freight, were doing so.

At the end of 1940, MGM produced *The Women*, a movie that shocked and amused the nation—at least the matinee audiences, made up mostly of women. Crawford insisted that she should play the role of Crystal, a cold-hearted bitch. Louis B. Mayer was appalled. The role was such a departure for her. What had happened to his "jazz baby"? George S. Cukor, the director, did not want Crawford at all as he had had "trouble with her" before. She would be in scenes with the greatest actresses in the MGM stable. Moreover, she would be playing the perfume salesgirl who steals Norma Shearer's husband. To her way of thinking, it would be superb casting.

Also in the cast were Rosalind Russell, Paulette Goddard, Joan Fontaine, Ruth Hussey, Virginia Grey, and Marjorie Main, as well as Hollywood gossip columnist Hedda Hopper. All of their parts were genteel; Crawford's was rude, bordering on vulgar. The project was considered daring because although men were the constant topic of conversation, not a single man was in the cast.

Crawford proved doubly shocking when, for one entire scene, she traded barbed insults with Rosalind Russell. Russell was fully dressed and impeccably groomed. Crawford sat insouciant and cool, immersed in a bubble bath. Oddly,

Crawford was the one that more women admired and longed to emulate. Her go-to-hell manner was their wish fulfillment.

"Can you beat that? He almost stood me up for his wife," was Crawford's triumphant, iconic line before she sailed off with, presumably, Norma Shearer's husband. Women in theaters everywhere laughed and clapped at her bravado.

When she and Shearer completed their last scene together, both left the set. They never spoke to each other again.

Crawford had one last chance to "take" from Shearer. Louis B. Mayer had bought the Broadway hit and high comedy *Susan and God* for Norma Shearer, who did not want to play a woman with a fourteen-year-old daughter.

Mayer passed the role on to Crawford, who had never attempted anything like it before. The film was directed by her directorial nemesis George Cukor. By that time she had developed a sixth sense working with Cukor. She could tell when he was pleased or displeased. Before long she won him over, and he began to direct her with a fair hand. The film was a splendid success against everyone's expectations.

Despite her triumphs, Crawford couldn't defeat the clock. Audiences were no longer interested in the stars of the thirties who had been on movie screens since the silent films. Judy Garland, Lana Turner, and Hedy Lamarr were moving upward in popularity as Greer, Norma, and Joan slipped. They were suddenly "box office poison." To finish out her contract, Crawford was given three of the worst scripts she had ever read.

Perhaps trying to counter the box office slide with a younger man on her arm, Crawford married for the third time. Phillip Terry was a former oil field worker who had played football for Stanford University. He was just another pretty face, but he was six years younger than the age she listed on the marriage license. In reality he was probably ten years younger than Crawford. When they walked onto the set of her last movie for MGM, *Reunion in France*, her costar John

Wayne commented on the kind of marriage it was going to be: "First came Joan, then her secretary, then her makeup man, then her wardrobe woman, finally Phil Terry, carrying the dog."

Unfortunately, neither Wayne nor Crawford could save the World War I film. It was simply passé.

Biographers tell different stories about what really happened next. The story most flattering to Crawford is that rather than continue and wait to be fired, she went to Louis B. Mayer and asked for a release from her contract. He is supposed to have protested but finally agreed to give her the opportunity to make a fresh start.

In the summer of 1943 with World War II raging in Europe and the Pacific, Crawford left MGM, where she had worked and all but lived for eighteen years.

Warner Brothers made Crawford an offer because Jack Warner believed she would bring class to the studio he hoped to build. According to one biographer, she was delighted, gracious, confident that she could do the job. She was offered a three-movie contract for $500,000 and received a weekly salary, drawn against the total. It was not a bad contract, but it was much less than she was used to making.

No fool, she knew that she was being used to keep his number one dramatic actress Bette Davis "in line."

Almost two years passed and Joan made one cameo appearance in the World War II movie *Hollywood Canteen*. Made largely for propaganda purposes, the movie was a moderate success. She and Phil Terry adopted a son. Crawford exerted her influence for her husband to receive a contract with RKO. Terry lost it within a year. Crawford began to believe that she also was finished. She even asked her agent, Lew Wasserman, if she was washed up.

Tragically, she began to drink.

After a set-to that ended with Jack Warner's remark that "that broad must be crazy," she really expected her pink slip the next day. Instead, Jack Warner tossed the script adaptation of James M. Cain's novel *Mildred Pierce* into the lap of a studio hustler Jerry Wald and instructed him to produce it.

Wald wrote for the newspapers, for God's sake!

The script had been written by Budd Schulberg, a fine writer whose previous scripts had been "men's war movies." What was that about? The Breen office, which exercised complete control over the release of all films, had taken a very dim view of the idea of raw infidelity and murder. The studio would be lucky if it wasn't chopped to pieces by their edit. It had been bought as a vehicle for Bette Davis, who declined "regretfully."

Who would play this middle-aged drudge?

The casting of the title role told its own story. Joan Crawford had been let go from MGM after eighteen years. Though she claimed to be only thirty-seven years old, she was probably as old as forty-one. She was famous for playing jazz dancers, ladies of the evening, girlfriends, and bitches. Mildred Pierce was none of those. She was a mother, trying to make a living in a hard man's world. Throughout the movie, she suffered, she ached, she was willing to sacrifice herself.

The script called for Crawford to play the suspect accused of murder. Throughout the film, no one in the audience doubted she had done it, but the ending was a shocker—the big surprise, the twist no one in audience had seen coming. Some members of the publicity department even objected to the ending, thinking the audience might be offended by not being able to figure it out.

No one really realized that Crawford didn't have to act at all to be that woman. In her world where she created her own realities, she *was* that woman. Especially now. She saw herself rearing two little children—Christina, the daughter she'd adopted to make a family after she and Franchot Tone divorced, and Christopher, the boy she had adopted for Phil Terry's sake.

The studio mostly shook its collective head. This whole project was doomed. Crawford's last picture would be a bust. Even she had no faith in the movie. It was so opposite the type of character that she had always portrayed that she herself didn't know whether she could pull it off. Her self-confidence was in the dust. She'd probably never work again.

And yet Jerry Wald called Crawford's press agent, Hank Rogers, after reading the script. "Why don't you start a campaign for Joan to win the Oscar?"

"But the movie hasn't started filming yet."

"So what?"

Hank called Hedda Hopper, who sounded skeptical, but planted the story anyway as "her own prediction" based on an unnamed source.

Crawford herself had asked that her director be Hungarian import Michael Curtiz. From the first day, he was against Crawford. "Me direct that temperamental bitch! Not on your life!"

She agreed to test for him. He grudgingly liked the test but hated her shoulder pads. He screamed at her about them the first day. She had on a costume that he believed was designed by Adrian. She held her ground. "This dress is from Sears, Roebuck. There are no shoulder pads."

The cameraman had to be replaced because he refused to work with Crawford when she demanded "her" lighting. But when everything was to her specifications, Joan Crawford threw herself into the movie and suddenly it all began to work. It was mesmerizing—dark, intense, and, above all, real. Perhaps in the end she surprised herself.

In 1944, the year the picture was filmed, she was the year's best comeback story. And in 1945, she won one of the most coveted awards in the world. Hollywood gossip columnists Louella Parsons and Hedda Hopper praised her to the skies. Hedda gloated over the fact that she had predicted the win all along.

Crawford told everyone that from that time on, she would never do anything but "character roles." The scripts arrived at her house every day from producers who had been "on location" when she called before. She even involved her children in her publicity. Christina in particular, Crawford trotted out in matching mother-daughter outfits to pose for magazine and newspaper photographers. At Crawford's house, everyone and everything was calculated to advance her career.

She developed her own fan club and entertained the local members while she used them shamelessly to answer her bags and bags of fan mail. She created an entire persona for herself, from her favorite perfume—Jungle Gardenia—to her favorite color—green. Much of it was just hype intended to make the fans adore her as a perfect woman, mother, and actress.

Some part of it might have been real insofar as she began to live up to her own hype. She published much of her own contradictory fantasy autobiography in the form of letters she wrote to her fans in the "Joan Crawford Club News," mailed monthly from New York.

Thanks to the Academy Award hoopla and producer Jerry Wald's hustling, Crawford was able to do the two films to complete her contract in 1946 and 1947. *Humoresque* (1946) was a vehicle for "tough guy" John Garfield playing a concert violinist who Crawford tries to lure away from his art. The violin music was supplied by virtuoso Isaac Stern. Real pianist Oscar Levant was his foil, providing acerbic comedy relief. Crawford played a wealthy, destructive woman who tries to lure the violinist from his art. She suffered and emoted throughout, and when she walked into the ocean to drown herself, the audience was probably relieved.

The filming went well, and the movie was as successful as a dark, depressing film with a classical music theme could possibly be. Crawford was offered a new seven-picture contract that paid her $200,000 per picture. At the same time she began to have black moods.

Crawford refused to work during her menstrual period, excusing herself by saying that she did not photograph well then. By this time in her life there very well may have been no menstrual period, but she would never admit to such a possibility.

Since she divorced Phil Terry in 1946, she no longer needed the older children, Christina and Christopher, who were adopted "as extras" early in her career. They were now young teenagers who detracted from her Herculean efforts to retain the appearance of youth and vitality. She sent them away to strict private schools and trotted them home only occasionally—even leaving them at their respective schools during the holidays. According to Christina, her oldest adopted daughter, Crawford came to consider her and Christopher as nuisances. The presents they received from Crawford and her friends were arranged under the magnificent Christmas trees with which she decorated her home, and then stored in a separate room to be given to others or to be used as Christmas props for the next year. Crawford was seen only with the blonde baby girls she adopted in 1947, girls she swore were twins even though they looked nothing alike and were actually two months apart in age. Cathy and Cindy were seven years younger than Christina.

Around the same time she acquired Greg Bautzer, a new man to escort her around to all the parties. The former navy flier was quite different from Fairbanks, Tone, and Terry. World War II had put an edge on the men who survived it. A successful lawyer, he was handsome and accorded a perfect escort for beautiful movie stars. He was a superb dancer, so Crawford saw to it that they were photographed frequently at famous nightclubs. The movie magazines were full of the glamorous Crawford dancing and laughing.

Then in 1947 Bautzer sat at the end of the dinner table and laughed with Rosalind Russell, Crawford's longtime friend from *The Women* and MGM days. Crawford became irrationally infuriated. She sent Rosalind a three-page telegram that arrived at three o'clock in the morning. As Rosalind read it, she exclaimed to her husband, Henry, "She's gone crazy!"

Only a few weeks later after a party at Louis B. Mayer's, Joan drove Greg and herself home in her car. She smiled. "Greg, darling, the right-rear tire feels as though it's getting flat. Would you mind getting out and having a look?"

When he did, she drove off, leaving him to walk three miles back to his suite at the Bel Air Hotel at 3 a.m. in the cold.

Warner Brothers now had eight pictures to make with Crawford. All her pictures were in their film noir style with titles like *The Damned Don't Cry* and *This Woman Is Dangerous*. She suffered beautifully, but the scripts were interchangeable. One of the clauses in her contract was that she must be allowed to break off the relationship with her leading man; he must never leave her. During that time she made two other less-than-great films, one for 20th Century Fox and one for Columbia, in an effort to change her image from the constantly suffering tragedienne.

Finally, she told her agent to get her out of her contract with Warner Brothers before her career was completely destroyed. The move cost her close to a million dollars when youth and beauty were fading fast.

By this time she was drinking in her dressing room and carrying a bottle of champagne into the children's playroom when she showed them films. When staying at a hotel, she required four bottles of the very best quality gin, vodka, bourbon, and Scotch be stocked before she arrived, along with two bottles of chilled champagne and buckets of ice.

Ironically, after *Mildred Pierce* Crawford's most successful picture was an independent film, *Sudden Fear*. Her role was as a woman playwright who overhears a phone conversation between her new younger husband and his lover. They are plotting to kill her. She immediately insisted that Clark Gable be hired to costar. By that time Gable had his own career. He was "unavailable," even for Joan Crawford.

The producer planned to go with someone who could match Crawford's intensity and contrast with her "too beautiful mannequin face." The young man had his own intriguing face. He was Jack Palance.

When Joan was told, she screamed at the director. After she calmed down, he told her that since she refused to be anything but beautiful, he had to cast her with someone whose looks were so menacing that she appeared vulnerable compared to him. Seeing the sense of that reasoning, she agreed.

If Palance had a hard time acting opposite her, she had a worse time opposite him. He was a method actor from the Actors Studio in New York. He was relaxed, he was casual, he was offhand, he mumbled and threw away lines. All the leading men before him had been Hollywood trained. For Palance, no moves were natural, no stance relaxed. When he was off camera, he sat in a chair to throw her lines to her for her close-up shots. Crawford felt he was not showing the proper respect for her.

It was torture. She was also required to lie in a bed with sheets pulled down below her shoulders, the implication being that she slept nude. She objected strenuously, but in the end the director insisted, and she did it.

The picture was a relatively cheap $720,000 to make. Crawford took a percentage rather than demanding her $200,000 customary salary. The decision was a wise one. It was her most popular picture in years and won her both Oscar and Golden Globe nominations. She felt she was on her way again.

The ego boost from the adulation and excitement, unfortunately, cost her the role that might have won her the Oscar the following year. She was offered the role of Karen Holmes, the faithless wife who makes love with Burt Lancaster in *From Here to Eternity*. Crawford demanded so many compensations and special treatments that studio head Harry Cohn abandoned the idea of her in the project. He absolutely refused to be dictated to. Deborah Kerr took the part instead, and her scenes with the rugged sergeant rolling in the water on the beach are classic and bounced the cold English beauty's career into the top drawer.

Crawford's next movie offer was a sort of musical by MGM. *Torch Song* gave her a chance to come full circle and to dance again—if only briefly. Though she rehearsed a number and it was filmed, it was cut out of the script. She was back to suffering again.

In 1955 she married Alfred Steele, the creator of Pepsi-Cola. He was a southerner of humble beginnings, whose regional soft drink company had gone national. He was a self-made millionaire, whom Crawford charmed "the pants off." She was his ticket into a glamorous high life. He was her ticket into financial security. Though she had made fabulous salaries, she had spent fabulous amounts.

Despite Steele's early successes, he found himself not up to the task of being Joan Crawford's husband as well as being the chairman of the board for his burgeoning company. When he dropped dead of a heart attack four years after the marriage, many uncharitable persons said that he got out of the marriage more easily than Fairbanks, Tone, and Terry. At least she still respected Steele when he died.

In between movies she touted Pepsi-Cola and even served on the board for several years.

For five years she appeared in a series of less and less distinguished films for variety of studios. Attendance at her films fell steadily as her audience no longer cared about the "agonies she suffered." Though she still looked much the same, she was quickly approaching sixty years of age. Then she went through a three-year drought. No one was hiring her.

In 1962, desperate to get in front of the cameras again, she went to Jack Warner with a concept. He farmed it out to an in-house production company. Another actress with a fading career was Bette Davis. She had won two Academy Awards in the thirties, but had not made a movie in quite a few years. The two barely knew each other. Davis differed from Crawford in every aspect of her career. She was stage trained from an aristocratic Lowell, Massachusetts, family, and she didn't mind looking terrible on screen.

The movie idea came from a suspense novel by Henry Farrell—*Whatever Happened to Baby Jane?* It was a horror story of two sisters trapped alone in a dark gothic mansion. The production budget was $825,000, which it recovered within ten days of going national.

The two legendary divas of the screen played former stars that nobody remembered. The caricature title role went to Davis, who donned a long blonde wig curled like a child's hair from the turn of the century. Her eyes were heavily made up, her pancake makeup cracked and flaking, her lips drawn into an exaggerated cupid's bow. She was Baby Jane, whose star had flickered out long ago. At first Davis despised the entire idea. She "knew about" Crawford from her reputation. She knew the filming would be a miserable experience, but the chance to do something she had never done before intrigued her. "What the hell," she said as she resolved to play Jane full force. She was nominated for an Oscar after already having won two.

Critics agreed that Joan Crawford's portrayal of Baby Jane's sister, Blanche, turned in the better performance. With her real-life elegant makeup and perfectly coiffed hair, she portrayed all the desperation and horror that she was subjected to. Ironically, for the star of *Our Dancing Daughters*, she was trapped in a wheelchair, her legs paralyzed from an accident in a car supposedly driven by her sister.

At first they were polite and agreeable to each other's "suggestions," but later the sets on which they shot together turned into catfights. The movie ended after an hour and a half in which they tormented each other. The denouement on the beach is one of the great shockers in movie annals. Audiences could not believe their ears, and they loved it, in so much as one can love a movie with grotesque characterizations, murder, and madness.

It was an enormous success grossing $9,000,000.

Unfortunately, it did little for either of them. They were just too old. Over the last eight years of her career, Crawford did only five more movies, four in the horror movie tradition; the last, in 1970, was a "horror of a movie" named *Trog*, which featured Crawford playing opposite a creature in ape costume, supposedly a regenerated troglodyte or cave man.

That same year she returned to Stephens College to receive the first President's Citation given to a former student. She had not been back to the college that had asked her to withdraw forty-eight years earlier. She accepted it gratefully and gave a graceful speech, but she refused to reminisce with some women who remembered being in school with her.

Crawford spent the last five years of her life with members of her fan club, having more or less moved her four children out of her life. Her acting job was limited to one television appearance wherein she took her daughter Christina's role on a soap opera for four weeks. Christina consequently lost her job and left Hollywood forever.

Crawford's adherence to the principles of Christian Science did not save her from cancer. In 1977 she died in solitary "splendor" in her home.

She left her fortune, such as it was, to the adopted twins, but nothing to her blood relatives—her aunt and her niece. Both of her older children, Christina and Christopher, were purposefully omitted "for reasons which are well known to them."

The memorial service was exactly as Crawford would have wanted. Besides the beautiful flowers and the exquisitely performed tributes by her directors and her leading men, the theater was darkened and the audience of mourners viewed an epic montage of some of her greatest scenes, many with stars who had died before her: *Our Dancing Daughters*, *The Women*, *Grand Hotel*, and *Mildred Pierce*. Through it all, she had never looked lovelier—exactly as she would have wanted.

The next year Christina Crawford's tell-all book *Mommie Dearest* was published. Some people were surprised, but most believed every word of it, especially since Christina had carefully saved the often virulent notes her mother had written her over the years. Reprinted unexpurgated, they revealed a nearly psychotic woman transferring her own problems and punishing her daughter because Crawford refused to assume responsibility for her own shortcomings even though she recognized them.

She was, after all, an actress playing her greatest role to the very end.

THE KING AND THE BARON

What does a man do when he suddenly discovers that he is the grandson of one of the richest men in the world?

Baron Enrico di Portanova, who was always Ricky to his riotous friends, couldn't believe his luck. For twenty-four years, he had no idea he would ever be more than he was, an Italian "nobleman" with unproven and unprovable genealogy—hardly more than a gigolo on the fringes of polite society trying to revive la dolce vita in Rome. If he only had money, he was sure he could replace contempt with respect in the eyes of his own countrymen who were trying desperately to adjust to the socioeconomic problems of post–World War II Italy.

But who had money? He and his brother, Ugo, were all but resigned to lives of genteel poverty. Suddenly, in 1957, they began receiving $5,000 checks monthly. Manna from heaven?

Ricky didn't investigate immediately. After all, it came from faraway Texas on the other side of the world from Italy. He vaguely remembered the state had been the home of his mother whom he had not seen for over a decade and scarcely remembered. But this was too much like a fairy tale. He knew nothing of her family—his grandparents.

Perhaps, deep down, Ricky feared that if he questioned the person in charge of dispensing such largesse, that person might discover that a mistake had been made. Not only would the checks stop coming, but Ricky might have to pay the money back.

Of course, Ricky knew the story of his beginnings. His father, Baron Paolo di Portanova, had gone to Hollywood, California, in the early thirties. His looks, which Ricky had inherited, were his fortune, but unfortunately, Paolo couldn't speak English "so good."

Talking pictures were filling the movie houses even as silent films disappeared forever. Paolo with his heavily accented English was scarcely intelligible. He had arrived too late to be the next John Gilbert, a mustachioed silent-movie heartthrob. He learned that Gilbert's career had also ended when his speaking voice had sounded high and reedy when the microphone picked it up. The new movie stars needed more than looks to build their careers. They needed voices that sounded natural over the primitive microphones.

Paolo had one thing going for him that encouraged him to hang around for a while. American women were notorious for going crazy for a man of the nobility. He claimed that his baronial title dated back to 1740. True enough, but the documentation of his entitlement was obscure. Unexplainable breaks appeared here and there in his line of descent.

Nevertheless, the title and his obvious spectacular good looks impressed little Lillie Cullen, who had come to Hollywood with her "Aunt Louise," her father's half sister. While Lillie was trying to make a start in the movies, she met the handsome Italian with the charming accent. Instant attraction ignited between the baron and the little Texas girl, who seemed to have plenty of money. Her father was a cotton broker back in Houston.

Lillie was overwhelmed with not only his looks but his exquisite European manners. No man had ever treated her as politely and romantically as Paolo did. They married

December 16, 1932. Ricky was born eight months later to be followed soon afterward by Ugo.

With an heir to the title and a "spare," Paolo felt the ingenuous little girl had fulfilled her part of the bargain. When it was obvious that Paolo was not going to get jobs in movies, he departed, taking his sons back to Italy. Though his wife had some money, it was not enough to make it worth his time to hang around. Whether he asked her to return to Rome with him is unknown.

Lillie's family didn't disinherit her, although in the 1930s such a thing would not have been unusual. Polite society in those times looked askance at wayward women who had premarital sex. Divorce, while becoming more common, was still not accepted in the best circles. In the meantime, her father, Hugh Roy Cullen, had struck it rich in the oil fields. He and his wife, Lillie, continued to support their daughter with money, but no one is reported to have asked her to come home and be reintroduced into Houston society. She would have been something of an embarrassment. Cullen's other three daughters and his son had all married "well" and were leading happy lives.

Hollywood was not kind to the recently deserted Lillie di Portanova. She soon realized she was never going to be a star, nor even a bit player. She was not pretty enough; she had no training in dancing or singing; and her Texas accent was, in its own way, as unintelligible as Paolo's Italian one. Possibly too embarrassed or ashamed to return to Houston, she decided to move to New York. Perhaps she had some vague idea of trying her luck on the stage, but in the end she found it easier not to pound the pavements looking for work.

Her parents had an inexhaustible amount of money bubbling out of the ground with every new well her father drilled. In the matter of so many other stage-struck children with too much too soon, Lillie took up residence in a modest hotel on

Times Square and went to casting calls occasionally. At length, the rejections discouraged her. She gave up even that indifferent pursuit and wandered the streets dressed as a bag lady.

She bought good wool coats only to replace the collars with scraps of cheaper materials. She would cut the buttons off and fasten the fronts together with safety pins. Whether Lillie disguised herself with some purpose in mind or merely slipped gradually into a form of psychosis, no one can say. Certainly, no one would have ever targeted her for ransom or tried to rob her as she made her way down the streets.

So long as her father's checks of $5,000 a month kept coming, Lillie was able to pay her rent and keep herself in Coca-Colas and sweet cream, which soon became the sum total of her diet. Only the hotel employees where she lived believed she was a wealthy eccentric. They vied with each other to answer her call bell. And why not? She was famous for giving hundred-dollar tips to room service, even to those who simply brought her a Coke.

Eventually, the diet coupled with little exercise sent her into a fatal downward spiral. She became morbidly obese. At her death in 1966, Lillie weighed almost four hundred pounds. She had dressed in rags for twenty years. When she died, she had almost a million dollars in the bank plus much more in a trust fund established by her father for her care after his death.

All those years, Ricky and Ugo knew nothing about their mother's wealth, which they would have welcomed with ecstatic rejoicing. Then their grandfather died, and his estate was extended to include the heirs of his children. After some investigation the barons discovered they were among the legitimate and irrefutable heirs of a genuine Texas oil man. Nor was he any ordinary Texas oil man. Ricky's grandfather had been the fabulously wealthy Hugh Roy Cullen, whom newspapers all over Texas named the "King of the Wildcatters."

It couldn't be true. It was like a fairy tale. The grandfather, who had died, was a man so rich that before his death he had donated millions and millions to the arts, higher education, and medicine. Even oil-rich Houston was amazed at the fantastic amounts this self-made man had amassed and then used to set the example for charitable giving.

If the di Portanovas were Italian peers, the Cullens were Texas royalty. Roy Cullen's grandfather Ezekiel had come from Georgia in 1835 to join the "Texas Raiders," the illustrious volunteers who had followed Old Ben Milam into San Antonio. Theirs was the first victory in the war for Texas Independence and preceded the battles of the Alamo and San Jacinto.

Ezekiel Cullen had been at Washington-on-the-Brazos when the Texas Constitution was written. More important, he was the founder of the Texas public school system in the early days of the Republic of Texas. He had been appointed chairman of the education committee for the Third Congress of the Republic. From that position Cullen began the practice of land endowments for public schools and universities. Those endowments established the foundations for public education as it exists in Texas to this day.

Ironically, Ezekiel's grandson had little opportunity to take advantage of the system. Hugh Roy Cullen had quit school at twelve to take care of his mother when his father died. His formal education ceased, but he believed in it with all his heart and envied those who had it. He talked often about how determined he was that poor children should not miss their educations as he had.

Despite his limited learning, Roy Cullen moved quickly from cotton picker to cotton broker in San Antonio, a town steeped in a history that identified with tradition rather than fresh thinking. Eager, willing, and smart as a whip, Cullen looked toward Houston, which he believed was the direction the money flowed. He had a great eye for things that flowed, be they money, water, or oil.

When he was thirty, Cullen moved his family there. Though he had only a third-grade education, many in 1911 had no more and were becoming movers and shakers in the young vibrant city. Cullen gained a reputation for honesty and reliability as a cotton buyer. He acquired a seat on the Houston Cotton Exchange. His future looked secure if he wanted to accept it.

He was always a great one for research, and one project involved looking into ship channels all over the world. He was convinced that the Houston Ship Channel was absolutely essential to Houston becoming one of the world's major cities. Galveston Island had already proved—to its everlasting pain in 1900—that it was better suited to be an effective barrier island to oncoming hurricanes. With his research encouraging him, Cullen issued a statement calling for a bond drive to finish the work already begun, but lagging because of lack of support from many quarters. His final challenge to the voters was, "Shall we be content to stand still like the average city, or shall we continue to progress and be among the leading cities of our country?" The $3,000,000 bond drive passed three to one and the channel became a reality in 1914.

The town recognized him as one of its leading and most influential citizens.

Cullen might have been content to continue his success in agriculture, had he not found a new interest to pull him away. In 1917 he set out to discover oil—the easy way to quick riches. If a man could only find it.

All around him, men with crazy ideas were striking oil with nothing but wild dreams and used equipment. Spindletop, nearly twenty years before, had been found under a salt dome outside Beaumont. Salt domes seemed the most promising indicators of oil beneath. Prospectors looked there first, but sometimes salt domes yielded nothing but salt water.

Then "Little" Dad Joiner and "Big" Doc Lloyd, the industry's laughingstocks, moved their ramshackle rig fueled with scrap lumber and old tires two hundred feet to the west and accidentally brought in the Daisy Bradford No. 3 in the Piney Woods of east Texas, with nary a salt dome in sight. If they had moved the rig two hundred feet to the east, they would have drilled a dry hole. The oil business in the early days was mostly hit or miss.

Undeterred and undoubtedly a supremely confident individual, Cullen developed his own "scientific method," which he called "creekology." Explained simply, it was detecting oil through the study of surface geology and the paths of flowing water around land formations. He would walk the area, noting and patching together geological data such as the course of rivers, creek beds, and dry streams. As he studied and mapped, Cullen began to see—on a map in his mind—the formations of earth far below.

Others might call it "Cullen's luck," but luck had nothing to do with it so far as he was concerned. His fortunate move to Houston from San Antonio had been a matter of luck. His determination of where to set up his derrick and drill was scientific certainty.

From the coast of the Gulf of Mexico to the Cap Rock on the edge of the Panhandle, Texas had once been under salt water. Pools of it gathered just below the surface of the land. In some places near the coastline, the air stank of sulfur as bubbles slowly appeared and then burst in the tidal pools and tidelands on Varner Plantation, home of former governor James Stephen Hogg outside Columbia, Texas.

In the years since Spindletop, the oil business had become about discovering and sustaining wells. Many times wells had been drilled successfully, produced oil, and then quickly run dry. Cullen had a theory about why this happened. He maintained that the trouble with the oil business was that the first people in it had found oil easily on the surface, and they expected to find it that way always. When the oil stopped flowing, they abandoned the well and moved on.

Cullen believed that they had not dug deeply enough. Taking a chance against the prevailing thinking of the day, he bought their "worn-out" leases for a song and, to their disgust, began drilling again and discovered millions of barrels of oil in the fields, pumping it out of abandoned holes because he dug deeper.

Though his reputation was based on his pseudo-scientific creekology, he was really basing all his instincts on the hundreds of core samples he had seen pulled out of the depths of producing-and-then-suddenly-dry wells. One and all they demonstrated that the earth beneath the topsoil was layers upon layers of different kinds, textures, and colors of rock. And within them and under and above them oil seeped and pooled and was absorbed. He alone was prepared in these early days to break through the layers of rock—slate and shale and, of course, sand—that contained the earth's black gold treasure. In many cases he discovered the oil was not in pools, but present in the porous rock layers themselves forced there by the pressure of the earth above it.

The oil industry itself had a shameful reputation. The great discoveries were blackened by tales of men who had owned the land but had received nothing in oil royalties from what lay beneath it. Of men who had dug "slant holes" and sucked the oil from a neighbor's pools. Of men who had drilled oil wells side by side and pumped the oil out until the oil pressure was exhausted, rather than risk someone else tapping into their pools.

Roy Cullen also developed a reputation for honest dealings. The names of the fields he discovered are all part of Texas's great strikes. In 1928 he formed the South Texas Petroleum Company with a partner named Jim West. Together they found a billion-dollar pool of petroleum near Houston.

The first time Cullen tried his theories, he found oil on the land of a man named Hiland Lockwood. His land was in southeast Texas, where people had drilled before but without much success. Cullen and West had already obtained leases from Lockwood, but Cullen found oil on part of the land that he had not leased. Instead of drilling slant holes as many others in the business would have done, he pulled out a core, dropped it into a bucket, and called the man out of his house before breakfast to show it to him.

Both men knew that the value of the land had increased astronomically after a proven well had come in. Both men knew that the other one knew it. When Cullen asked how much the owner wanted for his leases, Lockwood proved he could be fair too. He quoted the same price as the rest of his land.

Cullen's partner was astonished. He would never have shown Lockwood the sand, but eventually, Lockwood would have found out and spread the word that West was dishonest. By the simple act of playing square with the owner, Cullen showed the world that he was completely honest. Shortly thereafter, Humble Oil came calling to buy the field. Jim West wanted to sell out and enjoy the money. Somewhat to West's amazement, Cullen agreed.

The deal was done. After all the papers were signed and West was on his way out the door, Cullen warned him acrimoniously that he would never partner with him again: "I'm not going to find any more oil fields for you to give away."

With West gone, Cullen set up his own offices in the same building where South Texas Petroleum Company had been. There he immediately formed Quintana Petroleum.

Cullen quickly became one of those legendary larger-than-life wildcatters, unbelievably wealthy even after the stock market crashed in 1929. To celebrate his success, he built an immense mansion on six acres in River Oaks west of downtown Houston.

The River Oaks land, all 875 acres of it, had been purchased in 1924 by the son of former governor James Stephen Hogg. Part of the acreage was first designated as a memorial park for the fallen soldiers of World War I. The rest of the land was sold for homes of wealthy Houstonians. Hogg's daughter Ima had asked John Staub, a conservative Houston architect, to create her home and gardens on fifteen acres at a bend in the Buffalo Bayou, which meandered through the city.

Between Ima Hogg and Hugh Roy Cullen, the reputation of River Oaks was made. Cullen's lot was a modest size by comparison, but he considered it was appropriate to the size of his family—his wife as well as his children and future grandchildren when they came to visit. It required "only" fourteen servants to maintain, and the family loved it. He had hired John Staub, Ima Hogg's own architect, to design and build the home. It was a symbol of their success against all odds. Not bad for a fellow with a third-grade education.

Cullen then proceeded to discover and drill in field after field. At Humble Field where oilmen and geologists had hit shale and been unable to draw oil for thirty years, he forced his drill bits through inch by inch. While others watched in consternation, his wells yielded five thousand barrels a day. The list of his strikes reads like a story of the oil industry. Cullen's Tom O'Connor Field south of San Antonio was one of the greatest strikes in Texas history.

Lillie Cullen, Roy's wife, had only one objection to the oil business: it was so dangerous. Fires were common since they were maintained in close proximity with oil and natural gas. Men worked within inches of heavy machinery with constantly moving parts including huge belts, pipes, and cables. Riggers climbed up on top of high towers and balanced on perilous monkey boards. Drill platforms were themselves temporary structures with the metal derricks sitting on top of them, sliding, tilting, swaying as the great horse heads pumped up and down.

Most dangerous of all were blow outs when the oil pool was finally reached. Many times, when the drill bit chewed through to the pool, the pressure of the earth itself blew the oil, carrying with it pipe, drill, bit, and shattered rock out through the top of the derrick with the speed of cannonballs. If a man were on the monkey board, the chances were good that he'd be blown off and killed instantly.

Young Roy Gustave Cullen had followed his father around the oil fields almost as soon as he could walk. He had devised and improved many pieces of drilling machinery. While his father and mother were in Europe on vacation, Roy had directed the drilling of the entire company. When he was thirty-one, he had been called in to troubleshoot on a rig near Edinburg, Texas. The pipe was frozen a mile and a quarter down in the well. Roy went up on the derrick and was working at the top, when the well received a call from Houston.

Knowing his son and knowing the danger of working with frozen equipment, Cullen was on the line ordering his son off the rig. If they had to drill another well beside the frozen one, so be it.

Too late! The big derrick began to crumble and then collapse. Roy was thrown to the ground and the tangle of steel and wood crashed down on top of him. He was pinned in the wreckage. Roy's leg had to be amputated, and the surgery, along with his other injuries as well as the strain on his system, was too severe. He only lived for two days. In 1936 surgical and postsurgical resources and procedures were severely limited. Even penicillin was ten years in the future. Despite the best medical care Cullen could provide—aspirin; quinine; and iodine, with catgut for sutures and a primitive antiseptic working area—his only son, the scion of the family, died in an oil field accident.

That same year saw the beginning of the Cullens' charitable giving. Cullen said simply that was he selfish enough to want to see his money spent before his death. Perhaps that was so. And perhaps he had no more reason to accumulate such a large fortune. The one who would have managed it and would have needed it to discover more and more oil in all the strange and dangerous places of the earth was gone.

William Marsh Rice had chartered and endowed Rice Institute for the Advancement of Literature, Science, and Art in 1891. The school had opened its doors in 1912. By 1937 it was already attracting some of the same students that would otherwise have attended MIT, Stanford, Yale, or Harvard. To this day it continues to deliver a first-class education for a price well beyond what most people in Texas can afford.

Hugh Roy Cullen, whose education stopped too early, led the city to create another kind of institution. He believed so strongly in education that people might have thought he had graduated cum laude from an Ivy League school. His ambition was to create an institution where every poor child in Houston would be able to afford a college education.

A small junior college was already attached to the Houston public school system. The roots were there. It could quickly grow into a first class four-year institution—the University of Houston.

Several wealthy Houstonians donated 108 acres of land three miles southeast of the city to be the site of a college for those sons and daughters who would not have enough money to go to prestigious and expensive colleges. The first fund-raising campaign began with Roy and Lillie Cullen's donation of $260,000, an enormous sum in those days, to erect the first building on the campus, the Roy Gustave Cullen Building, to house the College of Liberal Arts. It opened September 20, 1939, the first air-conditioned college building in the world.

More donations followed. The Ezekiel Cullen Building, named for Roy's grandfather, and the dormitory group were all built as a result of Roy and Lillie Cullen's donations and their fund-raising activities. At the same time, Cullen donated more than $11,000,000 to build the Cullen Nurses Home at Baptist Memorial Hospital and the Cullen Family Building at St. Joseph's Catholic Hospital. Other projects swiftly followed. In 1947 he established the Cullen Foundation and endowed it with $160,000,000 to finance worthy causes in perpetuity.

Only the Rockefeller and Ford Foundations surpassed it in capital.

During one forty-eight-hour period, Cullen gave Houston's four hospitals more than a million dollars apiece, with absolutely no strings attached as to how it should be spent. He gave away the largest amount of money ever given away in a single lifetime. In all, the King of the Wildcatters managed to give away 93 percent of his personal fortune.

Today, the Bill and Melinda Gates Foundation, also contributed to by Warren Buffett, has surpassed Cullen's generosity with $33,000,000,000 in capitalization, but inflation is partly responsible for their own astronomical amounts. Their stated goal is to liquidate the entire foundation within fifty years.

Half a century after the death of Roy Cullen, the foundation continues to provide for the people of Houston. In 1986, thirty years after Hugh Roy Cullen's death, the Houston Museum of Fine Arts dedicated a "most peaceful acre," a world of playfulness and peace in the heart of Houston—the Sculpture Garden—dedicated to Roy and Lillie Cullen and containing the first American works of internationally famed sculptor Isamu Noguchi. Entrance to this quiet haven is free.

Cullen's incredible legacy rightly continues to return the riches of Texas, drawn from beneath her land, to her sons and daughters in perpetuity.

In contrast Jim West, Cullen's partner who had sold out to Humble Oil, died with millions in the banks. He owned forty-one Cadillacs and kept $290,000 in silver dollars stored in his basement. He had truly buried his "talent."

As proof that no one can totally control his wealth nor spend it to the good of others after his death, Cullen's Italian grandson arrived on the scene. Assuredly, the King of the Wildcatters must have forgotten all about him.

In 1961 the Baron Enrico di Portanova flashed onto the "Petro Metro" Houston scene. His mother, the tragic Lillie, still lived on the streets of New York dressed in the rags of her choice. Neither Ricky nor his brother were believed to have made any effort to see or contact her. Instead, accompanying him was his wife Ljuba, a statuesque member of a Yugoslavian women's basketball team. Everyone who was anyone was impressed, especially so when somehow the news got out that Ljuba had been compared with that most fabulous of Italian beauties Sophia Loren. Houston society was fascinated and thrilled. Ricky was so un-Cullen.

His mother's three sisters, who had married bankers engaged in investing and dispensing the Cullen millions, treated Ricky well, although they did not welcome him as their long lost nephew. No one with any common sense, not to speak of business acumen, could doubt what he had come for. While they themselves lived in comparatively modest homes and lived restrained lifestyles, they had no way to conceal the true extent of the money Ricky was heir to.

He quickly found others who were less conservative. In the course of a few months, Ricky had hired himself a lawyer. While he and his wife were entertained by fascinated young Houstonians in their very best Texas style, Ricky went to court and won several relatively small financial victories. In 1965 his aunts gave him $841,425.

Unfortunately, he did not go away. Ricky and Ljuba created a new social scene that the "beautiful people" of Houston took to their hearts. It was all so exciting and exotic compared to their "whoopee-ti-yo" style parties. The titled peer and the sports goddess were sought after. While she was undoubtedly beautiful, the baron himself created the glamour. He had inherited his father's looks: chiseled features tanned á la George Hamilton, black wavy hair, dark eyes, and a Clark Gable moustache.

Both of them were addicted to jewelry, perhaps regarding it as capital that could be easily grabbed and stashed in a sock if one had to make a quick escape. Those who had known old

Roy Cullen could not help but remember what he thought of such utterly useless excess: "Jewelry is something people use in order to make out that they're better than other people."

In 1966, Lillie Cullen di Portanova died in New York City. Ricky and his brother Ugo inherited her $4,800,000 estate. Ugo too moved to Houston, although he did not want to move in society as his flamboyant brother had. Ugo was a rather fat man who was content with a more-or-less modest penthouse where he could continue the project dearest to his heart. He was rewriting the Bible to show that God did not punish people for their transgressions. His view of the Deity was that He was kind rather than vindictive. (Note: This writer did not try to obtain a copy of the Ugo di Portanova version of the Old Testament with its floods, plagues, fires, and brimstone, although, undoubtedly, it would have been instructive.)

While Houston watched with almost lascivious interest, the following year Ricky and Ljuba aired each other's dirty linen in a messy divorce. The Yugoslavian basketball player proved the exception to the rule that athletes are less than brilliant. She hired Percy Foreman, the superstar of the Houston courtrooms. He accepted three-star sapphires and a diamond necklace as a down payment on his fees.

When the dust settled, Ljuba came out rather well. She got over a million dollars, her jewelry, her townhouse, and her furs, which she would need should she return to Yugoslavia. Ricky had to pay her lawyer $300,000.

Texans shook their heads and thought about what the King of the Wildcatters would have thought of all these goings-on. Many who knew and loved him were glad that he wasn't alive to see the profligacy and waste, even if Cullen had been generous to a fault.

In some ways, Ricky proved himself the King's grandson in that he was clever with his money. Despite his early spending forays, Ricky kept most of the substantial fortune, which—invested—was earning more than he could spend initially. He also found he was very good at playing the stock market and multiplying his millions.

So, darn it all! Ricky couldn't keep up with all the spending he needed to do. The trusts were then paying him $64,000 a month. A single man again, he married his new love, Sandy "Buckets" Hovas, who overnight began the process of reinventing herself as the Baronessa Alessandra. Almost before the honeymoon was over, they were hard at spending their money. In fact, at one time, the couple was going through a million in a month.

Soon they were able to take their "taxi," as they called their Learjet, to their apartment in Rome; their 40,000-square-foot villa on the beach in Acapulco; and back to Hovas House, nominally the home of Sandy's mother, smack dab in the middle of River Oaks. The house was just down the street from Hugh Roy Cullen's old house, designed it will be remembered by one of the most conservative and respected of Houston architects.

Hovas House was another example of the baron's esthetic tastes that sent shock waves through Houston society. The couple planned to be in the white Mediterranean-style baronial palazzo only three months of the year. That was quite long enough because they didn't like Houston's muggy, oppressive climate, but while they were there, friends came to visit them. Suddenly, Houston was a destination as well as a starting point for the jet set. Baron Ricky di Portanova, newly rich, gave a tip of the hat to his Hollywood and Italian heritage to christen his private plane the *Barefoot Contessa*.

With unlimited funds at his disposal, Ricky renovated Hovas House to impress. He bricked over the front yard entirely and planted a cavorting-cupid fountain dead center. Not satisfied with more than an acre of red brick in an otherwise totally green expanse of front and back lawns stretching unbroken before and behind the houses on River Oaks Boulevard, he commissioned a forty-by-forty-foot swimming pool to be dug, enclosed the entire backyard in glass and steel, installed a megaton air conditioner, and hung two gigantic crystal chandeliers over the whole.

River Oaks, which had always prided itself on the conservatism of its architecture and the ambiance of the neighborhood "look," was in shock. They should have been prepared. Houston society was rich. With Ricky to lead them, they became decadent.

The di Portanovas added the European aristocratic panache that had been sorely lacking. Pavarotti was entertained at a sit-down dinner, and the "friends of Sandy" were invited. Those who were not invited were definitely déclassé. Here and there someone might have commented on Ricky's amazing menagerie: his pet snake, Katharina; his albino ferret; and his hedgehog. Then there was the commercial hot dog machine rotating in one corner of the dining room. When questioned, most Houstonians invited to sit in at his table thought the "pets" indicated Ricky really had a warm-hearted nature. They also thought the hot dog machine made the whole room eclectic rather than stilted and formal.

The apartment in Rome underwent a like transformation. The living room was extended to seventy-five feet, and all manner of expensive bibelots were added as Sandy and Ricky decorated according to their extremely eclectic tastes.

With unlimited funds at their disposal, Sandy and Ricky, along with Sandy's friends, who soon became Ricky's friends, jetted off for an evening in Paris, a gambling party in Monte Carlo, tea at the Beverly Hills Hilton in Hollywood. Nothing would do but that the couple maintain a luxurious suite in Claridge's in London. High tea with the di Portanovas was what everyone sought and everyone talked about. The couple received an invitation to, and attended, the wedding of the Prince of Wales and Lady Diana Spencer. To prove it, they brought home souvenir silver flasks, which Sandy prominently displayed.

Of course, guests would perhaps have trouble finding such small things among the excessive animal sculptures that the di Portanovas favored. Statues of sphinxes, jaguars, dolphins, and stags shouldered for attention among classical figures in marble and candelabra-hoisting Nubians in bronze. Besides the baron's menagerie, Baronessa Alessandra delighted in organizing Christmas parties with live camels, wise men, Santas, and gospel choirs.

In 1975 Ricky bought land for his dream house in Acapulco. He envisioned a winter villa on the Pacific coast of Mexico. He spared no expense. With his wife at his elbow, Ricky and an architect designed a house dedicated to the gods of outrageous excess. It was to be called the Villa Arabesque, which perfectly described the building that included a harem room with piano bar, a grand salon, and a rooftop terrace with a stucco-tented kitchen and bar area. No fewer than nine guest suites were available for special friends. Besides three swimming pools, there was a funicular railway that carried guests from the villa to the beach and back again.

A large portion of the villa housed the Poseidon Grill, which would seat as many as sixty guests. It was attached to, of all things, the Poseidon Discotheque, a nightclub large enough to accommodate two hundred guests. It was used by Ricky's European friends as well as Sandy's Houston pals, who were rich enough to buy their own Learjets or at least to charter a plane to fly in for a party. Perhaps he saw himself as becoming an entrepreneur in the manner of Conrad Hilton.

The Houston newspapers carried story after story of la dolce vita, Texas style, and wrote article after article in the society pages reporting the doings. They also carried the stories of Ricky hiring New York super-lawyer Roy Cohn to sue the Cullen family for $500,000,000 in punitive damages—presumably for denying him as much money as he wanted. The case dragged on for years. Even three years after Cohn's death, it had not been settled.

While the Houston papers reported all the lurid details at every social opportunity, nowhere was there any reporting of charitable giving. No di Portanovas thought about contributing to the health and education of the citizens of Houston. Ricky thought only about his next outrageous spending spree that seemed to include whatever might strike his fancy no matter what the price. As the house was being decorated, he bought lavishly and crammed it all together. The result was a wearisome outrageous mess wherever they went and lived for very long.

International print and more often electronic media continued reporting his life as an idle millionaire, who consumed pâté and flew bosomy party girls, including Anita Ekberg, from his apartment in Rome and his homes on the other side of the Atlantic in Houston and in Acapulco. Henry Kissinger, a notable jet-setter when he wasn't impressing the political class with his erudition, was often Ricky's guest.

The ordinary herd got to see carefully selected parts of the Acapulco villa in the James Bond movie *License to Kill*. With a tip of the hat to his father and mother's Hollywood years, Ricky rented the villa to Albert R. Broccoli's production company as a set for the film. Ricky's own guards armed with AK-47s and Kalashnikovs were no match for Pierce Brosnan's delivery of Bond's one-liners.

But nothing lasts forever.

No less than the *New York Times* published Ricky's obituary March 4, 2000, under the headline "Baron Enrico di Portanova, 66, Flamboyant Member of the International Jet Set." His wife died in the same year. They had no children. The article characterized his death as the end of la dolce vita. In April of 2004, Arabesque was for sale for $29,000,000.

Perhaps that money will go back into the Cullen family trust, since Ricky and Ugo left no heirs. The incredible and outrageous excess is a cautionary tale for all parents and grandparents who leave their fortunes to people who have no self-control. While it can be said that Ricky and Sandy hurt no one and provided employment for hundreds, perhaps thousands, of artisans, domestic servants, contractors, bartenders, furniture manufacturers, and the like, the outrageousness of their spending somehow outweighs everything else.

It would be good to think that the earning power of all that wealth that spouted from the deep heart of Texas would remain in Texas where it all began, that Texas children could be educated, that Texas's sick and old could be cared for properly, and that the purchase and maintenance of objects of fine art could continue so as to provide enrichment and beauty for all the people of the Lone Star State.

Hugh Roy Cullen, the King of the Wildcatters, had every intention that it should.

SUGGESTIONS FOR FURTHER READING
ABOUT OUTRAGEOUS TEXANS

Cartwright, Gary. *Blood Will Tell: The Murder Trials of T. Cullen Davis.* New York: Pocket Books, 1980.

Cary, Diana Serra. *The Hollywood Posse: The Story of a Gallant Band of Horsemen Who Made Movie History.* Norman: University of Oklahoma Press, 1995.

Crawford, Christina. *Mommie Dearest.* New York: William Morrow and Company, 1978.

Friedman, Kinky. *Elvis, Jesus, and Coca-Cola.* New York: Bantam, 1993.

———. *Kinky Friedman's Guide to Texas Etiquette, or How to Get to Heaven or Hell without Going through Dallas–Fort Worth.* New York: HarperCollins, 2001.

———. *'Scuse Me While I Whip This Out: Reflections on Country Singers, Presidents, and Other Troublemakers.* New York: HarperCollins, 2004.

———. *Ten Little New Yorkers.* New York: Simon & Schuster, 2005.

———. *You Can Lead a Politician to Water but You Can't Make Him Think: Ten Commandments for Texas Politics.* New York: Simon & Schuster, 2007.

Friedman, Myra. *Buried Alive: The Biography of Janis Joplin.* New York: Bantam, 1974.

Hutson, Jan. *The Chicken Ranch: The True Story of the Best Little Whorehouse in Texas.* New York: A. S. Barnes and Company, 1980.

Kennedy, Rod. *Music from the Heart*. Austin: Eakin Press, 1998.

Kilman, Ed, and Theon Wright. *Hugh Roy Cullen: A Story of American Opportunity*. New York: Prentice-Hall, 1954.

Knowles, Ruth Sheldon. *The Greatest Gamblers: The Epic of American Oil Exploration*, 2nd edition. Norman: University of Oklahoma Press, 1978.

Malsch, Brownson. *Captain M.T. Lone Wolf Gonzaullas, the Only Texas Ranger of Spanish Descent*. Austin: Shoal Creek Publishers, 1980.

Olien, Roger M., and Diana Davids Olien. *Life in the Oil Fields*. Austin: Texas Monthly Press, 1986.

Presley, James. *Saga of Wealth: The Rise of the Texas Oilmen*. Austin: Texas Monthly Press, 1983.

Roach, Joyce Gibson. *The Cowgirls*. Denton: University of North Texas Press, 1990.

Salerno, Steve. *Deadly Blessing: The Story of Troubled Texas Aristocrat Price Daniel, Jr., and His Death at the Hands of the Woman from the Other Side of the Tracks.* New York: William Morrow and Company, 1987.

Sheehy, Sandy. *Texas Big Rich: Exploits, Eccentricities, and Fabulous Fortunes Won and Lost*. New York: William Morrow and Company, 1990.

Shirley, Glenn. *"Hello, Sucker!" The Story of Texas Guinan*. Austin: Eakin Press, 1989.

Thomas, Bob. *Joan Crawford, a Biography*. New York: Simon & Schuster, 1978.

Thompson, Thomas. *Blood and Money*. New York: Dell Publishing Company, 1977.

Webb, Walter Prescott. *The Texas Rangers*. Austin: University of Texas Press, 1996.

Wendt, Lloyd, and Herman Kogan. *Bet a Million! The Story of John W. Gates*. New York: Bobbs-Merrill, 1948.

ABOUT THE AUTHOR

"My life is hectic, but what a great way to live!" So says Mona D. Sizer, author of thirty-two books of historical and contemporary romance, biography, history, true crime, poetry, and memoir. She is the editor of as well as a contributor to the popular *Tales Told at Midnight along the Rio Grande.* Her nonfiction articles appear regularly in *LifeTimes*, published by Blue Cross/Blue Shield. She reads eclectically and travels far and wide with her handsome husband, Jim. Their marriage has been a joy for forty-six years.